CRUDE AWAKENINGS

CRUDE AWAKENINGS

GLOBAL OIL SECURITY AND AMERICAN FOREIGN POLICY

STEVE A. YETIV

CORNELL UNIVERSITY PRESS
Ithaca and London

First published 2004 by Cornell University Press

Printed in the United States of America

Library of Congress Cataloging-in-Publication Data

Yetiv, Steven A.
  Crude awakenings : global oil security and American foreign policy / Steve A. Yetiv.
      p. cm.
  Includes index.
  ISBN 0-8014-4268-0 (cloth : alk. paper)
1. Middle East—Foreign relations—United States. 2 United States—Foreign relations—Middle East. 3. Saudi Arabia—Politics and government—1932- 4. Petroleum industry and trade—Middle East. 5. Security, International. I. Title.
  DS63.2.U5Y48 2004
  327.73056'09'045—dc22

                                                              2004005008

Cornell University Press strives to use environmentally responsible suppliers and materials to the fullest extent possible in the publishing of its books. Such materials include vegetable-based, low-VOC inks and acid-free papers that are recycled, totally chlorine-free, or partly composed of nonwood fibers. For further information, visit our website at www.cornellpress.cornell.edu.

Cloth printing   10 9 8 7 6 5 4 3 2 1

CONTENTS

FIGURES AND TABLES

ACKNOWLEDGMENTS

I spent five years writing this book in what proved to be a lengthier effort than I expected. It no doubt would have been much longer without the support that I received from many individuals whom I inhumanely punished with my pesky questions and fuzzy notions. For taking this punishment in good stride, I thank the colleagues who read part or all of this manuscript. They include Anouar Boukhars, Jill Crystal, Kurt Taylor Gaubatz, Gregory Gause, Eric Miller, and John Torcivia. I am especially grateful to Edward Morse, whose many critical comments strengthened this work.

I also thank a number of OPEC officials, Fatmata Deen of OPEC's library, and many former and current officials from the United States, China, Russia, France, and various nations in the Middle East. The information they provided filled key gaps in the record.

Last but hardly least, I extend a special thanks to editor Roger Haydon of Cornell University Press. His guidance was crucial, his intuition keen, and his input highly valuable through more drafts than I care to remember.

S.A.Y.

Norfolk, Virginia

ABBREVIATIONS

b/d	Barrels per day	MFN	Most Favored Nation
bb	Billion barrels	mb	Millions of barrels
CIS	Commonwealth of Independent States	mb/d	Millions of barrels per day
		NESA	Near East and South Asia
CDLR	Committee for the Defense of Legitimate Rights	NTR	Normal Trade Relations
		NPT	Non-Proliferation Treaty
CAFE	Corporate Average Fuel Economy	OAPEC	Organization of Arab Petroleum Exporting Countries
DOE	Department of Energy		
EIA	Energy Information Administration	OPEC	Organization of Petroleum Exporting Countries
FSU	Former Soviet Union	OECD	Organization for Economic Cooperation and Development
CCC	Gulf Cooperation Council		
G7	Group of Seven		
IAEA	International Atomic Energy Agency	PNTR	Permanent Normal Trade Relations
IEA	International Energy Agency	RDF	Rapid Deployment Force
IMF	International Monetary Fund	SPR	Strategic Petroleum Reserve
MECS	Middle East Contemporary Survey	UAE	United Arab Emirates
		UN	United Nations
MEED	Middle East Economic Digest	WMD	Weapons of mass destruction
		WTO	World Trade Organization
MEES	Middle East Economic Survey		

Chapter 1

INTRODUCTION

Oil is one of the most controversial and widely used commodities in history. It provokes many familiar rallying cries: No Blood for Oil; Oil Corrupts; Oil and the Environment Don't Mix; Oil Funds Terrorism; A Dangerous Appetite for Oil; End the Oil Addiction; The Axis of Oil.

As we can see, oil is linked to quite a noxious mixture of subjects. Indeed, a visitor from a faraway universe would be forgiven for concluding that oil was a disease, a scourge that needed to be eradicated and forsaken as soon as possible. Of course, our alien would be in for quite a surprise: namely, the voracious, nearly ubiquitous consumption of oil all over the world. Indeed, whatever we think of oil—and surely there are some big negatives—oil is the single largest sector of global trade. As long as we lack the technological prowess and the political will to produce a widely consumable and cost-efficient alternative, we are unlikely to alter our current course toward growing global dependence on oil.

This book is about the past, present, and future of the supply of global oil to the world economy, a subject that should concern leaders, scholars, and citizens around the world. Global dependence on oil at reasonable prices makes all states, both wealthy but especially poor, potentially vulnerable to intended or unintended disruptions in oil supplies, disruptions that could hinder global economic growth and, in turn, harm human welfare by producing a cascade of negative effects carried along the myriad connections of the interdependent global economy.[1]

Oil stability has been important for decades, but it has regained its urgency. Fears of spikes in the price of oil brought about by events in the Middle East surfaced throughout the 1990s. The terrorist attack in 2000 on the USS *Cole*

[1] *High Prices Hurt Poor Countries More Than Rich* (Paris: International Energy Agency, 20 March 2000), www.iea.org/new/releases/2000/oilprice.htm.

while the Navy destroyer was in port in Yemen and the Palestinian unrest that same year in the West Bank rocked global stock markets. Market gurus and political pundits, scholars and leaders repeatedly warned that Middle East unrest was a wild card that could raise oil prices, impede global growth, and hurt the stock market. Fears also arose that the Organization of Petroleum Exporting Countries (OPEC), which controls 35 to 40 percent of world oil production and 77 percent of world oil reserves, would curtail oil supply and push prices higher out of self-interest, out of an inability to agree on production levels, or in sympathy with the Palestinians.

On March 29, 2001, newly elected President George W. Bush dramatized oil instability when he referred to an American "energy crisis."[2] Echoing Bush, Energy Secretary Spencer Abraham asserted in April 2001 that the United States was facing its "worst energy crisis" since the 1973 Arab oil embargo.[3] To be sure, these remarks may have been intended in part to sell Bush's domestic energy plan—and the crisis itself was driven only partly by oil concerns—but the remarks nonetheless underscored a perceived danger of the growing dependence on foreign oil.

Against this general backdrop, the September 11 terrorist attacks on the World Trade Center and the Pentagon elevated concerns about oil stability. Fifteen of the nineteen hijackers came from oil-rich Saudi Arabia and were furious with the Saudi monarchy's overly accommodating relationship with the United States. The attacks and the support that the terrorists received within Saudi Arabia raised the prospect that U.S.-Saudi relations could unravel and highlighted the potential for instability within Saudi Arabia. Ongoing Palestinian-Israeli tensions ratcheted up the pressure and spawned fears of a regional war or an Arab oil embargo. In April 2002, in fact, Iraq cut off oil to the world economy for one month in what it portrayed as an act of solidarity with the Palestinians, and Iran and Libya threatened to follow suit.

The potential of a U.S.-led attack on Iraq further elevated the question of oil stability. In a September 19, 2002, letter to the United Nations General Assembly, Saddam Hussein argued that the United States wanted "to destroy Iraq in order to control the Middle East oil, and consequently control the politics as well as the oil and economic policies of the whole world."[4] He subsequently warned of a bloodbath for the infidel invaders; in turn, President Bush, like his father before him in the 1990–91 crisis, cast Saddam as a threat to global peace.

The White House sent a letter to Congress in late September 2002. It enumerated Iraq's failure to meet numerous UN Security Council Resolutions and asked Congress to pass a resolution allowing the administration to "use

---

[2] CNN, 29 March 2001.
[3] "Iran: The OPEC Factor and Price Prospects," APS Review 56 (9 April 2001).
[4] New York Times, 20 September 2002, A12.

all means" to "defend the national security interests of the United States against the threat posed by Iraq and restore international peace and security to the region."[5] Congress obliged, and the UN Security Council, after some political wrangling, passed Resolution 1441 on November 8, 2002, by a vote of 15–0.[6] The resolution required Iraq to admit inspectors from the UN Monitoring, Verification, and Inspection Commission (UNMOVIC) and the International Atomic Energy Agency (IAEA) and to comply fully with UN resolutions. More important, it created the potential for a U.S.-led war against Iraq if Baghdad failed to comply. After determining as much, the United States spearheaded an attack on Iraq that commenced on March 19, 2003, and resulted in the elimination of Saddam Hussein's regime three weeks later.

In the months and weeks prior to the Iraq War, politicians and academics, media personalities and ordinary citizens around the world raised concerns that war would further destabilize the Middle East. People largely took for granted, and seldom questioned, the notion that the region was unstable, even volcanic. On the oil front, some analysts were not discounting the possibility of an oil price spike to $70 to $75 per barrel (p/b), more than doubling already high oil prices.[7] Even the U.S. Energy Information Administration warned that oil prices could end up in that range as a result of war-related fears and developments. Others doubted that OPEC could even offset the loss incurred by Venezuela's oil strike, much less any war-related losses.[8] The belief that the Gulf region was unstable gained such currency that U.S. defense officials regularly referred to it as part of a broader "arc of instability."

The events of 1999 to 2003 underscored a fact of international life: there is no dearth of imagined, anticipated, potential, and real threats to and concerns about oil stability. Analysts have periodically argued that the Saudi regime could fall, to the detriment of the global economy, and that the region is broadly unstable.[9] Others have pointed to such things as regional

---

5   Matthew L. Wald, "Approval Is Seen for Military Action against Iraq," *New York Times*, 23 September 2002.
6   For the text of the resolution, see *Arms Control Today* 32 (December 2002), 28–32.
7   Stephen Wyatt, "The Great Threat to Global Growth," *Australian Financial Review* (4 January 2003).
8   "Saudis Pre-empt Opec Meeting With Extra Supply," *Oil Daily* (10 January 2003).
9   Some analysts argued that the Saudi regime could fall during an intelligence briefing in which this author participated (Washington, D.C.: Meridian International Center, 27 April 1996). See also Peter W. Wilson and Douglas F. Graham, *Saudi Arabia: The Coming Storm* (Armonk, NY: M. E. Sharpe, 1994), esp. 266–68. On such views held by others, see Michael Collins Dunn, "Is the Sky Falling? Saudi Arabia's Economic Problems and Political Stability," *Middle East Policy* 3 (1995), 29. *APS Diplomatic Operations in Oil Diplomacy* 43 (28 January 2002). Robert Baer, *Sleeping with the Devil* (New York: Crown, 2003). For a brief discussion of some of these views and works, see Mary Seikaly, "Kuwait and Bahrain: The Appeal of Globalization and Internal Constraints," in *Iran, Iraq, and the Arab Gulf States*, ed. Joseph A. Kechichian (New York: Palgrave, 2001), 177–80; Øystein Noreng, *Crude Power: Politics and the Oil Market* (London: I. B. Tauris, 2002), chap. 5.

wars, weapons of mass destruction under autocratic control, oil strikes in OPEC nations such as Venezuela, transnational terrorism against U.S. and global oil facilities, the Arab-Israeli conflict in its many dimensions, and oil blackmail against the West.[10] Endless variants of one or more of these threats have also been considered.

THE CENTRAL ARGUMENT OF THIS BOOK

To be sure, we should heed some of these threats to oil stability as we head into the twenty-first century. However, the real story of global oil over the past twenty-five years is not about the spillover effects of Palestinians fighting Israelis, or terrorist attacks on U.S. forces in Saudi Arabia and Yemen, or Iraq's stormy relationship with Kuwait. It is not even about periodic small- and large-scale U.S. attacks on Iraq. Rather, the real story is about longer-term developments that have changed the international relations of the Middle East, politics at the global level, and world oil markets. These developments have increased oil stability.

On the surface, it may seem bizarre to argue that oil has become more stable. Few observers would make this case, partly because oil stability is linked to Middle East events—and the region seems periodically on the verge of exploding. But as we assemble the disparate pieces of the argument, chapter by chapter, a picture emerges of developments that, taken together, constitute shock absorbers under the shifting and complex mosaic of global oil. Some of these developments are familiar to us, such as the rise of U.S. capability in the Gulf; others are less well recognized, or if recognized not viewed as germane to oil stability.

While each of these developments is important in its own right, the more intriguing question is what they mean for oil stability when considered together. The widespread focus on instability makes it easy to miss how these longer-run political, security, technological, and market developments interact in the crucible of history to yield a counterintuitive outcome: enhanced oil stability. In this sense, this book presents an argument that contrasts sharply with the concerns, fears, and sometimes hype regarding oil instability.

Despite appearances, the Iraq War underscored a key aspect of my argument. Many analysts believed that the U.S. strategic petroleum reserve

[10] On transnational terrorism, see "Time for Asian SPR, Says Former Senior U.S. Official," *Oil Daily* (2 April 2002) and Neal Adams, *Terrorism and Oil* (Tulsa, OK: PennWell Corporation, 2003). On oil blackmail, see "Report of an Independent Task Force," *Strategic Energy Policy: Challenges for the 21st Century* (New York: Council on Foreign Relations, 2001), 2 and Anthony H. Cordesman, "The One True U.S. Strategic Interest in the Middle East: Energy," *Middle East Policy* 8 (March 2001).

would have to be used, and President Bush faced pressure in Washington to do precisely that, both before and during the war. Yet despite the fact that the oil sector also faced heavy disruptions due to the oil strike in Venezuela and the ethnic and political strife in Nigeria, the United States did not have to resort to using the strategic petroleum reserve. This is no mere coincidence: the U.S. ability to avoid doing so is a direct result of some of the developments laid out in this book.

Oil Stability versus Price Stability: A Crucial Distinction

To argue that oil stability has increased presumes an idea of what "stability" means. Of course, different thinkers from different backgrounds and perspectives will define it in their own way. For the purposes of this book, oil stability is defined as a function of the ability to deter, mitigate, and contain threats to the supply of oil.[11] Simply put, the greater the ability to do so, the more stable oil supply is; the lesser the ability to do so, the less stable oil supply is.

Threats to supply stability fall into four categories. The first two are conventional. They are (1) political, economic, and strategic developments such as wars, revolutions, coups d'état, transnational and local terrorism, and labor strikes; and (2) the active policies of oil-producing states that have the power, independently or collectively, to increase or decrease the existing oil supply to the global economy. The second set of categories is less direct than the first. Although this book focuses far less attention on them, they add a broader perspective to any analysis of oil stability. They are the ability or inability (3) of discovering, producing, delivering, and conserving oil, chiefly through high technology and national and global energy policies and (4) of producing commercially viable alternative sources of energy. I view them as salient to stability because the extent to which they are executed successfully can affect the level of stress on the oil supply of the world. Thus, the better we are at discovering oil and finding alternatives to it, the less stress there will be on global oil supply.

While this book focuses chiefly on the supply of oil to the market, it is important to underscore a point about the price of oil. Supply stability is one factor that affects price. The more stable the supply, the more stable the price, all other things being equal. But "other things" are rarely equal. Some factors that affect price include the level of demand, market psychology, and the nature of increasingly important and publicized relations among OPEC

---

11 While my definition of oil stability is specific to the oil issue area, it may not differ significantly from the notion that the international system is stable when it is durable or enjoys a self-reinforcing equilibrium. See William C. Wohlforth, "The Stability of a Unipolar World," *International Security* 24 (Summer 1999), esp. note 11.

nations and between OPEC and non-OPEC nations at any given time.[12] Because so many factors affect price, it is perfectly possible that supply stability can increase at the same time that oil prices are increasing. This is especially true if we examine the volatility of oil prices, rather than just changes in the level of oil prices over a longer period.

Oil price volatility is defined as the speed and magnitude of price changes and should not be confused with stability as defined in this book. Measured on a day-to-day basis, volatility has clearly increased over time,[13] partly because oil is now a commodity subject to the caprice of markets. The stable oil prices of the mid-1970s to early 1980s gave way to greater fluctuations, largely because the OPEC states abolished price controls and indexed their sales to prices in the open market, while privatized Russian companies sold their oil on spot markets as other entities do.[14] In addition, at the start of the oil era, the world was not nearly as wired technologically as it would be at the outset of the twenty-first century, when OPEC announcements, transmitted around the world instantaneously, could shake markets like any major political or strategic event.

Oil Stability and the Middle East

While global oil is affected by numerous factors, the pursuit of all-important energy at reasonable prices also influences a broad swath of phenomena, including global stock markets, the proliferation of weapons of mass destruction, global economic growth, war and peace, and international terrorism. Indeed, some might argue that in seeking to secure global energy in the Middle East, the United States and its allies inadvertently contributed to transnational terrorism, including September 11.[15] Whatever one thinks of such an argument, it is clear that the story of global energy (with emphasis on the role of the Middle East) ties into core elements of world affairs and yields insight into what may become one of the organizing fault lines of global politics in the twenty-first century: the struggle to provide, protect, influence, and gain access to global energy. All major states in world affairs now fully understand the importance of energy to their plans. If the bipolar conflict of the Cold War defined twentieth-century world affairs, the geopolitics of

---

12 Interview with Javad Yarjani.
13 For evidence on volatility going back to 1870, see Philip K. Verleger Jr., *Adjusting to Volatile Energy Prices* (Washington, D.C.: Institute for International Economics, 1993), 23–28.
14 Michael C. Lynch, *Oil Market Structure and Oil Market Behavior* (Riyadh, Saudi Arabia: 7th International Energy Forum, November 17–19, 2000), esp. 5.
15 Al Qaeda did offer an approximately 3,700-word justification for the grotesque terrorist attacks of September 11 on April 24, 2002. See www.mepc.org/public%5Fasp/journal_vol10/alqaeda.html.

energy, as Michael Klare suggests, may do the same in the first half of the twenty-first century.[16]

To be sure, the debate rages about the extent to which world dependence on oil has increased.[17] But irrespective of that level, current estimates suggest that Persian Gulf production will increase significantly in quantity and, more important, as a percentage of world consumption through 2025, as one can gather from Table 1.[18]

The Persian Gulf supplies only a fraction of total U.S. consumption, but the United States, as Table 2 shows, has become more dependent on Gulf oil over the past two decades, as have China and Japan. The U.S. Department of Energy projections for 2020 show that U.S. dependence on Middle East oil will rise, and that overall global dependence on oil, especially in developing Asia and North America, will also rise, with the smallest projected increase in Western Europe from 2001–2025 (see Figure 1).[19]

The Persian Gulf not only supplies significant energy to the world economy, but holds two-thirds of the world's oil reserves—the estimated amount that can be produced from known reservoirs—compared to only 4 percent from the United States.[20] This concentration makes political, economic, and security developments in the region vital to the question of global energy stability. Energy sources other than oil, such as coal and nuclear power, provide over 60 percent of the world's energy, but interruptions in their supply are not a big concern. This is not the case for oil, and especially not the case for Gulf oil. Oil disruptions have occurred numerous times in history, for various lengths of time. In many of these cases, world oil supply was reduced

16   Michael T. Klare, *Resource Wars: The New Landscape of Global Conflict* (New York: Metropolitan Books, 2001).

17   See A. M. Samsam Bakhtiari, "The Price of Crude Oil," *OPEC Review* 23 (March 1999), 11–14. Some estimates suggest it will increase significantly in the early twenty-first century. See also *United States Security Strategy for the Middle East* (Washington, D.C.: Department of Defense, Office of International Security Affairs, May 1995), 3 and "Global Energy Wire: Hubbert's Pique" (Deutsche Bank: 9 June 2003).

18   *International Energy Outlook 2003* (Washington, D.C.: EIA, DOE, May 2003), www.eia.doe.gov/oiaf/aeo/. The DOE offers different estimates based on different market assumptions about oil demand. I refer here to the DOE estimate in the reference case, which assumes neither a very high nor a very low oil price. It is useful to note, however, that because of projected consumption increases in developing nations, the share of Persian Gulf imports to industrialized nations in particular is projected to fall by about 12 percent by 2025. *International Energy Outlook 2003* (Washington, D.C.: DOE, May 2003), 41, www.eia.doe.gov/oiaf/ieo/index.html. Also, see Adnan Shihab-Eldin, Rezki Lounnas, and Garry Brennand, "Oil Outlook to 2020," *OPEC Review* 25 (December 2001).

19   *Annual Energy Outlook 2002* (Washington, D.C.: EIA, DOE), 60. Of course, as DOE officials will assert, such predictions tend to be wrong, but they offer some sense of direction at the present time.

20   Beyond oil production, the Gulf also holds significant gas reserves. After Russia, four states—Iran, Qatar, the United Arab Emirates, and Saudi Arabia—hold the largest proven gas reserves in the world.

TABLE 1.
World oil production by region and country, reference case,° 1990–2025
(Million barrels per day)

Region/Country	History (estimates)		Projections				
	1990	2001	2005	2010	2015	2020	2025
OPEC							
Persian Gulf	16.2	20.6	21.7	24.8	29.2	34.6	40.5
Other OPEC	8.3	9.8	9.9	11.3	12.2	13.6	15.1
Total OPEC	**24.5**	**30.4**	**31.6**	**36.1**	**41.4**	**48.2**	**55.6**
Non-OPEC							
industrialized							
United States	9.7	9.0	9.0	9.2	9.0	9.4	9.4
Canada	2.0	2.8	3.1	3.4	3.6	3.8	4.1
Mexico	3.0	3.6	3.8	4.2	4.5	4.6	4.8
Western Europe	4.6	6.9	6.6	6.5	6.0	5.6	5.1
Other	0.8	0.9	0.9	1.0	1.0	0.9	0.9
Total industrialized	**20.1**	**23.2**	**23.4**	**24.3**	**24.1**	**24.3**	**24.3**
Eurasia							
China	2.8	3.3	3.5	3.6	3.5	3.5	3.4
Former Soviet Union	11.4	8.8	9.7	11.6	13.3	14.4	15.9
Eastern Europe	0.3	0.2	0.3	0.3	0.3	0.4	0.4
Total Eurasia	**14.5**	**12.3**	**13.5**	**15.5**	**17.1**	**18.3**	**19.7**
Other non-OPEC							
Central and South America	2.4	3.8	4.3	4.7	5.7	6.2	6.7
Pacific Rim	1.7	2.5	2.5	2.6	2.8	2.7	2.8
Other	3.5	4.8	5.4	6.1	7.3	8.1	9.4
Total other non-OPEC	**7.6**	**11.1**	**12.2**	**13.4**	**15.8**	**17.0**	**18.7**
Total non-OPEC	**42.2**	**46.6**	**49.1**	**53.2**	**57.0**	**59.6**	**62.7**
Total world	**66.7**	**77.0**	**80.7**	**89.3**	**98.4**	**107.8**	**118.3**
Persian Gulf production as a percentage of world consumption	**24.6**	**26.7**	**26.8**	**27.7**	**29.6**	**32.0**	**34.1**

Source: Energy Information Administration/*Annual Energy Outlook* 2003.
°The reference case presumes that oil prices will be neither high nor low.

by at least two million barrels per day (mb/d), contributing to global economic problems (see Table 3).

Reflecting commonly held views, Robert Priddle, the former director of the International Energy Agency, which represents oil-consuming nations, in 2002 repeatedly claimed that security of supply has returned to the top of the agenda and will likely remain there, calling it a "major pre-occupation of at least equal significance" to other global oil issues.[21]

[21] For instance, see *3rd International Oil Summit* (Paris, France: Institut Française du Pétrole, 25 April 2002).

TABLE 2.
Oil imports from the Persian Gulf as a percentage of total imports, 1983–2002°

	U.S.	Western Europe	Japan	China	France
1983	8.8%	41%	60%	—	—
1984	9.3%	39%	61%	—	—
1985	6.1%	35%	59%	25%	—
1986	14.7%	45%	58%	24%	—
1987	16.1%	43%	60%	27%	—
1988	20.8%	44%	58%	29%	—
1989	23.1%	47%	63%	30%	—
1990	24.5%	48%	65%	29%	49%
1991	24.2%	43%	64%	34%	39%
1992	22.5%	43%	66%	36%	36%
1993	20.7%	50%	68%	42%	43%
1994	19.2%	48%	68%	40%	39%
1995	17.8%	47%	70%	45%	38%
1996	16.9%	43%	70%	53%	38%
1997	17.3%	47%	74%	47%	35%
1998	19.9%	50%	76%	61%	39%
1999	23.0%	50%	74%	48%	33%
2000	22.1%	45%	75%	—	32%
2001	20.1%	—	76%	—	25%
2002	20.2%	—	74%	—	24%

Source: Energy Information Administration. For data on France from which the author derived calculations, see www.eia.does.gov/emeu/ipsr/t413.txt. In addition, see *Chinese Customs Statistical Review*,
2000.
° Imports include crude oil, natural gas liquids, and refined products.

Market forces, to be sure, may contribute to energy crises if demand out-
paces supply, a problem that would be exacerbated if we find that global oil
supplies will not last for another forty or fifty years, as some analysts predict,
and if other sources of oil and energy prove less promising than some anticipate.[22] Spikes in oil prices may also arise due to pipeline problems, refinery
bottlenecks, technical factors of production, or market structure.[23] However,
a bigger unknown is how political and security factors will affect supply and
pricing. As Edward Morse astutely points out, the "linkages between oil and
other factors of international life have become more extensive since the

[22] For predictions that demand will outpace supply, see *APS Review Gas Market Trends*, 58
(11 March 2002) and Cyrus H. Tahmassebi, "Effective U.S. energy policy," *Oil and Gas
Journal* 99 (2 April 2000), 21. On the possibility that oil reserves may not last another forty
years, see Richard A. Kerr, "The Next Oil Crisis Looms Large—and Perhaps Close," *Science*
281 (21 August 1998).
[23] See "OPEC on Top," *Middle East Economic Digest* (MEED) 44 (21 July 2000) and Abdul-
Razak Faris Al-Faris, *OPEC and the Market: A Study of Oil Price Rigidity, Determination,
and Differentials* (Boulder, CO: International Research Center for Energy and Economic
Development, 1994).

Figure 1. Increments in oil consumption by region
(1970-2001 and 2001-2025)

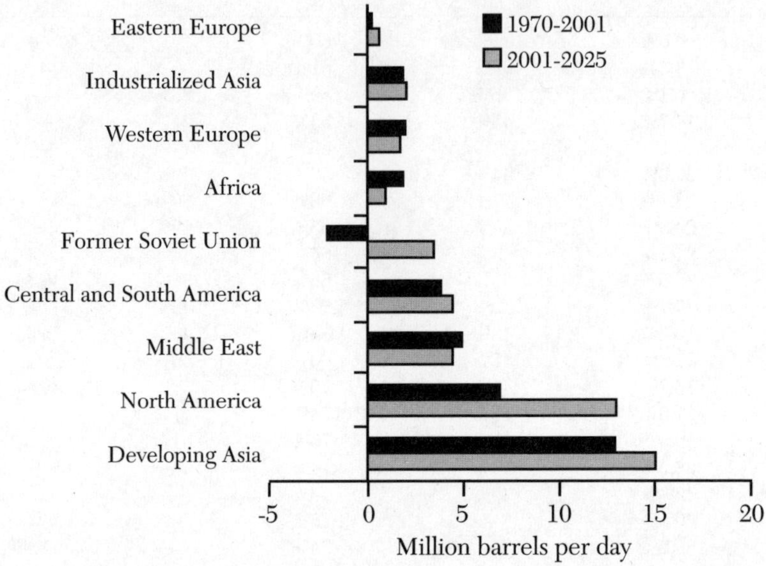

Source: Adapted from Energy Information Administration, *International Energy Outlook 2003.*

1970s."[24] It is increasingly important to study global energy holistically, and in doing so, to take an interdisciplinary approach based on a combination of market analyses, security studies, political economy, and area studies.

TEN KEY LONGER-TERM DEVELOPMENTS

Instead of reporting from the trenches, this book sets out to offer a panoramic view of ten longer-term developments, each meaningful in its own right and, more important, with respect to oil stability. These developments largely did not exist in 1973, when the Arab oil embargo threw the U.S. and global economies into recession by quadrupling oil prices. Nor did they exist to any great degree in 1979, when the Iranian Revolution generated great instability in the Gulf region and reduced Iran's crude exports to a trickle, or on September 22, 1980, when Iraq's invasion of Iran produced a sudden loss of 3.5 mb/d, or 15 percent of OPEC output. They were also insignificant in the early 1980s, when oil prices once again contributed to recession.

[24] Edward L. Morse, "A New Political Economy of Oil?" *Journal of International Affairs* 53 (Fall 1999), 15.

TABLE 3.
Global oil supply disruptions since 1951

Disruption°	Duration°°	Average gross supply shortfall+	Reason for disruption
3/51–10/54	44	0.7	Iran nationalizes oil fields
11/56–3/57	4	2.0	Suez War
6/67–8/67	2	2.0	Six Day War
5/70–1/71	9	1.3	Libyan price controversy
4/71–8/71	5	0.6	Algerian-French nationalization struggle
3/73–5/73	2	0.5	Lebanon unrest
10/73–3/74	6	2.6	1973 War/Arab oil embargo
4/76–5/76	2	0.3	Lebanon civil war/ Iraq exports disrupted
5/77	1	0.7	Damage to Saudi oil field
11/78–4/79	6	3.5	Iranian Revolution
10/80–12/80	3	3.3	Iran-Iraq War erupts
8/90–10/90	3	4.6	Iraq invades Kuwait
4/99–3/00	12	3.3	OPEC (excl. Iraq) cuts production to raise prices
1/02–1/03	12	3.5	Venezuelan and Nigerian crises
3/03–3/-	—	2.6	Iraq War

Source: Adapted from various EIA/DOE analyses, Interagency
Database and Projections Working Group. Author's estimates.
° Net oil supply
°° Months of net supply disruption
+ Millions of barrels per day

By the time of Iraq's invasion of Kuwait on August 2, 1990, they were strong enough to play a role, and they were outright vital in the Iraq War. I sketch these developments in the following ten sections.

Changes in Saudi Stability

Saudi stability has been widely questioned,[25] but a longer-run view reveals that, on the whole, it has neither increased nor decreased. In 1979, external threats to Saudi Arabia were far more significant. Not only was the general tenor of Middle East politics more radical, but Iran and Iraq had also not

[25] See note 9 of this chapter.

yet weakened politically, ideologically, and militarily as a result of their eight years of war that dominated the 1980s. Thus, both states had the ability and will to influence Saudi stability. The Saudis, moreover, faced major internal threats that were stoked in part by revolutionary Iran, but also by internal politics and repression. Over time, internal threats did increase, leaving Saudi Arabia less stable internally. The net result, taking into consideration external and internal threats, has been no major change in the level of stability from 1979 to 2003.

The Move toward Tripolarity in the Region

While Saudi Arabia has faced profound economic and political challenges, its capabilities at the interstate level have clearly increased. In fact, the power structure of the entire Gulf region shifted significantly well before Saddam's regime was eliminated in 2003. Power became more diffuse. In the past, Iran and Iraq were the two strongest states, but over time they weakened and Saudi Arabia became relatively more powerful, transforming our conceptions of the region as bipolar.[26] This fostered regional stability and, indirectly, oil stability, because the Saudis, despite their controversial station in relation to September 11, have been a key to stability, while Iran and Iraq have played a more disruptive role. The Iraq War of 2003 reinforced this trend, because not only were Iraq's capabilities further reduced but the nation also underwent something akin to a foreign policy lobotomy. Iraq will be far less aggressive toward the region than it was under Saddam, at least for the foreseeable future.

The Rise of American Power

If power has become more diffuse among regional states, it has become more concentrated at the global level. Since the end of the Cold War, the United States has emerged as the sole superpower in world affairs, and over the past two decades its commitment to and capability for protecting Middle East oil supplies has risen strikingly. Interestingly, the two most significant oil shocks of the past several decades—in 1973 and 1979—coincided with a weak U.S. position in the region.

A Global-Regional Military and Political Infrastructure

While the improvement in U.S. capabilities from 1979 to 2003 is quite dramatic overall, what I term a global-regional infrastructure has also evolved.

[26] On such conceptions, see Charles F. Doran and Stephen W. Buck, eds., *The Gulf, Energy, and Global Security: Political and Economic Issues* (Boulder, CO: Lynne Rienner, 1991), 4.

This infrastructure of strategic, political, and economic relations was much more limited in 1979 but developed in the 1980s and 1990s, partly because the states in the region increasingly realized that there are no serious military alternatives to the United States. The United States used the military dimension of the infrastructure to reverse Iraq's invasion of Kuwait in 1991 and to deal with the challenges of post-Saddam Iraq, and may utilize it in the future. Economically, Saudi Arabia and Kuwait also understand that they cannot sustain single-commodity economies forever, because the oil will eventually run out. Thus, they have been interested in diversifying their economic base, and the United States has become more important to that task and to the goal of incorporating their economies into the globalizing world economy.

Of course, such an infrastructure does not preclude serious disagreement and even disruptions in bilateral relations, as well as profound anti-Americanism in the Arab Street. September 11 certainly generated some serious cracks in this infrastructure in the case of Saudi Arabia. However, while the impact of 9/11 has been quite serious, U.S.-Saudi relations firmed up in the twenty years before 9/11 and their mutual interests provide enough ballast to at least diminish the negative effects of 9/11. And even if these relations weaken, improved U.S. ties to other Gulf states such as Kuwait, Qatar, Bahrain, and Oman offer the West stabilizing alternatives to Riyadh for regional cooperation. Overall, this infrastructure has developed slowly, benefited regional stability, and helped moderate the oil policies of key oil producers.

Asymmetries in Rising Global Interdependence

At the global level, important developments tie into the story of oil stability. For the first time in many decades, the Gulf region is largely free of intense global rivalry. Moscow has profoundly altered its role in the Gulf, as well as its interactions with the rest of the world. This has clearly worked to the advantage of oil stability.

By looking at snapshots of interaction over time, we can also see that cooperation among outside states in dealing with major threats to oil stability has largely increased from 1979 to 2003. One key explanation is that Russia increasingly has needed the United States; in technical terms, Russia has suffered asymmetrical interdependence in the post–Cold War world.[27]

---

[27] The classic formulation underlying the concept of asymmetrical interdependence is in Albert O. Hirschman, *National Power and the Structure of Foreign Trade* (Berkeley: University of California Press, 1945). For a modern formulation, see Robert O. Keohane and Joseph S. Nye, *Power and Interdependence*, 3rd ed. (New York: HarperCollins, 2001), 11–19. Also, on the salutary effects of interdependence, especially when at play with international organizations and democracy, see Bruce Russett and John Oneal, *Triangulating Peace: Democracy, Interdependence, and International Organizations* (New York: W. W. Norton, 2001).

Before the collapse of the USSR, Moscow needed Washington far less for trade, economic support, high-technology transfers, and assistance in dealing with international institutions such as the International Monetary Fund (IMF), the World Bank, and the World Trade Organization (WTO).

The China Factor

Like Russia, and perhaps even more significantly, Beijing faces asymmetries of interdependence with the United States—a tectonic development of the past two decades. China is abundantly aware of its increasing dependence on the United States and on Gulf oil, both of which make it more inclined to help ensure oil stability and yield Washington some leverage as the security guarantor of the region. These developments are unlikely to reverse themselves and, for the foreseeable future, will make China more likely to take actions that benefit oil stability.

The Oil Weapon

So far we have explored how developments outside oil markets affect oil stability, but it is affected by much more than global and Middle East events. One special threat to oil stability is the use of the oil weapon in unilateral or collective embargoes. Several key developments have, however, made embargoes less likely and will continue to do so in the foreseeable future. Oil producers have learned that it does not pay to use the oil weapon for political reasons, and they have been shorn slowly of leaders that would spearhead such an effort. Furthermore, the Arab-Israeli conflict, which has driven Arab states to use the oil weapon in the past, remains problematic but for several reasons has become much less likely to trigger use of the oil weapon.

The Rise of Oil Supply Cushions

While the potential for the use of the oil weapon has decreased, the ability to deal with oil crises has increased. The global economy has been able to count more and more on sources of oil that can be put on the market to contain the negative effects of a disruption in supply caused by political and security events. These sources of oil can buy time for leaders to deal with supply disruptions and, thus, to mitigate their negative effects.

Oil Market Dynamics

The oil weapon is a dramatic and rare threat to oil stability, but the oil policies and strategies of oil-producing states can also threaten oil stability. OPEC has become increasingly constrained by factors ranging from the rise of non-OPEC oil and oil industry privatization to the status of post-Saddam Iraq to the reality of global interdependence. Such factors have not undermined OPEC cooperation but they have placed some limits on OPEC's ability to coordinate policy, increased competition for market share, and placed a loose ceiling on how far OPEC can cut the supply of oil to raise oil prices. Global economic interdependence, moreover, has increased the extent to which an oil crisis negatively affects OPEC as much as it does its customers. High prices can trigger economic recession, damage the interdependent global economy, and lower the demand for oil.

Oil, Technology, and the Environment

Finally, new technologies and environmental pressures to reduce dangerous fossil fuel emissions create some potential for stemming the urgency over the supply of oil at any particular time, or over time. These pressures are important because they now affect the exploration for and production and delivery of oil, as well as the short- and longer-run strategies of oil-producing states.

COMPLEX STABILITY AMID SEEMING CHAOS

The story of increasing oil stability is a tale spanning over two decades, a tale that shows how elements of stability can coexist with chaos—and sometimes even neutralize it. Predictions about world politics are often unwise, but the notion that longer-run developments can buttress stability in an environment that is so often referred to as tension-bound, unpredictable, chaotic, anarchic, and Hobbesian, deserves our attention.

Of course, the idea that order can exist amid seeming chaos is hardly an epiphany. It has echoed on the fringes of academia for decades, with each generation dressing it up in its own particular garb.[28] In this book I sift through a combination of surface chaos, real political debris, and ever-present threats; we will see a synergy of factors at play that on balance favors stability.

Indeed, a central theme of this book revolves around what I term "complex stability." It provides some insight into how stability can arise. Complex stability means simply that longer-run developments that create stability reinforce and augment each other. And if one of them falters, weakens, or reverses, the others can still play stabilizing roles. In this sense, oil stability

---

[28] On modern chaos theory, which is more suitable to the sciences than to the caprices of world affairs, see John L. Casti, *Would-be Worlds* (New York: John Wiley, 1997); Roger Lewin, *Complexity: Life at the Edge of Chaos* (New York: Macmillan, 1992); and James Gleick, *Chaos: Making a New Science* (New York: Viking, 1987).

is "complex" and hard to break down, and what really matters for understanding stability is the bigger picture rather than any specific area within it.

On that score, at least some observers might argue that the rise of American power has been enough to bolster oil stability, that Washington can control Middle East politics and the levers of global oil markets. However, while the American factor is a crucial development in the story of oil stability, it is not sufficient to explain that stability.[29]

Contrary to some conspiratorial notions, the United States is not a political impresario invested with vast powers to conduct world affairs. A number of threats to oil stability cannot be addressed easily, if at all, by the United States. U.S. power and presence itself often exacerbates problems, including local and global resentment and potential efforts to challenge and undermine Washington. Balance of power theorists, for instance, would predict that hegemony will provoke counterbalancing efforts by others who abhor, and are imperiled by, the concentration of power in one state.[30]

While the U.S. role is important in its own right, the multiple longer-run developments sketched in this introduction work together in order to bolster stability. Thus, for instance, I would argue that American power, when combined with asymmetrical interdependence, produces more stability than the rise of American power alone, partly because such asymmetries make others less likely to balance against the United States and to seek to undermine it.[31]

---

[29] This lends support to hegemonic stability theory inasmuch as the United States is a hegemon that provides for the public good of world oil supply. In simple terms, this theory postulates that stability is more likely when one state is preponderant, rather than when the distribution of power is bipolar or multipolar. On various international public goods and the challenges of protecting them, see Inge Kaul, Isabelle Grunberg, and Marc A. Stern, eds., *Global Public Goods: International Cooperation in the 21st Century* (New York: Oxford University Press, 1000). Unfortunately, the debate about American hegemony deals chiefly with the international distribution of power and largely ignores issue areas and regions of the world.

[30] John Ikenberry, ed., *America Unrivaled: The Future of the Balance of Power* (Ithaca: Cornell University Press, 2002), introduction. For a good review of works that doubt the stability of unipolarity, see Barry R. Posen and Andrew L. Ross, "Competing Visions for U.S. Grand Strategy," *International Security* 21 (Winter 1996/97), 5–54.

[31] Scholars have focused much attention on explaining why, contrary to the predictions of balance of power theory, most states have not balanced against the United States in the post–Cold War period. See Ikenberry, ed., *America Unrivaled* and Ethan B. Kapstein and Michael Mastanduno, eds., *Unipolar Politics: Realism and State Strategies after the Cold War* (New York: Columbia University Press, 1999). But there has not been much investigation into the role of asymmetries in interdependence in diminishing balancing. Future work may consider theoretically that hegemony and interdependence offer much more explanatory power when considered together than can either alone. It may be that being the strongest actor in an arena will likely stabilize it when other key actors depend on that actor, but will likely destabilize it when they do not. This is because they will be reluctant to balance against an actor on whom they are dependent.

THE BROADER ENERGY MARKET: OIL, GAS, AND NATURAL GAS

While this book focuses on the oil dimension of global energy, it is worthwhile distinguishing among oil, gas, and natural gas.

Oil is a central fossil fuel because it can be converted into gasoline, which is needed to run automobiles. Seventy-five percent of global oil is used in the transportation sector, which means that efforts to decrease global oil dependence must focus on this sector. Over the past several decades, oil has been the world's primary source of energy, and that is not projected to change anytime soon. Its share of world energy was 39 percent in 2001 and, in the latest prediction by the U.S. Department of Energy, is expected to be 38 percent in 2025.[32]

Gasoline prices, however, are not simply a function of global oil prices. Sometimes people wonder why gasoline prices can remain high even when oil prices drop. Gasoline prices are affected by certain factors that are unrelated to the supply of oil. These factors include the refinery capacity in any country, existing gasoline stocks, the price of oil delivery, potential price gauging at local gas stations, and the time required to deliver oil. From the Middle East, it takes approximately one to two months for oil to arrive to the United States. It takes only about one week from Venezuela and even less from Mexico. Thus, even if OPEC increases supply and oil prices drop, part of the effect on price will likely be immediate because the market adjusts for future changes in supply and demand, but other parts will be delayed until actual oil is converted into gasoline and hits the market.

Natural gas is used chiefly to run power plants, to heat homes, and to make chemicals. It is viewed as a clean-burning and environmentally friendly source of electric power.

Natural gas and oil are affected by different factors and exist in different markets. Federal Reserve Chairman Alan Greenspan illustrated this point adroitly in testimony in front of the Congressional House Energy and Commerce Committee on June 10, 2003. He predicted that tight natural gas supplies and high prices will persist into 2004 and possibly beyond because the U.S. natural gas market is unable to draw on world supplies easily to meet surges in demand. While the oil market has become global, with the same price prevailing across regions, the natural gas market is still affected largely by local factors. These include the cost of production, which has increased as new discoveries have become harder to make, and the level of natural gas stocks in local storage, which, for the United States, was 28 percent lower in 2002 than the five-year average. They also include the capacity of import terminals and storage facilities, which are particularly important because

[32] *International Energy Outlook 2003.*

natural gas, while cleaner than either oil or coal, is harder to transport, handle, and store.[33] At present, the United States cannot process and manage the level of global natural gas supplies needed to meet local demand, thus splitting off the U.S. market from the market for natural gas worldwide. To add to the challenge, the United States produces about 3 percent of the world's natural gas but accounts for 25 percent of worldwide consumption.

Finally, these factors include the limited but improving commercial and technical prospects for using liquefied natural gas. It is easier to deliver and to store than its non-liquefied counterpart, and if developed in a cost-efficient manner, it could begin to transform natural gas into a global market, and help ameliorate localized problems.[34] Other important factors include the nature of local laws and regulatory barriers to exploration and development, and weather conditions—unusually hot summers and cold winters both decrease stocks.

THE ORGANIZATION OF THE BOOK

The organization of this book is straightforward. Chapters 2 through 11 develop the central argument by laying out the ten longer-term developments sketched here. Chapter 2 explores threats to Saudi stability. It shows how these challenges could prove troublesome in the future, but balances that analysis with a much-needed longer-run corrective.

Chapter 3 shows how power shifts have redounded to the benefit of regional stability and, in turn, of oil stability, while chapter 4 demonstrates how the United States has emerged as a key player in protecting oil stability, and discusses what this means. Chapter 5 lays out how a global-regional infrastructure has developed over time, and shows that this provides yet another piece of the puzzle of oil stability.

Chapters 6 and 7 are based on the notion that in an interdependent world, we cannot understand questions of oil stability without considering global currents. Chapter 6 underscores the impact of the fall of the Soviet Union on the region, and both chapters 6 and 7 explore changes in Russo- and Sino-American relations over the past two decades, showing how they are related to oil stability.

Chapters 8 through 11, rather than exploring regional stability or global political factors, focus on longer-run developments that have affected oil markets and the actors involved in them. These include OPEC, the rise of non-OPEC producers, privatization in the oil industry, and post-Saddam Iraq.

[33] Jerome B. Davis, *Blue Gold: The Political Economy of Natural Gas* (London: George Allen and Unwin, 1984).
[34] James T. Jensen, "The LNG Revolution," *Energy Journal* 34 (2003), 1–45.

Chapter 12 concludes the book by identifying existing and potential threats to oil stability as we head into the twenty-first century. While the body of the book illuminates how the ten key developments outlined in this introduction independently help to deter and contain some of these threats, chapter 12 shows how they work together to do so. It aims for integration in order to highlight the evolution of oil stability as a result of interacting and complementary developments.

Chapter 2

THREATS TO SAUDI STABILITY

In the broad scope of time, world interest in the fate of Saudi Arabia is certainly a sign of change. The modern state of Saudi Arabia was founded in 1932 by Abd Al-Aziz Al-Saud (also referred to as Ibn Saud). Massive oil resources have allowed the country to create a developed infrastructure, economy, and military, although its wealth has come with a price.[1]

Whatever one thinks of the House of Saud, Saudi Arabia is important to the story of the evolution of oil stability.[2] It is the only state with the proven oil reserves—one-quarter of the world's total—the potential to produce consistently above its market production, and the field production and pipeline capacity to add significant amounts of oil to the world market. Saudi spare capacity alone, which it keeps in reserve, would be large enough to replace the lost production of another major oil-exporting state. This yields Riyadh enormous power in times of crisis or high global demand, when the world counts on Saudi Arabia's ability to put oil on the market.

Over the past two decades, the global economy has been able to count on increasingly diverse sources of energy outside of Saudi Arabian oil. But while that is important for oil stability, few events would more greatly affect the world economy than the fall of the Saudi royal family to extremists, who would make the current ruling family look moderate by comparison. Although many human rights activists and other anti-Saudi enthusiasts might hail the fall of the regime which they view as irrevocably corrupt, most leaders around the world would shudder at the thought because the

---

[1] Kiren Aziz Chaudhry, *The Price of Wealth: Economies and Institutions in the Middle East* (Ithaca, NY: Cornell University Press, 1997).

[2] On twentieth-century Saudi history and oil, and for good bibliographic references to this literature, see Nathan J. Citino, *From Arab Nationalism to OPEC* (Bloomington, IN: Indiana University Press, 2002).

potential disruption in oil supplies could undermine their oil-dependent economies.

Even though Saudi Arabia was important well before 9/11, the attacks elevated it like never before to the forefront of global public attention, especially in the United States. This was inevitable once it was revealed that Osama bin Laden was born and raised in Saudi Arabia, as were fifteen of the nineteen hijackers.[3] They were uneasy products of the Saudi cultural, political and religious milieu, one largely shaped, controlled, or tolerated by the Saudi royal family.[4] These realities made it easy to conclude that the profound anti-Americanism of the attackers had deep roots in a state that the United States considered an ally and on which the world counted for oil stability. Americans, along with many others around the world, were shocked that these individuals could work quietly and assiduously inside America as part of its society in order to prepare for an unparalleled act of collective murder on American soil.

September 11, however, was more than a grotesque shock. It raised profound questions that were linked to the broader issue of oil stability: If the terrorists were also reactionaries against the Saudi regime, and if they had widespread sympathy and possibly support from within Saudi Arabia, then how stable could the regime be? Was Saudi Arabia a wobbly anchor of global oil stability?

As noted in the introduction, even before September 11, analysts argued that the Saudi regime could, or even was likely to, fall eventually. After 9/11, such concerns were raised anew with added vigor, partly because 9/11 put a much needed spotlight on how the Saudi domestic context helped breed terrorism and on the corrupt and repressive policies of the state.[5] Indeed, while some scholars have tried to explain why regimes have been stable in the Gulf, it became more common among scholars and analysts to predict trouble for the House of Saud.[6] One scholar, representing broader views, even described Saudi Arabia's current phase as a "pre-revolutionary mode,"

3 On Bin Laden's views, see Yossef Bodansky, *Bin Laden: The Man Who Declared War on America* (New York: Random House, 2001). On how the Saudi context helped shape his views, see Mamoun Fandy, *Saudi Arabia and the Politics of Dissent* (New York: St. Martin's, 1999), chap. 6.

4 For a lucid analysis, see F. Gregory Gause III, *Oil Monarchies: Domestic and Security Challenges in the Arab Gulf States* (New York: Council on Foreign Relations, 1994), 94–98. Also Joseph A. Kechichian, *Succession in Saudi Arabia* (New York: Palgrave, 2001), chap. 3; Ayman Al-Yassini, *Religion and State in the Kingdom of Saudi Arabia* (Boulder, CO: Westview, 1985), 70–76.

5 See *APS Diplomatic Operations in Oil Diplomacy* 43 (28 January 2002) and John E. Peterson, *Saudi Arabia and the Illusion of Security* (London: Oxford University Press for the International Institute for Strategic Studies, 2002).

6 Jill Crystal, *Oil and Politics in the Gulf: Rulers and Merchants in Kuwait and Qatar* (New York: Cambridge University Press, 1995), 75–78. Lisa Andersen coined the term "resilience" for use in this context.

while others wondered if the regime would suffer the same fate as the Shah of Iran.[7] Threats to the regime are certainly important to understand, but over the longer view external threats to the regime's stability have decreased, while internal threats have in some ways increased. This results in little net change in the overall level of stability from 1979 to 2003.

THE DECREASE IN EXTERNAL THREATS TO SAUDI ARABIA

The Persian Gulf has not become *Mr. Roger's Neighborhood*, but it was far more dangerous to the Saudis in 1979 than it would be in 1991 or 2003. Indeed, in 1979, a plethora of threats raised questions about whether Saudi Arabia might be invaded, surrounded, subverted, or constrained. Clearly, such a state of affairs indicated potential problems with oil stability.

The Iranian Revolution of 1978–79 increased the level of external threat to Saudi Arabia. The Saudis were already concerned about Tehran's increasing military strength and regional ambition prior to the revolution. However, they still shared an interest in preserving the status quo, despite Iran's increased pressure for higher oil prices. So the two states engaged in a good deal of tacit cooperation.[8] The revolution did not initially lead to tensions between Iran and Saudi Arabia. Although some extremists in Iran's government entertained a more ambitious foreign policy vis-à-vis the Arab Gulf states, Iran's overall threat was confined as long as the Gulf states appeared not to challenge the fundamental bases of the revolution. Indeed, Tehran sought to maintain relations with Arab states.[9] However, the underlying incompatibility of Iran's foreign policy with the policies of the more moderate Arab Gulf states eventually manifested itself.

The revolution put Saudi-Iranian relations on a path toward heightened tensions, and, in the 1980s, open conflict. Saudi legitimacy rested on the regime's role as the guardian of the two most holy sites of Islam, namely

[7] Quoted in Heidi Kingstone, "Trouble in the House of Saud," *Jerusalem Report* (13 January 2003). For a discussion of speculation on the potential demise of the Saudi regime, see Nawaf E. Obaid, "In Al-Saud We Trust: How the Regime in Riyadh Avoids the Mistakes of the Shah," *Foreign Policy* 128 (January/February 2002); Eric Rouleau, "Trouble in the Kingdom," *Foreign Affairs* 81 (July/August 2002); and Robert Baer, *Sleeping with the Devil* (New York: Crown, 2003).

[8] For a good discussion of the twin pillars, see Richard Haass, "Saudi Arabia and Iran: The Twin Pillars in Revolutionary Times," in *The Security of the Persian Gulf*, ed. Hossein Amirsadeghi (New York: St. Martin's Press, 1981), chap. 8. See also James A. Bill, *The Eagle and the Lion: The Tragedy of American-Iranian Relations* (New Haven: Yale University Press, 1988), esp. 200–204.

[9] See *Middle East Economic Survey* (MEES) 22 (6 August 1979), 3. Iran praised the Gulf states for rejecting the Omani plan, which called for increased cooperation with Washington. See "AL-RAY'Y AL-'AMM," in *Joint Publications Research Service: Near East and North Africa*, 23 September 1979, 23.

Mecca, the birthplace of Islam, and Medina, where the prophet Muhammad launched his mission in Allah's service. Unlike Pahlevi Iran, revolutionary Iran challenged Riyadh's claim as the champion of Islam by offering an alternative Islamic model that rejected the monarchical Islamic state and offered a theocratic one in its place. The clash between these two approaches to Islamic governance and between Sunni Saudi Arabia and Shia Iran, caused great friction in Saudi-Iranian relations, which were dramatized by the Iran-Iraq War and erupted in earnest in July 1987 when, during the annual pilgrimage to Mecca, Saudi security forces clashed seriously with disruptive Iranian pilgrims, believed to be inspired by Iran's regime.

Moreover, the revolution produced effects that undermined Iran's relations with Iraq, relations that previously had been relatively stable. In 1975, the two states signed the Algiers accord, in which Tehran pledged to curtail its support of Kurds in Iraq in return for concessions on the border along the disputed Shatt al-Arab waterway. Iraq renounced the agreement on October 30, 1979. On September 20, 1980, Iraq attacked Iran—partly, we can surmise, because it feared the revolution and partly because Saddam saw an opportunity to strike at Iran while it was in revolutionary chaos. Indeed, Saudi King Fahd claimed that prior to Iraq's attack on Iran in 1980, Saddam told him that "it is more useful to hit them [the Iranians] now because they are weak. If we leave them until they become strong, they will overrun us."[10]

Furthermore, the fall of the Shah created an opening for Saddam to assume the mantle of Gulf and Arab world leadership. Iraq's influence over Saudi Arabia increased from 1978 to late 1979, partly because of Baghdad's growing influence in general, but also because Iran's threat to Saudi Arabia made Iraq more vital to Riyadh.[11] This further limited Saudi action. Though the Saudis feared Iraq less than they did Iran under its supreme leader the Ayatollah Khomeini, Iraq was still viewed as a military and political threat. The Saudis were clearly subordinate in bilateral relations with Iraq and saw themselves as subject to the balance of forces between Iran and Iraq.[12] Baghdad was feared by other Arab states, including Kuwait, Saudi Arabia, and even Oman, which felt it necessary to mollify Iraq after allowing the U.S. access rights.[13] And most Gulf states quickly accepted Iraq's February 1980 Pan-Arab Charter, which among other things embodied Saddam's regional ambitions and called for a "new Arab order," as Iraq's Foreign Minister Tariq

---

10 See text of interview with King Fahd, in London *AL-HAWADITH*, FBIS:NES, 14 February 1992, 21.

11 See *Middle East Contemporary Survey (MECS)* 3 (1978–79), 236.

12 See Jacob Goldberg, "Saudi Arabia: The Bank Vault Next Door," in *Iraq's Road to War*, ed. Amatzia Baram and Barry M. Rubin (New York: St. Martin's, 1993), 130–31.

13 Ibid. See also Hermann Eilts, "Security Considerations in the Persian Gulf," *International Security* 5 (Fall 1980), 102.

Aziz would later describe it in September 1990, during the Gulf crisis.[14] In part, this charter called for the rejection of any foreign military presence in the Gulf and represented an effort to decrease or even eliminate U.S. regional influence. Iraq's growing status in the Arab world was enhanced by its success in tapping Arab disaffection with the 1979 Egyptian-Israeli peace treaty. Perceptions differed in the Arab world on the treaty, but many saw President Anwar Sadat's peace with Israel as selling out the Arab cause, breaking with Arab multilateral pressure on Israel, and appeasing the Americans and Zionists. As a sign of Iraq's power, the two emergency Arab summits aimed at dealing with Egypt's break with the Arab world were held in Baghdad.[15]

While the Iranian Revolution was generating turmoil chiefly in the Middle East, dynamics were also changing at the global level, which in turn affected Middle East politics. In 1978–79, the USSR substantially enhanced its influence in South Yemen and Ethiopia, which the Saudis interpreted as a long-term communist design to encircle their country.[16] The Saudis and Omanis even feared military action by the Ethiopians, directed by Moscow and aimed at controlling the strategically vital Strait of Bab el-Mandeb, which lies at the mouth of the Red Sea and sees major oil tanker traffic.

The Soviet invasion of Afghanistan in December 1979 further elevated these fears and laid the basis for an occupation that lasted nearly a decade. Moscow might well have invaded and occupied Afghanistan only to ensure the stability and pro-Soviet orientation of the Marxist Afghan government that it had propped up with a coup in 1978. But Soviet troops did come about 320 miles closer to the Gulf, placing them on Pakistan's doorstep. This generated fear that Moscow's ambitions stretched beyond Afghanistan. The perception of Soviet political and military gains in Angola, Ethiopia, South Yemen, and Afghanistan, coupled with Washington's loss of Iran as an ally, damaged U.S. credibility.[17] Analysts feared an increase in Soviet influence; a Soviet military invasion of the region; the spread of Islamic fundamentalism; the ascendance of Iran or Iraq to regional hegemony; an alignment of anti-American radical forces around Syria, Libya, and Iraq; and the weakening or collapse of the generally pro-American Saudi regime.[18]

14   Aziz interview in *London Al-Tadamun*, in FBIS: NES, 26 September 1990, 31.

15   David W. Lesch, *1979: The Year that Shaped the Modern Middle East* (Boulder, CO: Westview Press, 2001), 82–94.

16   For a good, brief discussion of Saudi weakness during this period, see *MECS* 4 (1979–80), 736–37. On Oman's perceptions, see *Salalah Domestic Service*, in FBIS: Middle East and Africa (MEA), 27 August 1981, C1.

17   Interview with Prince Bandar. See *Kuwait AR-RAY AL-AMM*, 9 January 1979, in FBIS: Middle East and Africa (MEA), 12 January 1979, C1. See also *MECS* 3 (1978–79), 22. Even the Shah blamed Washington for his demise. Gary Sick, *All Fall Down: America's Tragic Encounter with Iran* (Boulder, CO: Westview Press, 1985), 179. On America's loss of credibility, see *MECS* 3 (1978–79), 751. and *Middle East Economic Digest* (hereafter *MEED*) (9 March 1979), 13.

18   Ibid.

The Saudis were disappointed and unnerved enough by the loss of Iran and the weakened American position that they reportedly floated the idea of re-establishing diplomatic relations with Moscow.[19] Although some members of the Saudi family, among them Defense Minister Prince Sultan, continued to praise relations with the United States, they were strained by a Saudi loss of confidence in the United States and by U.S. doubts about Saudi stability in 1979, following domestic challenges to Saudi rule.[20] Moreover, when Riyadh called on U.S. military support in 1979 to signal post-revolutionary Iran of Washington's commitment to its security, the U.S. response was curiously divided. The United States flew high-performance aircraft to the Gulf in an apparent show of force—and then surprisingly announced while the planes were in en route that they were unarmed, evidently so as not to offend the new Iranian government of Shahpour Bakhtiar, which it hoped to court.[21] That further increased doubts about U.S. resolve, making the Saudis concerned about "casting their lot" with the United States.[22] It may have also contributed to the Saudi decision later in 1979 to reduce oil production in hopes of making inroads with Iran under Bakhtiar's replacement, the Ayatollah Khomeini, against the wishes of the United States.[23]

Saudi Arabia was also confronted with the rise in influence of the Arab rejectionist front, which was composed of hard-line Arab states such as Syria and Libya. They took a strong anti-American position in line with Moscow, rejected any accommodation with Israel in favor of open hostility, advanced a spirited form of pan-Arabism, undermined U.S. relations with key Arab states, and sought to remove the United States as a serious player in Middle East politics.[24]

EXTERNAL THREATS OVER TIME: A REVERSAL

External threats to Saudi Arabia were significant in 1979 and in the 1980s, but they decreased over time. The Afghanistan intervention lasted for about a decade and undermined Moscow's policy in the Gulf, where it was viewed

19 Jacob Goldberg in *The U.S.S.R. and the Muslim World*, ed. Yaacov Ro'i (London: Allen and Unwin, 1984), 264–68. Igor Belayev, the Soviet author of this controversial article, further confirmed this point in a discussion with the author.
20 *Riyadh SNA*, in FBIS: MENA, 30 May 1979, C2. On Riyadh's lack of confidence in America, see *MEED* (9 March 1979), 13.
21 Interview with Prince Bandar.
22 Interview with former National Security Adviser Brent Scowcroft in *Road to War: American Decision Making during the Gulf Crisis* (Films for the Humanities and Sciences, Part I of II).
23 Parker T. Hart, *Saudi Arabia and the United States: Birth of a Security Relationship* (Bloomington, IN: Indiana University Press, 1998), 300–303.
24 Nadav Safran, *Saudi Arabia: The Ceaseless Quest for Security* (Cambridge, MA: Harvard University Press, 1985), 238–39.

as anti-Muslim, colonial, and threatening, and it also absorbed the USSR's human and material resources. The clear result was that it hurt Moscow's relations with Iran and Saudi Arabia, both of which strongly supported the Afghan rebels, and it decreased Moscow's ability to pressure the Saudis, either directly or through its position in Ethiopia and South Yemen. The aggressive position of the USSR also had the effect of bringing Riyadh and Washington closer together.[25]

For its part, the Iran-Iraq War produced a military imbalance of power between Iraq and Iran, but the 1991 Gulf War and its aftermath largely eliminated Iraq as a major external threat to Saudi Arabia. Washington subsequently kept Iraq in a tight military box of containment and eliminated Saddam's regime in 2003.

Over the longer term, Tehran's threat to Saudi Arabia also decreased. Saudi Arabia and many states outside the Gulf feared an Iranian victory in the war, particularly after its significant success in early 1986 at the strategic Faw Peninsula. But victory proved elusive, as Iran and Iraq fell back into a military stalemate that further absorbed their energies, which otherwise could have been focused on gaining power over Saudi Arabia and the rest of the region. Even though the Iran-Iraq War devastated Iran economically and gave it much reason to assume a more conciliatory short-run stance toward its neighbors and the West, the Iraqi invasion of Kuwait gave Iran's neighbors and the West more reason to value Iran's regional role. The invasion made very clear to the Saudis the importance of Iran's potential balancing role against Iraq. It also gave Iran the opportunity to shore up its relations with Arab Gulf states and to make the case that the real threat to the Gulf had always come from Iraq.

After the Gulf War, Iran continued to claim that the U.S. role of "domination and intervention" was the "main source" of instability in the region.[26] However, there emerged a more pragmatic tone as well. Iran called for increased economic and political cooperation with the West, perhaps recognizing the undisputed rise of the United States in the region and world, and closer ties to Arab Gulf states.[27] Together with the waning Iranian Revolution, this suggested that Iran could be in a position to play a more constructive regional role.

---

25 For extensive analysis, see Steve A. Yetiv, "How the Soviet Intervention in Afghanistan Improved the U.S. Strategic Position in the Persian Gulf," *Asian Affairs: An American Review* 17 (Fall 1990).

26 See Mohammad Javad Larijani, "Iran's Foreign Policy Principles and Objectives," *Iranian Journal of International Affairs* (Winter 1996), 754–63.

27 On Iran's views of U.S. pre-eminence, see Akbar Mahdi, "Islam, the Middle East, and the New World Order," in *Islam, Iran, and World Stability*, ed. Hamid Zangeneh (New York: St. Martin's, 1994). On the closer ties to Arab Gulf states, see FBIS: NES, December 23, 1991, 5–6 and *Tehran IRNA*, FBIS: NES, 2 June 1992, 49.

Iran's revolution has continued to moderate in the twenty-first century. The clerical regime has increasingly been viewed as, if not an outright anachronism, at best out of touch with the majority of Iranians who seek greater freedoms and economic opportunities. Pressures for change in Iran are strong enough, as reflected in the elections of moderates to the Majlis (the Iranian parliament) as well as in public demonstrations, that they will not be easily reversed. Even if they are temporarily reversed, it will be hard to contain the energies of a more voluble, active, and youthful opposition to the regime's oppressive policies.[28] Iran is unlikely to be shorn of its religious underpinnings, but that element will likely play a smaller role as time passes. If the trajectory continues toward greater openings at home and more moderation in foreign policy, then Iran may well evolve into a more pro-western state and a potentially more stable partner for ensuring Gulf security. In turn, it may well become more cooperative on issues ranging from the fight against international terrorism to oil policy.

Iran's more moderate foreign policy, especially over the past five years, has allowed for improved Saudi-Iranian relations. Although both states have remained competitive in the region, they have become more interested in cooperation. From 1998 to 2000, Iran was even described as having undertaken a "charm offensive" with Riyadh, a move that was opposed by the hardline clerical ideologues represented by the Ayatollah Ali Khamenei. In December 1997, Crown Prince Abdallah, the heir to the Saudi throne who replaced the ailing King Fahd as the de facto ruler of the country in 1996, traveled to Iran for a meeting of the Organization of the Islamic Conference. By May 1999, Prince Sultan, architect of U.S.-Saudi military relations from the Saudi side, became the first Saudi defense minister to visit Iran in three decades. While he sidestepped Iran's desire for military cooperation between the two countries, a move that Washington opposed, his visit signaled vastly improved relations.[29] These were built, in part, on the need to cooperate on oil pricing in 1999. Saudi-Iranian cooperation helped push depressed oil prices higher, but it also underscored a decreased threat from Iran and a cautious rapprochement that is still thriving as of this writing, in late 2003.[30]

Overall, the record clearly suggests that external threats to Saudi Arabia have diminished greatly since 1979. In the past, Saudi Arabia faced serious

[28] For an interesting account by Manouchehr Ganji, Minister of Education under the Shah of Iran, see *Defying the Iranian Revolution: From a Minister to the Shah to a Leader of Resistance* (Westport, CT: Praeger, 2002).

[29] Nawaf E. Obaid, *The Oil Kingdom at 100: Petroleum Policymaking in Saudi Arabia* (Washington, D.C.: The Washington Institute for Near East Policy, 2000), 13–14, 79–83.

[30] For a good overview of the rapprochement, see Gwenn Okruhlik, "Saudi-Iranian Relations: External Rapprochement And Internal Consolidation," *Middle East Policy* 10 (Summer 2003), 113–25.

and, at times, simultaneous threats from Iran, Iraq, and the U.S.S.R, or from its perceived regional clients. By contrast, by 1991, Iran had moderated its foreign policy, its nuclear aspirations notwithstanding, and Iraq, while still belligerent, was seriously weakened militarily and by 2003 was in the process of being re-engineered as a country. For its part, Moscow remained active politically and, to some extent, economically, but it was largely relegated to the sidelines of the Gulf security landscape for the first time since the 1970s.

A CHANGING DOMESTIC CONTEXT

While external threats to Saudi Arabia have decreased in key ways, internal threats have largely increased. We can divide them into threats that tend to find their roots abroad or at home, though the two are sometimes linked. As I discuss below, internal threats generated from abroad have become less serious since 1979. However, those arising from within Saudi Arabia have become more serious.

Foreign-Inspired Internal Threats

The Iranian Revolution increased the internal threat to Saudi stability from Iran, partly by bedeviling Saudi-Iranian relations. Relations were complex at many levels, but at the core, Saudi Arabia's monarchical form of government, roughly pro-western tilt, and conservative outlook clashed with Iran's post-revolutionary clerical rule, anti-western bent, and revisionist foreign policy. Indeed, the Saudis viewed Khomeini as a heretic with a proclivity for vio-lence.[31] Several notable efforts were made to undermine Saudi authority in 1979. The first was in November 1979 when the Grand Mosque in Mecca was seized by several hundred armed zealots, who launched an Islamic upris-ing to protest the corruption in the royal family. The protests may have been small, but they were important in that they represented the first open attack on the credibility and improper conduct of the royal family since the reign of Ibn Saud in 1927.[32] This prompted predictions that the royal family would fall. With outside assistance, the Saudi National Guard successfully sup-pressed these zealots. But the Al Saud ruling family was concerned enough over the 1979 Mecca crisis to agree to a set of resolutions condemning the United States for its role at Camp David, in the hopes that this would bol-ster its credentials in the Muslim world.[33]

---

31   Al-Yassini, Religion and State in the Kingdom of Saudi Arabia, 123.
32   Madawi Al-Rasheed, A History of Saudi Arabia (Cambridge: Cambridge University Press, 2002), 144.
33   Safran, Saudi Arabia, 358–59.

Eight days after the seizure of the Grand Mosque, while the Saudi National Guard was still battling the zealots at Mecca, disturbances erupted in Saudi Arabia's oil-rich eastern al-Hasa province. They constituted the first political challenge posed by the Shia to the Sunni Saudi regime and were viewed as serious enough by the royal family to prompt the dispatch of 20,000 troops to the area.[34] The Mecca incident in 1979 further cast into doubt Saudi stability as well as its role as a pillar of Gulf security.[35]

Further clashes broke out in September and October 1981 in Medina and Mecca, respectively, between Iranian pilgrims and Saudi police. Iranian officials claimed that these disturbances were indeed an export of the Iranian Revolution, aimed at destabilizing the Saudi regime.[36] Shortly thereafter, in December 1981, Bahraini authorities arrested and subsequently convicted seventy-three individuals for plotting a coup against the regime. Bahrain also stated that the coup was part of a broader strategy to overthrow the House of Saud, and that the coup plotters had direct connections to Tehran.[37] This came as no great surprise, since Khomeini had repeatedly assailed the Gulf monarchies for being illegitimate and corrupt.

Riyadh faced the ongoing potential for Iranian-inspired subversion, but it was not until 1987 that this was manifested in stark relief. The annual pilgrimage to Mecca was disrupted by a riot touched off when Saudi security units moved in to stop a forbidden political demonstration by Iranian pilgrims in front of the Grand Mosque. Despite considerable evidence to the contrary, Iran's President Hashemi Rafsanjani, a close friend of Khomeini's from his early days in exile and later a key adviser, denied that Iran had instigated the subversion.[38] Insisting that the Saudis were to blame, he called on Iranians to act as "implementers of divine principles" and overthrow the Saudi royal family in revenge.[39] This caused alarm across the Gulf and in certain quarters in the West. Iran, which was in competition with Saudi Arabia for leadership of the Islamic world, wanted once again to destabilize Saudi Arabia and challenge its rule over Islam's holy sites.[40]

The Mecca crisis pushed the Saudis to sever relations with Iran and very nearly put the two states in military conflict.[41] Ironically, the crisis helped

34 For a factual record of the Mecca crisis, see *MECS* 4 (1979–80), 682–88.
35 For details on Saudi instability during this period, see *MECS* 3 (1978–79), 358–59, 736–55.
36 See Joseph A. Kechichian, "Trends In Saudi National Security," *Middle East Journal* 53 (Spring 1999), 225.
37 See *Manama WAKH*, FBIS: MEA, 25 February 1982, C-3.
38 Anthony H. Cordesman, *The Gulf and the West: Strategic Relations and Military Realities* (Boulder, CO: Westview Press, 1988), 370–71.
39 Quoted in John Kifner, "Iranian Officials Urge 'Uprooting' of Saudi Royalty," *New York Times*, 3 August 1987, A1.
40 On the link between the Haj and U.S. reflagging, see Shahram Chubin and Charles Tripp, *Iran and Iraq at War* (London: I. B. Tauris, 1988), 175–76.
41 Ibid., 1.

strengthen the Saudi position. It moved some Arab Gulf states closer to Saudi Arabia and away from Iran, further legitimized U.S.-Saudi security cooperation, and pushed the Saudis to appease discontented internal elements such as the Shia. Contrary to common interpretation, many Shia may very well have resented the Iranian actions in Saudi Arabia and remained largely loyal to the regime.[42] These actions help explain why Iran increasingly lost the ability and will to foment instability in Saudi Arabia, but— more important—the Iran-Iraq War contributed to the cessation of Iran's overt efforts to undermine Riyadh internally.

Initially, in Khomeini's view, it was through this war that Iran "consolidated the roots" of its revolution and told "the world about the power of the revolution" and of Iran's "cultural and ideological values in relation to Western values."[43] Be that as it may, Iran's war failures also gave moderate elements in Iran a chance to advance their political agenda. By arousing fear and focusing attention on Iran's revolution, the war made it more difficult for Khomeini to spread Islamic fundamentalism without provoking further alarm. Had Iraq not attacked Iran in 1980, Tehran could have spread Islamic fundamentalism in a non-military and less provocative fashion, keeping the military threat entirely tacit.[44] The war forced Iran to play this hand and to deplete its military arsenal.

By 1987, Iran became more concerned with consolidating and protecting the revolution within its own borders than with exporting its brand of Islam, and the Saudis were clear beneficiaries of that trend.[45] By the late 1980s, Iran's political and economic agenda was dominated by talk about the importance of attracting foreign investment, enhancing foreign trade, and improving relations with the West.[46] These concerns were driven by the imperatives of postwar reconstruction and by Iran's dependence on oil revenues.

THE GULF CRISIS AND THE 1990S: INDIGENOUS THREATS ON THE RISE

The 1991 Gulf War produced countervailing effects on Saudi stability. At one level, it contributed to and helped stimulate movements, both secular and religious, that challenged aspects of Saudi royal family rule. In December

---

[42] David E. Long, "Saudi Arabia in the 1990s: Plus ça Change ... " in *The Gulf*, ed. Doran and Buck, esp. 94–95.

[43] Quoted in Baqer Moin, *Khomeini: Life of the Ayatollah* (New York: St. Martin's Press, 2000), 251, 285.

[44] In Khomeini's view, other Islamic peoples would overturn their own governments. Richard W. Cottam, "Revolutionary Iran and the War with Iraq," *Current History* 80 (January 1981), 9.

[45] Gary Sick, "Iran's Quest for Superpower Status," *Foreign Affairs* 65 (Spring 1987), 714.

[46] Anoushiravan Ehteshami, "The Foreign Policy of Iran," in *The Foreign Policies of Middle East States*, ed. Raymond Hinnebusch and Anoushiravan Ehteshami (Boulder, CO: Lynne-Rienner, 2002), 288–92.

1990, in the midst of the Gulf crisis, King Fahd received a "Secular Petition" from forty-three religious and secular leaders; three months later came a "Religious Petition" from scores of top religious leaders.[47] The ultraconservative religious forces expressed their strong concern over royal family corruption, nepotism, and monopoly control over decision-making. Meanwhile, liberal forces pushed for reforms as well.[48] A limited but increasingly voluble and growing Islamic reform movement developed, which sought more influence over policymaking. New technologies, especially means of communication like the Internet, empowered this movement and allowed it to air grievances with less fear of retribution from the regime.[49]

The regime faced a series of antigovernment demonstrations in 1994, which, if not profoundly serious, were uncommon and pushed the regime to imprison some radical clerics. The peaceful demonstrations at Buraydah were organized by the Committee for the Defense of Legitimate Rights (CDLR) of Saudi Arabia in 1995. They were significant in their defiance of the Fahd regime by highlighting its repressive tactics and fostering further social ferment.[50] The CDLR, which was immediately banned by the regime after its formation in 1993, has sought more influence over policymaking, though it has dressed its tactics in the vestments of reform rather than revolution.[51] Its ranks include some individuals who had historically supported King Fahd and come from his tribal and cultural hinterland. Understandably, it was these people about whom King Faud was most concerned. Some are elder tribal leaders with whom he regularly consorted and whom he needed to handle carefully in order to maintain his legitimacy.[52] Indeed, the term "King" in the Saudi context is misleading because he is not only chosen by the core elites of the country but he also cannot act unilaterally without their consent.

At the same time, however, the House of Saud took measures to appease its critics. It had been under pressure to establish a Consultative Council of commoners appointed by the king in 1962, and promised to do so, but this did not come to pass. It was only after the Gulf War, which had created greater domestic pressures for some semblance of a political opening, that the Consultative Council was finally established.[53] In addition to calling for a Consultative Council, the royal decrees called for adherence to the rule of

---

47 The text of these letters appear in "Empty Reforms: Saudi Arabia's New Basic Laws," *Middle East Watch* (May 1992), 59–62. On the reforms, see Gause, *Oil Monarchies*, 94–98.
48 Al-Rasheed, *A History of Saudi Arabia*, 168–87.
49 Fandy, *Saudi Arabia*.
50 For the CDLR's description of the event, see *London CDLR MONITOR*, in FBIS: NES, 3 April 1995, 25.
51 See Al-Rasheed, *A History of Saudi Arabia*, 176–86.
52 Interview with Prince Bandar.
53 See *MECS* 2 (1976–77), 570.

law. King Fahd linked these measures directly to the Gulf War, describing them as a "kind of partnership between the grassroots and the leadership."[54]

The debate over reforms was not particularly divisive. King Fahd was widely viewed as the legitimate arbiter. But the reforms represented at least modest concessions to Saudi "democratic" forces, some of which were better described as anti-regime than as pro-democratic. At the same time, they were accompanied by increased state control and the use of violence against suspected dissidents, which was quite contrary to the spirit of reform. Nonetheless, these democratic forces had been pushing for reforms prior to the Iranian Revolution, but their efforts gained some momentum only after the Gulf War, which had given them impetus.[55] The royal measures did not accommodate the desire of conservative forces for the strict imposition of Islamic laws, but they did accommodate their demands for some greater participation in decision-making and new regulations to eliminate corruption, among other measures.[56] In this sense, the reforms contributed to Saudi domestic stability by charting a potential path for more meaningful reform and by helping assuage domestic discontent in some quarters.

However, in other Saudi quarters, the reforms were perceived as devoid of content in that they did not "presage any political reform or bring any change to the method of government."[57] It is true that they did not reflect any serious intention on the part of the regime to cede power. Nor did they represent a Saudi embrace of western-style democratic practices. King Fahd stated that the "democratic systems prevailing in the world are systems which in their structure do not suit this region and our people" and that "the system of free election is not part of Islamic ideology."[58]

The regime remained concerned about these new pressures for political change, as reflected by its decision in 1993 to treat the CDLR as an extremist group and in its efforts thereafter to undermine the CDLR's position through a series of security crackdowns and arrests throughout the decade. The attack on the U.S. barracks at the Khobar Towers in Saudi Arabia in 1996 in which nineteen Americans were killed, in some quarters reignited questions about Saudi stability. Furthermore, in April and June 1995 the Movement for Islamic Change sent faxes to the U.S. embassy in Riyadh

54 See text of interview with King Fahd, in London AL-HAWADITH, FBIS: NES, 14 February 1992, 22.

55 On a letter to King Fahd outlining the democratic reforms sought, see Amman AKHIR KHABAR, in FBIS: NES, 29 April 1991, 9.

56 For the text of the royal decrees, see "Empty Reforms." On the reforms, see Madawi Al-Rasheed, "God, the King, and the Nation: Political Rhetoric in Saudi Arabia in the 1990s," Middle East Journal 50 (Summer 1996).

57 See interview with King Fahd, in London AL-Quds AL'-ARABI, in FBIS: NES, 26 March 1992, 9–10.

58 Quoted in MEES 35 (6 April 1992), C3.

demanding the withdrawal of all U.S. forces by midsummer of the same year.[59] Prince Abdallah, widely viewed as a devout and uncorrupted Muslim, was effective in mending bridges with the regime's critics and in projecting a more austere example of royal family rule.[60] He was recognized as less beholden to western-educated technocrats, the business elite, and pro-American princes than he was to conservative tribal chiefs, which further enhanced his credentials with the extreme clerics and similar groups. On the whole, his efforts to mend fences served to decrease opposition to the regime significantly in the late 1990s, though the very presence of such internal pressures meant he would have to be more careful in avoiding perceptions of being too close to Washington.

To be sure, however, in the 1990s, Saudi domestic instability was compounded by unprecedented economic strains.[61] The Gulf War temporarily bankrupted the state, if not its wealthy princes. In the past, the regime had plenty of money to reward its domestic allies and to placate its adversaries or detractors. The inability to maintain the level of services provided to a growing population quite accustomed to the quintessential welfare state contributed to domestic discontent.

Decreasing oil revenues and high defense expenditures further forced the regime to reduce the size of the welfare state in the 1990s, thus making it harder to keep political opponents from causing unrest.[62] For a state whose oil revenues made up approximately 90 to 95 percent of its total export earnings and 35–40 percent of its GDP, falling oil prices took a serious toll. Prince Abdallah emphasized the seriousness of the problem in a 1998 speech in which he warned that the regime might have to cut social services. In most countries, fiscal problems can be addressed through tax increases, but such an action is practically unmentionable in Saudi Arabia, a country where the government is supposed to dole out money rather than collect it; the religious establishment in particular sees taxes as a sacrilege, which will make any such move in the future even more difficult.[63]

In addition to the impact of economic problems on political stability, the regime has had to deal with a growing population that is better educated and more connected to the world—especially to the Arab world. This creates

59 For a good brief on this period, see Anthony H. Cordesman, *Saudi Arabia: Guarding the Desert Kingdom* (Boulder, CO: Westview Press, 1997), 41–43.
60 On the views of such critics, see Fandy, *Saudi Arabia*, esp. 63–72.
61 See Rayed Krimly, "The Political Economy of Adjusted Priorities: Declining Oil Revenues and Saudi Fiscal Policies," *Middle East Journal* 53 (Spring 1999).
62 See Gary G. Sick and Lawrence G. Potter, eds., *The Persian Gulf at the Millennium* (New York: St. Martin's Press, 1997), esp. chap. 3. On Saudi economic, political and social problems, see Peter W. Wilson and Douglas F. Graham, *Saudi Arabia: The Coming Storm* (New York: M. E. Sharpe, 1994), esp. chaps. 5 and 6. On human development trends, see *Arab Human Development Report 2002* at www.undp.org/rbas/ahdr/bychapter.html.
63 Interview with Chas W. Freeman Jr.

greater potential for political activism and the expression of anti-regime sentiment. The disparity between the beliefs of the ruling family and the educated middle class, especially the younger Saudis, has also slowly been growing.[64] That Saudi domestic reforms were not extensive enough also irritated opposition groups, chiefly Sunni religious militants, disgruntled Shia, and anti-regime groups stationed abroad. While most political groups have simply wanted the Saudi regime to reform itself and become less corrupt, others seek its outright overthrow. In fact, until the Gulf War, most Islamists refrained from directly challenging the government and instead attacked liberal officials. However, the war revealed the country's core dependence on the West and Saudi weakness relative to Iraq, which focused greater attention on the government.[65] As Madawi Al-Rasheed points out, it exposed the contradiction between the "regime's ideology of self-reliance and the reality of total dependence."[66]

From September 11 to Postwar Iraq

U.S.-Saudi relations added another element to the picture. Anti-American views were prominent in Saudi Arabia well before 9/11, but that awful day exacerbated them. The attacks threatened to reveal growing fissures in Saudi society and accentuate anti-regime fervor. For his part, Osama bin Laden had repeatedly asserted his opposition to the presence of "infidel" forces in the land of Mecca and Medina. In his words, it was "not permitted for non-Muslims to stay in Arabia."[67] That the Saudi regime allowed U.S. forces entry in 1991 and even let some forces stay thereafter motivated Bin Laden and other Saudis who opposed the regime.[68]

Throughout history, Islamic rulers have faced the potential of being challenged by those who portray themselves as better or "purer" Muslims. Bin Laden's austere existence, his invective against western corruption, and his puritanical position on excluding "infidels" from Saudi land, contrasted sharply with the profligacy of Saudi princes, the royal family's connection to Washington, and the allowed presence of U.S. forces on Saudi territory. It

---

[64] Phebe Marr, Washington intelligence briefing in which this author participated. On destabilizing factors, see Gwenn Okruhlik, "Excluded Essentials: Ethnicity, Oil and Citizenship in Saudi Arabia," in *The Global Color Line: Racial and Ethnic Inequality and Struggle from a Global Perspective*, ed. Pinar Batur-Vanderlippe and Joe R. Feagin (Stamford, CT: JAI Press, 1999).

[65] R. Hrair Dekmejian, "The Rise of Political Islamism In Saudi Arabia," *Middle East Journal* 48 (Autumn 1994), 630.

[66] Al-Rasheed, "God, the King, and the Nation."

[67] This section is based on several Osama bin Laden videos shown on CNN in the period of 15 September to 15 October 2001.

[68] Baghdad INA, in FBIS:NES 10 October 1990, 27.

is no doubt true that his sentiments, extreme as they were, struck a chord in the Saudi body politic, which exhibited quite negative views of the United States. Indeed, in a nine-nation poll of Muslim countries released on February 27, 2002, only 16 percent of Saudis had a positive view of the United States; 64 percent viewed it negatively, and 3 percent saw it as trustworthy.[69] Such views are not surprising, given that most Saudis are raised on a strict diet of religious education anchored in the extremist Wahhabi sect of Islam, sometimes referred to as "Saudi Islam," an education that is perpetuated and enforced by the state. Since this extreme sect draws inspiration from the teachings of Muhammad bin Abd al-Wahhab, who spread his message throughout the eighteenth century until his death in 1787, it is worth briefly examining.

In 1744, al-Wahhab made an alliance with Muhammad ibn Saud, a local ruler of a small Arabian oasis town who took in the reformer and gave him protection.[70] The brutal fundamentalist Wahhabi tribesmen known as the Ikhwan proved central to Ibn Saud's military conquests, including the capture of Islam's two holiest sites, Mecca and Medina, and to the formation, contrary to what most might have predicted, of the Saudi nation.[71] The alliance between Ibn Saud and al-Wahhab was congealed through generations of intermarriage, providing the royal family with a religious legitimization for its rule.[72] Descendants of the royal family and those of al-Wahhab would rule both the governmental and religious spheres of life, often combining them. Thus, to return to contemporary matters, when Iraq invaded Kuwait, King Fahd turned to and gained reluctant support from the Wahhabi clerics, as he had several times in past situations, for his considered decision to allow non-Muslim troops on Saudi soil. The clerics, for their part, benefited from almost entirely free reign in religious practices—an arrangement that, as it happens, was shaken by the effects of 9/11.

Wahhabism takes different forms, but prominent among them are the beliefs that non-Muslims should not be present on Saudi soil and that jihad against non-Muslims for this reason can be justified, even mandated. This does not mean that Wahhabism must necessarily spawn terrorism, a notion widely rejected by Saudi authorities whose brand of Wahhabism differs from that of Bin Laden, but we do know that in interviews Bin Laden quoted generously from Wahhab's teachings.[73] There is little doubt that these teachings influenced his views and actions.

69 See www.usatoday.com/news/attack/2002/02/27/usat-pollside.htm.

70 Al-Rasheed, *A History of Saudi Arabia*, 15–20.

71 The Ikhwan helped Ibn Saud expand the kingdom but eventually turned on him. He defeated them in the 1920s.

72 See Christine Moss Helms, *The Cohesion of Saudi Arabia* (Baltimore: Johns Hopkins University Press, 1981) and Safran, *Saudi Arabia*.

73 See Fandy, *Saudi Arabia*, 190–92.

The impact of the Bin Laden movement and the war on terrorism on Saudi religious extremism is important. However, while a weak opposition movement has emerged in Saudi Arabia and may or may not become energized over time by the lagged effects of September 11, that movement lacks unity, organization, and a common purpose. Nonetheless, transnational terrorism and the appeal of Islamic extremists like Bin Laden represents an ongoing risk factor. Of note is the fact that of Saudi Arabia's estimated 21 million people, more than half are under eighteen. In June 2003, Saudi security forces discovered a plot to attack Mecca. Half of the twelve suspected Al Qaeda militants were minors, more susceptible to recruitment and manipulation through the Internet, mosques, and other venues. And in the summer of 2003, the House of Saud discovered that Al Qaeda operatives were better organized and more thoroughly insinuated into the kingdom than they had suspected and that they were targeting Saudi officials.[74]

For their part, opposition forces share a disdain for the Saudi regime or for aspects of its governance and policy. But that is generally not enough to cement a strong, unified movement. Following his earlier initiatives, King Faud appointed a new Consultative Council in July 1997, an important move. It suggested an ongoing commitment to the Saudi experiment begun in 1992 when the Consultative Council was established and, as R. Hrair Dekmejian put it, an apparent determination on the King's part to "institutionalize the consultative process" and to forge a "new openness" in the Saudi political system that would be "difficult to reverse."[75] At a minimum, the appointment of the new Consultative Council may act as a safety valve to help deal with some portion of the malcontents.

However, the fact that Kuwait, Bahrain, and Qatar, and, in 2003, post-Saddam Iraq have adopted some elements of democratization has alarmed some in the Saudi regime by creating the potential that pressures for liberalization will mount internally.[76] Such pressures, possibly buttressed, directly or indirectly, by American foreign policy initiatives and actions, may spread into Saudi Arabia more quickly than the regime can handle. Such a process may well bring greater long-term stability. After all, Bahrain, Qatar, and Kuwait are the states on which the United States feels it can rely the most militarily and which it sees as most stable, and they are also the farthest along in the Arab Gulf on the path to democratization.

However, hasty democratization or the type of public dissent that could accompany it could be destabilizing, especially in the short run. This is

---

[74] See Faiza Saleh Ambah, "Saudis hint al-Qaida presence," *Associated Press*, 30 July 2003; "Bush denies Saudi request to release 9/11 information," *Knight Ridder New Service*, 30 July 2003.

[75] See R. Hrair Dekmejian, "Saudi Arabia's Consultative Council," *Middle East Journal* 52 (Spring 1998), 204, 218.

[76] See *APS Diplomatic News Service* 57 (4 November 2002).

largely because Saudi public opinion may well be less moderate than that of the Royal family on issues ranging from relations with the United States to the fight against transnational terrorism. Even if a radical government did not emerge, a regime that reflected public opinion could lead to internal strife between moderates and radicals, and heightened tension with other states in the Middle East and around the world. Such a threat cannot be dismissed, especially given the impending question, due to the age and health of the existing leadership, of succession within the royal family. Unlike in Latin America, in the Arab Gulf coups occur within family ranks, and rivalries may erupt once King Fahd and 79-year-old Prince Abdallah pass from the scene, though, as I discuss below, such serious rivalries are not especially likely.

Weighing Internal Sources of Stability

While indigenous threats to Saudi stability have increased to some extent, it is hard to understand how threatening they are without exploring factors that can help check them. A number of them are at work in important ways.

First, while a nasty and destabilizing struggle for succession is possible, Saudi norms militate against it. Differences are usually reconciled within the ruling elite of the royal family, divided between the Sudeiri family and the other sons of Ibn Saud, equaling twenty-four living sons in total. The Sudeiri are all brothers of the same mother, and include most importantly King Fahd; Prince Nayef, the interior minister; and Defense Minister Sultan who, after Abdallah, appears in line for the throne, even though he is almost eighty years old. There are many Sudeiri grandsons, including Prince Bandar, Saudi Ambassador to the United States and son of the defense minister.[77] In essence, the country is governed by about four hundred key senior princes with varying levels of importance depending on their lineage, position, and access. Decision-making is rarely unilateral, but rather is done through the custom of consensus and consultation, which plays a central role in most serious matters of domestic as well as foreign policy.

Second, although the royal family was split on certain issues, ranging from how to deal with domestic turmoil to managing relations with the West, the longevity of the regime has remained by almost any standard quite enviable. This is a result of a good sense of self-preservation, a habit of mind that very much remains a factor. While current domestic problems are serious, the Saudis have faced similar difficulties in the past too. As one leading official put it, the "Ikhwan revolted against my grandfather, but he knew how far he could go with modernizing without losing his royal butt."[78]

[77] This despite the fact that his mother was a house servant, thus putting him lower on the royal rankings for succession.
[78] Interview with Prince Bandar.

In addition to traditional forms of oppressive state control, the regime has used a variety of strategies to quell domestic opposition and decrease potential internal conflicts. King Fahd, for instance, took effective steps to shore up his relations with the other tribal leaders from the Nejd, his historical base.[79] Abdallah has been well situated to reconcile tribal and traditional pressures with the pressures of modernization and western ties. This results from a combination of factors: his command of the National Guard, his strong support among the large Bedouin tribes of the Nejd, his reputation as a potentially critic of western intervention in the region, and his powerful tribal connections. In the view of one Saudi official, "critics underestimate us. Unlike the Shah, we know how to modernize without excessively westernizing, to handle relations with religious forces, to accommodate our critics, and to have evolution and not revolution."[80] Unlike in Iran in 1979, the Saudis have benefited from the fact that geography makes it hard for a large opposition to unite. The Shia of the eastern al-Hasa province have been a source of antiwestern fervor, but they represent 10 percent of the population and are not only religiously but also geographically distant from other Saudi groups.[81]

Third, that the royal family sits atop the world's largest known oil reserves led one Saudi official to assert jokingly that "every state should have such economic problems."[82] Riyadh faces short-term and possibly longer-run economic problems, but these reserves should, over time, work in its favor. Short-term rises in oil prices also have worked and could continue to work sporadically to generate big revenues. Indeed, the Saudis were able to offset some of the heavy Gulf War costs by capitalizing on the increase in oil prices created by the UN-imposed economic embargo of Iraqi oil. The Saudis also benefited in 1999 and 2000 from the significant spike in oil prices brought about by the decreasing supply of oil on the world market. In addition, net country deposits in western banks have been near $40 billion. Deposits in western banks are enough to allow Riyadh to guarantee its external financial obligations, and the government ministry could also draw on the royal family's massive, undisclosed international investment portfolio, which may exceed half a trillion dollars.[83] Moreover, it appears that inflation is largely under control, reflecting slowing demand and lower import prices. The annual average inflation rate has been estimated at just 0.1% in 1998 and is not projected to increase substantially.[84]

---

[79]   Ibid.
[80]   Ibid. On the regime's effective measures to resolve domestic instability, see Michael Collins Dunn, "Is the Sky Falling? Saudi Arabia's Economic Problems and Political Stability," *Middle East Policy* 11 (1995), 36–39.
[81]   Nawaf E. Obaid, "In Al-Saud We Trust: How the Regime in Riyadh Avoids the Mistakes of the Shah," *Foreign Policy* (Jan.-Feb. 2002).
[82]   Interview with Prince Bandar.
[83]   See Moin A. Siddiqi, "Saudi Arabia: Financial Report," *The Middle East* (January 1999).
[84]   Michael A. Gordon, "Devaluation? Who Needs It?" *The Middle East* (January 1999), 19.

The Saudis, despite their economic problems, have amassed major financial reserves of nearly $100 billion. The purpose of the fund is to allow the country to weather any period of low oil prices, and can help stabilize domestic politics through difficult times.

Fourth, opponents and even lukewarm supporters of the royal family also must consider that toppling the regime could leave them worse off. They could face internal chaos, be outmaneuvered by other forces filling the political void, and lose present contacts with the existing regime from which they benefit. It is one thing to topple a regime, quite another to create a workable alternative. Democratic forces must fear that non-democratic forces could hijack any movement toward greater democracy, and each segment of society, including competing factions within the religious establishment, must wonder how its interests will fare in such an upheaval.

Concerns about what type of regime would replace the royal family and the absence of any clear and preferred alternative creates a compelling logic of vested interests that works against significant shifts in the status quo. Bin Laden may have the sympathies of a dangerous number of Saudis, but it is hardly clear that many of them would want him, a violent man with no experience in governance and with a price on his head the world over, running their lives.

The regime has also been careful not to threaten the interests of substantial segments of the population. This has made it harder for an anti-regime coalition that crosses tribal, class and religious boundaries to arise. Key religious, technocratic, and tribal leaders and factions have been allowed to maintain their positions of influence and to offer informal input into the decision-making structure. The September 11 attacks and the campaign on terrorism, however, have forced the regime to crack down on Al Qaeda, even at the risk of angering Saudis who are sympathetic to the terrorist organization.

The pressure for political reform will undoubtedly continue, as will the challenges of dealing with such questions. These pressures can produce the positive outcome of forcing the regime to liberalize slowly, without threatening a violent and destabilizing upheaval. But, in any case, the Saudis do not have to be as concerned as in the past that such political challenges will be stoked and intensified by revolutionary Iran.

Fifth, ousting the royal family would require a revolution or coup. Yet, the military, like all institutions in the country, is controlled by the thousands of princes that constitute the broader backbone of the royal family, over seven hundred of which are direct descendants of Ibn Saud and approximately 400 of which are key. Potential revolutionaries must both penetrate that hierarchical structure and develop serious alternatives for governance. It may well be that Al Qaeda sympathizers exist in the military, but penetrating it enough to gain substantial influence will be no easy feat. It is doubtful, in any case, that the foot soldiers of revolution currently even exist, despite rising socioeconomic and political dislocation and despite the fact that 50 percent of the Saudi population is under the age of eighteen.

A new generation of more politically active and disgruntled Saudis has emerged, but even many of its members have little enthusiasm for radical or violent change.[85] Even if they were to pursue such scenarios, it is not clear that they could muster the numbers to make a difference. In that respect, Saudi Arabia is not like Iran. While the forces of extremism are no doubt present, regimes are not overthrown by rhetoric, demonstrations, or even terror. Usually, coordinated activity by military officers must exist or a grassroots Iranian-style revolution must develop if a military coup is to be successful. And for such widespread grassroots activity to emerge, the regime almost certainly has to be widely viewed as illegitimate at its very core. And unlike the Shah of Iran, who was viewed as enabled, controlled, and propped up by the United States, the Saudi royal family has the dubious distinction of having forged the state on the bloody anvil of brutal conquest.

Comparing multiple snapshots of both internal and external threats to the Saudi regime is a revealing exercise. It suggests that the Saudis face significant economic problems and new political challenges at home, which they must address with dispatch and determination to avoid serious internal instability, but that external threats to stability have decreased. The result, contrary to what many believe, is no real overall change in the level of stability from 1979 to 2003. It is important to stress that this is not a normative argument. It does not address the nature of the Saudi regime, of its internal repression and corruption, and of its direct or indirect export of radical Islam. Rather, it is an argument focused exclusively on the evolution of oil stability.

---

[85]   See Mai Yamani, *Changed Identities: the Challenge of the New Generation in Saudi Arabia* (London: Royal Institute for International Affairs, 2000).

Chapter 3

POWER SHIFTS

The balance of power is clearly important in understanding the dynamics of world affairs, just as it is in exploring changes within economic markets. Over time, we want to know which firms in a broader market have done well or poorly in terms of sales, market share, and innovation, and how these changes in the position of individual firms have altered the balance of power within a given market. The fate of firms can hinge on how well they understand their position in the market and the dynamics of market power. Similarly, in international relations, the balance of power indicates where capability lies in reality, which is of obvious importance to the leaders of states, because it underscores the capabilities that others might bring to bear in an inter-state dispute, and can alter decisions and outcomes.

In the past, the Gulf region was regionally bipolar, with Iran and Iraq predominant. However, indicators of military and economic capability clearly show that by the late 1980s Saudi Arabia had emerged as the weak third leg in a tripolar structure, together with Iran and Iraq. The diminishment of Iraq and Iran in relation to Saudi Arabia was important at various junctures when regional history could have gone down a dangerous path. This is chiefly because since the mid-1970s, Saudi Arabia has been far more likely to protect and refrain from threatening oil stability than Iran or Iraq. But beyond the military arena, Saudi Arabia, as chapter 9 will discuss, has become more likely since the mid-1970s to take action to stabilize oil markets.

In the following sections of this chapter, I first demonstrate the move toward tripolarity and then, to put this move in perspective, discuss existing limitations in Saudi military capability. I then turn to an analysis of the economic dimension and close with an evaluation of what these changes have meant for Saudi foreign policy. The role of the Iraq War of 2003 is then incorporated more fully into the analysis.

STRATEGIC POWER SHIFTS OVER TIME

Contrary to popular perception—and to his determined stance in the Iran-Iraq War—the Ayatollah Khomeini was not militarily oriented. In contrast to the Shah of Iran, whose military expenditures were extraordinary, Khomeini severed the extensive arms relationship with Washington, shut down U.S. military facilities on Iranian soil, and even spurned Soviet arms offers. In addition, he executed or imprisoned many of his top officers and placed much less trust in Iran's regular, better-trained military than in the ideologically motivated Revolutionary Guard. Although Khomeini used force internally, he asserted that even the export of Islam was to be conducted through non-military means.[1]

The military balance shifted to some extent in the 1980s, but the region remained bipolar. Iraq's September 1980 invasion of Iran was based partly on the notion that it was better to undermine Iran while it was vulnerable and in revolutionary chaos than to face it later when it regained strength.[2] But Iraq miscalculated Iran's steadfastness and its own military capabilities, and as the war proceeded Iran threatened to shift the balance to its favor. Iraq managed to check Iran with indirect support from America and from Arab states and direct arms sales from Russia and France. But this balancing behavior against Iran also helped strengthen Iraq and contributed to a profound imbalance in military capability by the 1990 cease-fire. In military terms, Iraq grew immensely from the outset of the Iran-Iraq War to the period preceding Iraq's invasion of Kuwait in August 1990. The 1991 Gulf War helped restore the power balance, and by 1994, Iraq was weakened significantly (see Table 4).

After the Gulf War, the UN commission examining the matter gave Kuwait a larger portion of the Rumaila oil field, over which Kuwait and Iraq lay joint claim. Kuwait also retained control over Warba and Bubiyan islands, which had constituted Iraq's only access point to the Gulf and which Kuwait has considered its rightful possession, one usurped by Iraq in 1932 and 1973.[3] Moreover, UN Resolutions 687 and 707 called for UN sanctions against Iraq, which impeded its ability to restore its military capabilities. Passed on April 2, 1991, Resolution 687 mandated full disclosure of all of Iraq's ballistic missile stocks and production facilities (covering missiles with a range of 150 kilometers or greater), all nuclear materials, chemical and biological weapons and facilities, and cooperation in the destruction of such

---

[1] Richard W. Cottam, "Revolutionary Iran and the War With Iraq," *Current History* 80 (January 1981), esp. 5–9.

[2] See text of interview with King Fahd, in *London AL-HAWADITH*, FBIS: NES, 14 February 1992, 21.

[3] On Kuwait's position, see FBIS: *Cairo MENA*, 24 April 1992, 13. Also, see FBIS: *Cairo MENA*, 7 May 1992, 15–16.

TABLE 4.
The military balance of power, 1980-1994.

Year	Total men[a]	Army	Tanks	Combat aircraft
1980				
Iran	240	150	1735	447
Iraq	243	200	2750	339
Saudi	44	35	350	178
1987				
Iran	645	305	1000	60–160
Iraq	1000	955	4500	500-800
Saudi	73	40	550	179
1990				
Iran	504	305	500	185
Iraq	1000	955	5500	689
Saudi	68	40	550	189
1992				
Iran	600–750	500–530	700–800	200–230[b]
Iraq	600–800	400–500	2900–3100	330–360
Saudi	104	70	770	292
1994				
Iran	513	345	1295	294[c]
Iraq	382	350	2200	325
Saudi	104	70	770	292[d]

Source: Various author interviews; U.S. Department of Defense, *Conduct of the Persian Gulf War* (April 1992), 154, 157; *The Military Balance* (London: International Institute for Strategic Studies, various editions). These numbers conform with classified data (off-the-record interview).
[a] Includes Revolutionary Guards forces and Popular Army forces.
Number in (thousands).
[b] Excluding the 112 aircraft flown to Iran in the 1991 Gulf War.
[c] Probably less than 50% of Iran's U.S. aircraft are functionable.
[d] Excludes 72 F-15s and 48 Tornadoes that were on order.

materials. Paragraphs 10 through 12 furthermore required Iraq to "unconditionally undertake not to use, develop construct, or acquire" weapons of mass destruction (WMD). Resolution 687 also forced Iraq to accept the UN demarcated border with Kuwait, the inviolability of Kuwaiti territory, UN peacekeepers on the Iraq-Kuwait border, and intrusive UN arms inspections aimed at ridding Iraq of its ability to produce WMD.[4] Iraqi compliance with Resolution 687 was a prerequisite for lifting or reducing sanctions against it, one that, according to the United Nations, it failed to meet prior to the U.S.-led attack on Iraq in 2003.

UN sanctions also deprived Iraq of oil revenues and a role in affecting the decision-making process in global oil markets. Although Baghdad

---

[4] For the texts of major UN resolutions adopted in 1991, see *U.N. Security Resolutions on Iraq: Compliance and Implementation*, Report to the Committee on Foreign Affairs by the CRS (Washington, D.C.: GPO, March 1992).

circumvented this ban to some extent, it lost an estimated $15 billion per year with which it could have rearmed.[5] UN sanctions prohibiting arms transfers and related materials further hindered Iraq's extensive rearmament efforts.

Moreover, Saddam's internal problems were worsened by economic deprivation. He not only had to quell the troublesome Kurds and Shia but also had to keep his own officers content. Iraq's living standards were cut to half the prewar level and inflation reached 250 percent over prewar levels.[6] Iraq's economic plight created dissatisfaction among the people, the army, and even within Saddam's Tikriti ruling family.

The March 1995 coup attempt against Saddam further underscored Saddam's problems. It is believed to have been engineered by Wafiq Samaraii, head of Iraqi military intelligence, and was the first time since the rise of Saddam's Baath Party in 1968 that a Sunni tribe traditionally loyal to Saddam attempted a coup.[7] The high-level defections to Jordan in August 1995 of Lt. Gen. Hussein Kamel Hassan Majeed, the architect of Saddam's war machine and military buildup, and Lt. Col. Saddam Kamel Hassan Majeed, the head of his personal guards, further raised doubts about Saddam's internal position. Saddam regained his position in part through purges, which also had the effect of reducing the cadre of experienced Iraqi leaders. They were replaced by loyal but much less competent operatives, the likes of which Saddam had to count on in the disastrous Iraq War of 2003.

Finally, Desert Storm and postwar UN sanctions weakened Iraq in the conventional and nuclear arenas. The world's sixth largest air force was dramatically reduced, Iraq's army was roughly halved, and Iraq lost an estimated 2,633 of 5,800 tanks, 2,196 of 3,850 artillery pieces, and 324 of an estimated 650 to 700 fixed-wing combat aircraft. Postwar UN sanctions also significantly reduced Iraq's operational readiness. Initially, Iraq did retain about 50 to 60 percent of its prewar conventional military capability and reconstituted a total of 28 of its prewar 57 divisions, thus maintaining its position as the strongest military in the Gulf region.[8] Over time, however, it lost more operational tanks and airplanes, as well as losing military cohesion. On paper, Iraq remained the largest military in the Gulf region, but its most crucial component, the Special Republican Guard divisions run by hand-picked

[5] The UN Security Council allowed Iraq to sell Jordan 70,000 barrels p/d. In addition, very small amounts of oil were sold illegally across the Turkish and Iranian borders, and by use of oil-smuggling barges that proceeded undetected along the Gulf coastline.

[6] *Developments in the Middle East, July 1993*, Hearing Before the Subcommittee on Europe and the Middle East, Committee on Foreign Affairs, House of Representatives, 103rd Congress (Washington, D.C.: GPO, 1993), 26.

[7] This paragraph is based on a personal correspondence with Iraqi expert Dr. Amatzia Baram.

[8] On Iraq's conventional capability, see *Conduct of the Persian Gulf War: Final Report to Congress* (Washington, D.C.: GPO, April 1992), 148–59.

loyalists, were transformed into Saddam's personal protective force in Baghdad. Rather than focusing on projecting power and confronting the type of military forces that Iraq faced in the Iraq War, they increasingly were tasked with internal security. This may help explain the rapid fall of Saddam's military in 2003, though this may have also been a deliberate strategy to transform Iraq's doomed military into a postwar guerrilla force, if not simply the result of mass betrayal.

Before the 2003 conflict there was lengthy and contentious debate about Iraq's nuclear potential. After the Gulf War, the best estimate was that all major parts of Iraq's program had been destroyed or seriously damaged, either by Desert Storm or by UN inspection teams. This included Iraq's nuclear reactor, major nuclear labs, calutron project, and centrifuges. Its uranium mine was also located and its processes for turning uranium ore into oxide controlled. Iraq, however, retained the human intelligence capability to support a nuclear program, substantial dual-use technology, working designs for a centrifuge system, and experience in how to defy internal inspections and defend its program from external attack.[9] After UN inspectors were ejected from Iraq in 1998, Saddam had a number of years to pursue WMD entirely unfettered. By 2002, some estimates suggested that Iraq had the ability to produce a nuclear weapon within months, if it could obtain fissile material necessary to this task.[10] But these estimates were based largely on speculation, and the aftermath of the Iraq War raised serious doubts about Saddam's WMD potential, above all his nuclear program, which appeared all but defunct.

Ironically, Saddam may have attacked Kuwait in 1990 partly to pre-empt what he perceived to be an impending era of U.S. regional hegemony,[11] but his actions produced something closer to the opposite outcome. Iraq's military was drastically reduced and its armed forces could not even move below the 33rd parallel within Iraq without risking U.S. retaliation. Its economy was in shambles, set back years if not decades by the Iran-Iraq and 1991 wars, and it remained under global scrutiny for any indiscretion. This state of affairs pushed some observers to argue that war was not necessary in 2003 because Saddam could be successfully contained.

9   This paragraph is based on off-the-record interviews with Department of State and Defense officials.

10   The prestigious London-based International Institute for Strategic Studies argued as much in a report released in September 2002.

11   See Shibley Telhami, "Middle East Politics in the Post Cold War Era," in *Beyond the Cold War: Conflict and Cooperation in the Third World*, ed. George Breslauer, Harry Kreisler, and Benjamin Ward (Berkeley: Institute for International Studies, 1991). That view was threaded throughout a speech Saddam made in February 1990. See "Saddam Hussein's Speech to the Arab Cooperation Council," in FBIS: NES, 27 February 1990. For further support of this interpretation, see "Iraqi Transcript of the Meeting between President Saddam Hussein and U.S. Ambassador April Glaspie," *New York Times*, 23 September 1990.

Of course, the Saddam problem was not over. "Smart bombs" did not kill him during the Gulf War, nor was he undone by postwar uprisings by the Kurds and Shia. In fact, in the years following the Gulf War, Saddam responded with characteristic brutality and efficacy to a range of challenges, including those orchestrated by the CIA, a variety of Iraqi defectors, and detractors in Saddam's own Sunni base of power at home. Iraq, moreover, periodically took suspicious actions that very strongly suggested that it was trying to hide some key elements of its weapons programs from postwar UN arms inspectors in defiance of UN resolutions. This came to a head first in 1998 when, under the threat of joint U.S.-British air strikes, Iraq agreed to provide UN inspectors with unconditional cooperation. But Baghdad failed to comply, forcing UN inspectors to leave the country and prompting Operation Desert Fox, which involved four days of United States and British air strikes. The Iraq War closed this chapter in U.S.-Iraqi relations and Saddam's ignominious capture without a fight in December 2003 finally ended the myth that the dictator could elude all enemies.

In the broader scope of time, the Iranian Revolution and the Iran-Iraq War, on the whole, produced military imbalances in the region by leaving Iraq far stronger than Iran. However, the Gulf War helped restore the military balance by weakening Iraq. Meanwhile, over two decades of revolution and war, Saudi Arabia was growing in capability. While Riyadh has faced a number of political and economic problems in the post–Desert Storm period, the Saudis went to great lengths, even in peacetime, to develop military capability that could deter key elements of Iraqi and Iranian capabilities.

As demonstrated in Table 4, Saudi Arabia gained, in terms both absolute and relative, in virtually every military category. Although Riyadh was building its military even before the Iranian Revolution, regional conflict pushed it to accelerate and diversify this effort. Conflicts in the region also made the United States more willing to contribute to the development of Saudi capabilities. Saudi acquisition of AWACs capability and its development of major command, naval, and defense facilities represented quantum leaps in military sophistication. Riyadh also developed its own armed forces and engaged in military maneuvers and cooperation with America and Arab Gulf states.[12]

By 1994, the Saudi air force had developed significantly, and the delivery of seventy-two F-15s and forty-eight Tornados further closed the regional military gap. It is quite possible that, given the sophistication and number of Saudi aircraft, the increased training and experience of Saudi pilots, and

[12]   For details, see *Manama WAKH*, in FBIS: MEA, 7 February 1984, C1. Also, see "Witness Statement before the Senate Armed Services Committee," General H. Norman Schwarzkopf, Commander of U.S. Central Command, 8 February 1990, 55 (hereafter called "Schwarzkopf Statement").

ongoing U.S.-Saudi technical and logistics cooperation, by year 2000 Riyadh had developed the best air force in the Gulf region. In terms of ground forces, important gaps remain. However, with the full integration of an additional 315 M1A2 tanks, the Saudis now have more M1A2 tanks than the U.S. military does.

To be sure, assessing military capability based on numbers alone can be misleading. The quality of weapons varies and differences in experience and strategic expertise can result in great variations among nations in the level of using military capability for political purposes. Yet more sophisticated techniques that measure actual war-fighting ability also suggest that by 1992, Saudi military capability exceeded that of Iran. Iraq still remained the most militarily capable state in the Gulf, despite Desert Storm, something that would change decisively in 2003.[13]

Saudi defense expenditure as a percentage of central government expenditure has always been high. Although Iraq exceeded Iran and Saudi Arabia in this category in the 1970s, Riyadh outpaced Tehran, leading one Iranian politician to observe that "nobody is concerned by the fact that a neighbor of Iran—Saudi Arabia—has a military budget 10 times that of Iran while its population is six times less."[14] This basic trend continued throughout the 1980s. The Saudis poured tens of billions of dollars into developing a major military infrastructure. This was largely to accommodate the entry of U.S. forces in the event that the USSR or Iran threatened to overrun the Gulf.

Moreover, Arab Gulf states were unable to develop an effective collective military force with the participation of Syria and Egypt in the post–Gulf War period. Instead, Riyadh moved ahead to develop its own military forces. King Fahd spent billions of dollars on sophisticated weaponry to enlarge the Saudi army and to improve its combat readiness.[15] In fact, from 1985 to 1991 the Saudis led the region, far surpassing Iran in military spending; Saudi per capita expenditure, or expenditure as a percentage of GDP, also increased substantially after Desert Storm.[16]

At a less tangible level, Riyadh obtained increasing external political and military support. In 1980, for instance, the Saudis could not count on the six-member, Saudi-led Gulf Cooperation Council (GCC), composed of Saudi Arabia, Kuwait, Oman, Qatar, the United Arab Emirates (UAE), and Bahrain,

---

[13] For a discussion of these measures and a histogram comparing the capabilities of Saudi Arabia, Iran, Iraq, Israel, Egypt and Syria, see James W. Moore, "An Assessment of the Iranian Military Rearmament Program," *Comparative Strategy* 13 (October-December 1994), 381.

[14] Quoted in *Moscow Interfax* in FBIS: SOV, 12 April 1997.

[15] *Berlin Neues Deutschland*, in FBIS: NES, 27 February 1991, 1.

[16] U.S. Arms Control and Disarmament Agency, *World Military Expenditures and Arms Transfers* (Washington, D.C.: U.S. ACDA, various editions), table 1. For graphs that compare regional defense expenditures, see Moore, "An Assessment," 377–78.

which was first formed in May 1981.[17] Saudi-Egyptian relations were
derailed over the Camp David agreement. Riyadh also lacked political and
military experience interacting with European states, which would come only
after the reflagging of Kuwaiti tankers as a result of Desert Shield and Desert
Storm. As we shall see, U.S.-Saudi relations also improved in the 1980s and
were raised to a new high after the joint cooperation necessitated by the
Gulf crisis, though they would be complicated by September 11 and the consequences of the Iraq War of 2003.[18]

LIMITATIONS ON SAUDI MILITARY CAPABILITY

While Riyadh increased its relative military capability, this development must
be kept in perspective. Despite key improvements, the Saudis have faced
major problems that limit their military effectiveness. They lack the requisite
manpower to handle major military threats on the ground and the training to
utilize effectively their large inventory of sophisticated weapons.[19] Moreover,
they lack a joint military planning scheme, because the Al Saud prefer a balance of forces to prevent a potential military coup d'état. This raises questions
about a total force concept that can integrate the various services in effective
ways for actual combat. Compartmentalized military forces do not usually perform very well in combat, unless specifically organized to do so ahead of time.

Riyadh, moreover, has understandably put far greater emphasis on its air
force than on its navy or army. The uneven development of the Saudi armed
forces also poses problems of interoperability, which are compounded by the
effort to compartmentalize the military services already mentioned. The
Saudis also lack major military experience; in some cases their pilots have
not demonstrated a commitment to the task of developing their flying skills.[20]
They have not fought an extended war, as have Iran and Iraq, although the
air force has flown significant numbers of sorties and the Iranian pilots who
were tested in the Iran-Iraq War are past their prime.

Beyond the question of military experience arises the question of the
Saudi political culture. Saudi Arabia is not a militarized society and lacks a
tradition of warfare. Unlike Iran, it is questionable whether Riyadh could
sustain military operations for very long and impose serious casualties on its

---

17 On the GCC, see R. K. Ramazani, *The Gulf Cooperation Council: Record and Analysis*
   (Charlottesville: University Press of Virginia, 1988).
18 For details, see *Manama WAKH*, in FBIS: MEA, 7 February 1984, C1. Also, Schwarzkopf
   Statement.
19 On Saudi military strengths and vulnerabilities, see Anthony H. Cordesman, *After the
   Storm: The Changing Military Balance in the Middle East* (Boulder, CO: Westview, 1993),
   561–600.
20 Off-the-record interviews with pilots that have flown with the Saudis.

armed forces. The GCC offers a means by which Saudi capability can be
enhanced, but the efficacy of the GCC remains unclear. The Saudis opposed
the Omani plan aimed at developing a large GCC joint military force partly
because they didn't want to pay for it.

The perception of most high-level U.S. and Arab officials prior to the
2003 Iraq War was that in the foreseeable future the Saudis could not defend
themselves on their own, but could at least form a sort of trip wire to buy
time for American rapid deployment. The Saudi regime has sought to do
that, and in the postwar period has a better chance to do so.[21]

THE ECONOMIC DIMENSION

At the economic level, Saudi Arabia also made gains over Iran and Iraq,
though Riyadh also weakened over time. The Saudi position was quite strong
prior to the Iran-Iraq War, despite the rigors of the modernization process.
The war, however, imposed serious costs. The Saudis loaned Iraq billions of
dollars to fend off the Iranians, loans which were never repaid. In addition,
from 1983 to 1991, Saudi had a trade deficit of approximately $120 billion.[22]

The 1991 Gulf War was not only costly, it also produced profound economic dislocation. Although King Fahd described the Saudi economic situation as being stronger than ever in the post–Gulf War period, in fact the
war imposed severe opportunity costs.[23] While it is true that Saudi oil income
in 1991 was over $40 billion due to windfall profits from increased prices
and production related to the Gulf crisis, Saudi war expenses have been estimated at $60–70 billion.[24]

Riyadh's financial woes were further exacerbated by a downturn in the
global economy in this time period. That slowdown decreased the demand
for oil and contributed to falling oil prices, a problem that would recur in
2000 and 2001. Budgetary problems even pushed the Saudis to stretch out
payments for billions of dollars of U.S.-made weapons. The combination
of high military spending per capita, an enormous welfare state, a rising
population, sporadic drops in oil prices and revenue, and budget deficits led
the IMF to assert strongly in 1994 and 1995 that without major reform,
Saudi Arabia would have difficulty dealing with its economic problems.[25] As

---

[21]   Interview with Prince Bandar.
[22]   *International Financial Statistics Yearbook* (Washington, D.C.: International Monetary
       Fund, 1994), 630–31.
[23]   Quoted in *Saudi Arabia: The Monthly Newsletter of the Royal Embassy of Saudi Arabia*
       (Washington, D.C.: September 1992), 3.
[24]   David Ottaway, "Saudis Said to Owe $64 Billion, Scrape to Meet Obligations," *Washington
       Post*, 3 April 1991, A25.
[25]   *MEED*, 5 April 1996, 30–43 and IMF Article 4 Report, 1994 and 1995.

Gregory Gause notes, the massive decrease in oil revenue was not matched by changed spending habits and cutbacks in its huge welfare state; as a result, the Saudis had to scramble for ways to pay off their international loans of $4.6 billion and to shore up their financial position.[26] At home, they have had budget deficits since 1983, and high unemployment, which is estimated to have reached a high of almost 30 percent.[27] Inefficient industries, government corruption, and a glacial move toward privatization have caused additional economic problems.

Desert Storm severely hurt the Saudi economy, but regional wars utterly devastated the economies of Iran and Iraq. Iraq's GNP (GDP plus net income from abroad) peaked during 1979 and 1980, with totals of $118 and $120 billion, respectively; by the end of the Iran-Iraq War in 1988, it had fallen to $65.8 billion. And in the post–Desert Storm period, it was further cut by at least two-thirds and then radically changed, of course, by the Iraq War. Based on GDP comparisons, the Saudis made major strides against both Iran and Iraq. Even before the Iran-Iraq War erupted, the Saudi GDP compared well against Iran and Iraq. However, in the ten-year period following the Iran-Iraq War, the Saudi GDP, which remained relatively stable from 1979 to 1993, substantially outpaced the GDP of Iran and Iraq (see Table 5), thus elevating Riyadh in the balance of power. This trend largely continued through 2001—Iraq's GDP showed some improvement in that period, but it was moving up from such a low base that it made little difference.[28]

GDP is perhaps the best quantifiable indicator of economic strength, but other factors, such as foreign debt, are also useful, particularly when examining war-ridden regions where defense expenditures represent a high percentage of GDP. While the Saudis did incur serious debt as a result of Desert Shield and Desert Storm, several factors militate in favor of the Saudi economy.

The Saudi economic crisis in the mid-1990s was itself largely exaggerated by the U.S. Department of Defense, which sought to emphasize the serious nature of Riyadh's financial problems to other branches of government, which had previously ignored it. Defense department officials believed that this neglect was problematic in that it prevented Washington from taking coordinated action to help Saudi Arabia through a potentially destabilizing economic downturn. As a result, they exaggerated Saudi problems in order to draw attention to the problem, but once they did so, the story gained a

---

26 On Saudi economic problems, see F. Gregory Gause IV, "Saudi Arabia over a Barrel," *Foreign Affairs* 79 (May/June 2000), 82–86.

27 *International Financial Statistics Yearbook* (Washington, D.C.: International Monetary Fund, 1994), various issues.

28 For a different set of numbers that yield similar interpretations, see *2001 Annual Statistics Bulletin* (Vienna, Austria: OPEC 2002), 3.

TABLE 5.
The economic balance of power, 1979-2001.

GDP[a]	Iran	Iraq	Saudi Arabia
1979	84.7	38.6	97.3
1980	112.0	54.0	147.6
1981	92.8	31.8	165.9
1982	104.7	34.6	153.0
1983	99.7	30.6	119.9
1984	157.0	27.0	105.4
1985	163.0	46.8	93.7
1986	147.0	36.5	77.4
1987	369.0	39.0	71.1
1988	447.3	46.09	75.3
1989	53.1[b]	58.5	83.0
1990	59.5	40.8	87.9
1991	68.2	24.5	109.1
1992	54.2	20.0	121.1
1993	57.8	19.0	124.8
1994	59.8	18.5	128.1
1995	62.5	15.0	125.0
1996	67.3	15.0	136.0
1997	85.0	17.0	146.0
1998	89.0	19.0	133.0
1999	93.0	20.0e[c]	141.0
2000	73.0	15.4e[c]	185.0
2001	82.0	15.0e[c]	176.0

Source: The Military Balance (London: International Institute for Strategic Studies, various editions); Brassey's (all editions). In addition, interviews with International Monetary Fund (IMF) officials, and the International Financial Statistics Yearbook (Washington, DC: IMF, various editions). These figures are educated conjecture (indeed, figures from The Military Balance, which are based on IFSY data, differed after 1985 from IFSY figures based on this author's calculations), and reflect data revisions.
[a] Based on information from governments; not fully accurate, particularly given exchange rate fluctuations. Figures are in U.S. $ billions; constant 1988 prices.
[b] The figure is not an error, but requires evaluation in context.
[c] Designates estimates rather than government-provided figures.

life of its own and other branches of government may very well have over-estimated the seriousness of the problem.[29]

In addition, the Saudis did take some fiscal measures in the 1990s to address structural economic problems, including austerity measures recommended by the U.S. government. This helped offset the costs of the 1990–91 crisis somewhat, although those same measures also created greater potential for political instability by decreasing the regime's ability to use its largesse to appease some of its malcontents. Huge oil reserves and financial investments have also offered the Saudis a key source of financial strength well into the future.

[29] Off-the-record interview with DOD official.

To be sure, Riyadh still faced problems in the mid-1980s when oil prices collapsed and revenues fell to less than a quarter of what they had been at their peak after the October War in 1973. As Figure 2 below shows, oil prices rose again only to suffer another major fall in 1998.[30] Since Saudi Arabia relies on oil for about 80 percent of government revenue, the oil price collapse of 1998 caused havoc, bringing oil prices in constant Year 2000 dollars to lows last seen in the early 1970s, and triggering the first recession in Saudi Arabia since 1992.

Yet while such problems represented a weakening of the Saudi economic position over time in absolute terms, Iran and Iraq in fact were far more devastated economically in the period covered in this book. Indeed, unlike Saudi Arabia, they endured inestimable war-related damage to infrastructure and incurred serious debt, which was much harder to service. Iran rescheduled about $9 billion in debt in 1994, but borrowed another $20 billion in 1994 and 1995 and has thereafter held unprecedented foreign debt.[31] The final Iranian government report placed the direct economic damage of the war as equal to twenty years of the country's oil revenue at the 1983 earning level of $20.5 billion; 52.85 percent of the economic damage was indirect.[32] That Iran has had little success in harnessing the energies of its economy, despite efforts at privatization, has compounded its problems. In the last twenty years, nearly two-thirds of its overall annual state budget has been used to prop up unprofitable state industries and banks.[33] While the Saudis also suffered in the 1990s from structural economic problems and government rigidity, the ongoing effects of war and revolution have exacerbated Iran's problems.

Predictably, Iraq was in even worse shape than Iran. Raw estimates suggest that Desert Storm not only halved Iraq's GNP but also left it with debts totaling $83 billion, excluding liabilities of up to $80 billion for war reparations.[34] Iraq's Minister of Trade Mohammed Mahdi Saleh asserted that Iraq had lost more than $140 billion in revenue in the decade since

30 Note that Brent crude oil prices differ from West Texas Intermediate (WTI), Dubai, and the OPEC Basket. For useful graphs tracing the differences from 1992–2001, see *2001 Annual Statistical Bulletin* (Vienna, Austria: OPEC, 2002), 117.

31 Based on personal correspondence with Jim Placke, one of the directors of Cambridge Energy Research Associates, 15 July 1996. Also, on Iranian economic problems, see Massoud Karshenas and M. Hashem Pesaran, "Economic Reform and the Reconstruction of the Iranian Economy," *Middle East Journal* 49 (Winter 1995), 89–111.

32 For extensive data on war damage, see Hooshang Amirahmadi, "Economic Destruction and Imbalances in Post-revolutionary Iran," in *Reconstruction and Regional Diplomacy in the Persian Gulf*, ed. Hooshang Amirahmadi and Nader Entessar (London: Routledge, 1992).

33 "Now for the Hard Part," *MEED* (13 March 1998), 2.

34 These estimates are based on various editions of *The Military Balance* (London: Oxford University Press, 1995).

Figure 2. Oil prices (1980-2003)

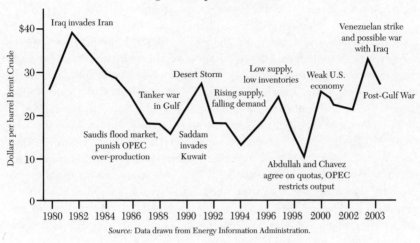

Source: Data drawn from Energy Information Administration.

UN sanctions were imposed on it in 1990.[35] The UN tried to alleviate the plight of the Iraqi people by offering Iraq the chance to sell $1.6 billion worth of oil in 1992 to pay for the import of food and medicine. But Iraq, which did not like the violation of its sovereignty and wanted to control the funds of its oil sales, rejected this offer until 1996 when it finally agreed to the terms of UN Resolution 986. Iraq could now sell oil on the open market, under UN supervision, in order to feed its food-strapped population, pay war reparations, fund UN operations in Iraq, and later also to buy spare parts and equipment to help upgrade Iraq's oil-producing capacity.

In the last fifteen years, Iran and Iraq have also incurred incredible opportunity costs from defense expenditures, partly in the form of foregone economic growth.[36] In a July 1989 speech, former Speaker of the Parliament and later President Hashemi Rafsanjani revealed that Iran spent "some 60 to 70 percent of the country's income" on the war.[37] Rafsanjani's election as president following the death of the Ayatollah Khomeini brought to power the more pragmatic branch of the fundamentalist camp that eschewed efforts to

35 "Iraq has Exported $23bn worth of Oil under UN Programme since 1996," *OPEC Bulletin* (May 2000), 22.
36 On the tendency for defense spending to limit growth in the broader Middle East, see James H. Lebovic and Ashfaq Ishaq, "Military Burden, Security Needs, and Economic Growth in the Middle East," *Journal of Conflict Resolution* 31 (March 1987), 106–38.
37 Quoted in Amirahmadi and Entessar, *Reconstruction and Regional Diplomacy*, 79.

redraw the region's political map.[38] Despite Iran's assertive postwar actions, Rafsanjani, while hardly a moderate, did put relatively greater emphasis on economics over ideology. Radical elements in Iran argued for a more confrontational foreign policy, but the regime had little support for renewed conflict with its neighbors, although Iran, in keeping with its nationalist ambitions, has continued to want to be recognized as the dominant power in the region.[39] Overall, Iran's economic problems circumscribed the nature of its foreign policy and put limits on how ambitious it could be in the region.

Saudi military expenditures also increased greatly. Unlike Iran and Iraq, Saudi Arabia did not suffer other economic strains associated with the Iran-Iraq War, did not have to reconstruct its infrastructure and economy, and was thus more able to service its debts. Iran's economic reconstruction program has faced domestic and international obstacles, including the effects, some of them lagged, of poor economic policies, U.S. economic sanctions, the freezing of its assets by Washington, the Iran-Iraq War, the vagaries of the oil market, and a world-class regional arms race.

SAUDI FOREIGN POLICY

While chapter 2 examined the evolution of threats to Saudi stability, this chapter has shown that Saudi capability has clearly increased relative to its immediate neighbors. Both of these developments have made it easier for Saudi Arabia to play a role in protecting regional oil supplies, as has the development of the GCC.

The Iranian Revolution produced interest in forming the GCC, but the influence of Iran and Iraq, both of which wanted to dominate any such union, was a major stumbling block to its formation.[40] The Iran-Iraq War, however, not only gave Arab Gulf states added incentive to create the GCC in order to deal with the Iranian threat but it also removed the Iran-Iraq obstacle by absorbing the energies of both states. The GCC was formed and developed largely in reaction to the Iranian threat, which was dramatized by

---

[38]   On Rafsanjani's views, see Mohsen M. Milani, "Iran's Gulf Policy: From Idealism and Confrontation to Pragmatism and Moderation," in *Iran and The Gulf: A Search for Stability*, ed. Jamal S. Al-Suwaidi (London: I. B. Tauris, 1996), esp. 89–91, 93–95.

[39]   Iranian moderates did well in elections for Iran's Fourth Islamic Majlis in April and May 1992. The elections were a resounding victory for Rafsanjani, whose supporters won an absolute majority in the Majlis. Farzin Sarabi, "The Post-Khomeini Era in Iran: The Election of the Fourth Islamic Majlis," *Middle East Journal* 48 (Winter 1994), 104. On regional security, see Daniel Byman, Shahram Chubin, Anoushiravan Ehteshami, and Jerrold Green, *Iran's Security Policy in the Post-revolutionary Era* (Santa Monica, CA: RAND, 2001), 74–77.

[40]   Nadav Safran, *Saudi Arabia: The Ceaseless Quest for Security* (Cambridge, MA: Harvard University Press, 1985), 373.

the Iran-Iraq War. In December 1981, the attempted coup in Bahrain was attributed by GCC leaders to revolutionary Iran, and was interpreted as a collective attack on the GCC.[41] The coup attempt motivated several GCC states to sign bilateral security agreements, and Bahrain proposed the formation of an independent GCC rapid deployment force (RDF).[42] Interestingly, the events of December 1981 would seemingly repeat themselves in May 1996, when Iran would again be identified as supporting efforts to overthrow the Bahraini government, and GCC leaders would again convene to discuss proper security measures.

While the 1981 Bahrain coup attempt largely motivated efforts to improve GCC protection against internal threats, Iran's ability to put Iraq on the defensive in 1982 largely catalyzed initial GCC efforts to deter external threats. Bahrain's proposal for a GCC RDF gained currency in 1982, and by October 1983 the Peninsular Shield joint GCC military exercises commenced. These exercises, while militarily unimpressive, represented a novel attempt to coordinate GCC military maneuvers and to develop the Gulf RDF as a shock absorber that could buy time for regional or "over the horizon" reinforcements. Finally, the eruption of the tanker war between Iran and Iraq in 1984 intensified efforts to integrate GCC air defenses: The Saudis agreed to share AWACs intelligence with geostrategically exposed Kuwait, and later with other Gulf states.[43] By underscoring regional dangers, the Iraqi invasion of Kuwait stimulated increased interest in GCC security, and in political and economic cooperation.[44]

To be sure, Saudi Arabia and other GCC states continued to fear not only Iran but also South Yemen, with which they had serious border conflicts, even after the development of the U.S.-backed GCC. This fear might have predisposed Oman, the UAE, and Bahrain to establish diplomatic relations with the Soviets in 1985, one of the USSR's major gains from the Iran-Iraq War. But the GCC, while hardly a significant military actor, nonetheless promoted regional stability by seeking to ensure the stability of its member states through intelligence and security cooperation, and by enhancing Riyadh's ability to pursue a leadership role in the Gulf. Prior to the war and

---

41   See *Manama WAKH*, FBIS: MEA, 25 February 1982, C-3.

42   For a description of the bilateral agreements, see *Manama WAKH*, in FBIS: MEA, 22 February 1982, C-3. See also *Riyadh Domestic Service*, in FBIS: MEA, 24 February 1982, C-5. For more on the RDF, see *Manama WAKH*, in FBIS: MEA, 23 December 1981, C-1.

43   A good discussion of the tanker war's effect on GCC security appears in R. K. Ramazani, "Iran's Islamic Revolution and the Persian Gulf," *Current History* (January 1985), 41.

44   See interview with Saudi Defense Minister Prince Sultan on the nature of postwar GCC relations. *Riyadh SPA*, FBIS: NES, 15 January 1993, 29. Also, see Saudi Arabia, *The Monthly Newsletter of the Royal Embassy of Saudi Arabia* 9 (Washington, D.C., February 1992), 1–2 and *Kuwait KUNA*, in FBIS: NES, 16 November 1992, 5.

the GCC's formation, the smaller Arab Gulf states were reluctant to become too dependent on Saudi Arabia for their collective security, partly because they doubted its stability.[45] Saudi weakness made them all more vulnerable to influence by Iran, Iraq, and even the Soviets. This, in turn, compromised U.S. interests, as suggested by the fact that the Saudis agreed in 1979 to diminish their cooperation with Washington in exchange for Soviet moderation concerning the Yemens.[46]

The Saudis tended to be timid in foreign policy, with two clear exceptions. When they found themselves up against a wall, they did confront Nasser's Egypt in the 1960s, and certainly in Yemen; in the 1973 Arab oil embargo they did play an assertive role.[47] However, by and large, they preferred to accommodate regional and international aggressors rather than to oppose them.

A strategy of accommodating adversaries tended to make sense in the late 1970s, because the Al Saud faced internal and external threats, were weak militarily, had strained relations with the United States, and lacked significant experience in confronting adversaries. Thus, they were not in a position to assume an assertive foreign policy, or, in other words, a policy based much more on challenging other actors than on accommodating them for purposes of meeting foreign policy goals. It was preferable for the Saudis to accommodate real or perceived adversaries in order to avoid conflict. However, as the Iran-Iraq War progressed into the 1980s and as the political-strategic landscape began to change, Riyadh became more assertive. In part, this was because U.S.-Saudi relations began to improve at the global level and Iran and Iraq increasingly became bogged down in the Iran-Iraq War. Increased Saudi assertiveness was demonstrated in several cases.

Of all Muslim states, the Saudis and Iran took the strongest stance against the Soviet invasion of Afghanistan. Throughout the 1980s, Riyadh supported the Afghan rebels politically, economically and militarily, and, as already noted earlier in this chapter, refused to have meaningful relations with the USSR while it was in Afghanistan. The Saudis also exhibited increased assertiveness during the Iran-Iraq War. With AWAC guidance, the Saudis managed to intercept an Iranian F-4 in 1984 and to protect their airspace and later to deter an Iranian naval attack on their offshore oil fields in 1987, with U.S. forces again playing an indirect role.[48] In late 1987, Riyadh also foiled Iran's attempt to drive a wedge between Arab states in order to increase its influence with them.[49] The Saudi reaction to the 1987 Mecca

45 Anthony H. Cordesman, *The Gulf and the West: Strategic Relations and Military Realities* (Boulder, CO: Westview Press, 1988), 402.
46 Safran, *Saudi Arabia*, 235.
47 I owe the observation about Yemen to Gregory Gause.
48 Interestingly, the 1984 action was met with a conciliatory tone in Iran. Shahram Chubin and Charles Tripp, *Iran and Iraq at War* (London: I. B. Tauris, 1988), 167.
49 On this attempt, see *Christian Science Monitor*, 13 October 1987, 9.

incident also reflected an increasingly assertive policy. In the past, it would have been unimaginable for the Saudis to have taken such a strong stance against Iran. These actions extended beyond self-defense and reflected greater confidence in challenging Iran.

The development of Saudi capability in the 1980s was felt when Iraq invaded Kuwait in 1990. Saddam faced a more steadfast and experienced opponent in Riyadh than he was used to. Presented with the choice of appeasing or opposing Saddam, Riyadh chose the latter course. This is important because old tendencies were still at play. For instance, Washington had solid intelligence after Iraq invaded Kuwait in August 1990 that the Saudis were considering pocket-book diplomacy.[50] The Saudi Defense Minister, among others, either opposed or was exceedingly wary of the U.S. deployment to Saudi Arabia and promoted the notion of appeasing Saddam—a viewpoint that was not adopted by the regime of course.[51]

While the Saudis did not become bold thereafter, they did appear more able to contribute to protecting regional stability in the post–Gulf War period. Thus, in August 1999, some U.S. officials noted with satisfaction Riyadh's deft handling of repeated Iranian overtures, and in particular its stated reluctance to engage in any military cooperation with Tehran.[52] The Saudi initiative in putting forth a Middle East peace proposal in 2002 was also important, especially given the hardened atmosphere in the Arab world against Israel. While the proposal may well have aimed at diverting attention from global attention on 9/11, it also did underscore an important Saudi regional role.

THE IRAQ WAR OF 2003

Until the Iraq War, the Gulf region moved toward a tripolar power structure, with Saudi Arabia emerging as the weaker third leg. This development was quite important to the story of the evolution of oil stability. As we shall see in the conclusion of this book, it helped constrain Iran and Iraq while elevating the ability of the Saudis to support regional and market stability.

The Iraq War has played its own important role. What is key is that it left Iraq not only much weaker than Saudi Arabia but also with far less intent to be aggressive. Iraq's air force was all but eliminated, and its army dispersed. In the postwar period, Iraq began to develop the nucleus for what could become a military force of between 40 to 50 thousand troops. Of course, Iraq has retained the knowledge base, albeit scattered around the country, to build weapons, as well as an experienced but aging cadre of

---

soldiers. It could in the future rebuild a strong military. But clearly, for the foreseeable future, its armed forces will be limited and its foreign policy at least influenced by Washington. Iraq's weakened military posture is important to note. The region has been more stable when a balance of power has existed between Iran and Iraq, which suggests that Iraq's weakness could embolden Iran. However, examining the balance of power can only tell us so much. The intentions of the actors are also crucial.[53] Thus, it is preferable to have a defanged Iraq, as is the case in the post-Saddam era, and a stronger Iran than it is to have both a strong Iraq and Iran. This is especially the case because important developments over the past two decades have decreased the salience of Iran's military advantage over Iraq. The Iranian Revolution has mellowed, both Iran and Iraq have learned the savage lessons of war, Iran has engaged in a rapprochement with Arab Gulf states, Saudi military capability has increased significantly, and U.S. military capability in the region has developed to the point where Washington can check Iran's regional power if not its nuclear aspirations.

The balance of power in the Gulf has changed in important ways over time. Based on an evaluation chiefly of economic and military indicators, Saudi Arabia clearly rose in power compared to Iran and Iraq. That has benefited regional stability at critical points when history may have gone down a more dangerous route and into the twenty-first century. As we shall see later in the book, these changes also translated into positive outcomes in global oil markets.

---

[53] Randall L. Schweller, *Deadly Imbalances: Tripolarity And Hitler's Strategy of World Conquest* (New York: Columbia University Press, 1998).

Chapter 4

THE CHIEF GUARANTOR OF OIL STABILITY

The struggle for power, security, and welfare in the Persian Gulf region has not occurred in isolation from the broader global setting. Regional events have had an enormous effect on outside states, and these states have altered the trajectory of regions and of actors within them. On that score, no outside state has done more to affect regional and oil stability over the past two decades than the United States.

The United States has evolved from a period in the 1940s when its ability and will to affect regional politics was minor, to a period in the twenty-first century during which it has become the primary external protector of global oil supplies from large-scale threats. The rise of the United States in this role took place mostly in the past two decades, and it represents an important anchor of oil stability, despite the fact that its presence in the region also stokes controversy and generates problems that need to be considered. Overall, the strong U.S. role has served a real and perceived goal. In real terms, Washington has developed the capability and will to deter, contain, and reverse some key threats to oil stability. On a perceptual level, many more actors now *believe*, as compared to past periods, that the United States has the direct and indirect ability to protect oil stability. That in itself decreases the potential for market instabilities. This chapter sketches the American trajectory from the 1970s into the post–Iraq War phase starting in 2003, as a basis for making further arguments in subsequent chapters about what this has meant in the bigger picture of oil stability.

SLEEPING GIANT

Even before oil was discovered in the region, the Gulf was prized by kings, emperors, and dictators as an area, which, if controlled, could consolidate their power. That rivalry would not end in the nineteenth or twentieth centuries. While Americans were in the process of shaping a nation through civil war, conquest, and exploration in the nineteenth century and quietly developing the underlying capability and institutions to become a superpower, Britain and tsarist Russia vied for influence across Asia in what Rudyard Kipling referred to as the "Great Game."[1]

In the post-Napoleonic era, the British feared that tsarist armies, which had already overrun Central Asia, would use Afghanistan to threaten Persia and Britain's lifeline to its primary overseas possession, India. Given the great distance between Britain to India, its lifeline to this prized colonial possession was highly vulnerable, despite the prowess of the vaunted British navy. And Russia showed an enormous appetite for territorial aggrandizement, having increased the size of its empire between the seventeenth and nineteenth centuries by astounding proportions. Britain's fears of Russian intentions heightened in the 1830s, and even pushed it to invade Afghanistan twice in an effort to stave off Russian influence there, only to trigger two Afghani wars between these great powers. Both states jockeyed for influence at the expense of local actors such as Egypt and, later, Iran. Indeed, in 1907, Russia concluded a treaty with Britain dividing Iran into spheres of influence, with Russia controlling the north and Britain the south, and Iran in the neutral center. For its part, while Russia was concerned primarily with British expansion in Afghanistan and in other parts of Asia, it also sought a desperately needed warm water port, preferably in the Gulf. And military influence in the region, furthermore, was seen as a way of not only allowing Russia to protect its expanding borders in the south but also helping it project an image of boldness that might translate into expanded power. Thus, these two great powers, each pursuing its own goals, ran afoul of each other over similar terrain where there was not enough room for two developing empires. With time the great game evolved, assuming new dimensions and different players, albeit carrying a not dissimilar pedigree. The USSR assumed tsarist Russia's role as the counterweight to perceived western ambitions, and the United States replaced Britain.

THE EVOLUTION OF THE U.S. POSITION

The Cold War pitted the United States against the USSR in an intense period of hostility without actual warfare between the superpowers themselves. As a colossal struggle of irreconcilable ideologies, it also assumed

[1] For a good discussion of the "Great Game," see George N. Curzon, *Russia in Central Asia in 1889 and the Anglo-Russian Question* (London: Frank Cass, 1967) and Milan Hauner, "The Last Great Game," *Middle East Journal* 38 (Winter 1984).

interesting dimensions in the Gulf region. Partly as a result of this rivalry, but also because of other factors, America's commitment to the region increased significantly over time, as did its capability for regional contingencies. I argue that this evolution occurred in five phases from 1945 to 2003, which are discussed in the balance of this chapter.

Phase I: Initial Commitment

It is perhaps fitting that the United States would end the century as the major protector of Middle East oil, because it began the century as the key pioneer in the global oil industry. In fact it is the oldest major global oil producer, producing more oil, cumulatively, than any other country (180 billion barrels from 1918 to 1999).[2] In the Persian Gulf, the United States and its oil companies rivaled their British counterparts for position in the burgeoning oil industry over the first decades of the century, but it was not until after World War II that Saudi Arabia became more vital in U.S. global machinations.

During that war, it became clear to Washington that Middle East oil could in the future be important for fueling its military machine and growing population, and that it could not rely forever on its domestic oil supplies. The Cold War added to these concerns. As early as 1945, the United States began to appreciate the vital role of Saudi oil not only as an economic resource but also as a potential political weapon for any actor that controlled it—namely the Soviet Union, whose troops had not yet withdrawn from Iranian Azerbaijan, despite the end of the war and promises from Moscow to do so. This recognition pushed President Harry S. Truman on September 28, 1945, to approve the completion of the air base at Dhahran, Saudi Arabia. We now know that the United States was formally committed to Saudi security at least as early as 1947, when Truman and King Ibn Saud made a pact, described in a State Department cable, which pledged that if Saudi Arabia were attacked by another power or under threat of attack, Washington would take strong measures under the auspices of the United Nations to address the threat.[3]

However, while the United States did make certain commitments to the Saudis in this first phase from 1945 to 1971, America remained unable to protect the region, whether by proxy or independently. Rather, Britain was chiefly responsible for regional stability, with the United States playing a distant secondary role.

[2] According to the DOE, EIA.
[3] This paragraph is partly based on Michael A. Palmer, *Guardians of the Gulf: A History of America's Expanding Role in the Persian Gulf, 1833–1992* (New York: Free Press, 1992), 27–29, 46–47 and Daniel Yergin, *The Prize: The Epic Quest for Oil, Money, and Power* (New York: Simon and Schuster, 1992), 391–400.

Phase II: The Proxy Phase

In 1968, Britain announced that it would withdraw "East of Suez." By 1971, Britain had made good on this declaration, thus leaving core responsibility for regional stability to the United States. Washington, however, did not assume this responsibility directly. Rather, Iran and, to a much lesser extent, Saudi Arabia formed the anchors of the twin pillar policy, which was an outgrowth of the Nixon doctrine and which aimed at protecting the U.S.-favored status quo in the Gulf during the 1970s.[4] One month after the USSR and Iraq signed a historic agreement of cooperation, President Nixon and National Security Adviser Henry Kissinger visited Iran and made an agreement in which Washington promised to provide the Shah with unrivaled access to U.S. weapons, in exchange for his role in protecting U.S. regional security.[5] The twin pillar policy, while hardly perfect as statecraft, absolved post-Vietnam America of the need to develop its own military capability for Gulf contingencies. It could rely primarily on Iran, and secondarily Saudi Arabia, in exchange for U.S. arms and technical support.

While the United States counted on Iran in the 1970s, U.S.-Iranian relations faced problems. At times, the Shah appeared more interested in accepting U.S. arms than in cooperating with the United States on other matters. Nor was Washington particularly stingy in its arms transfers, which provoked serious criticism from Congress. The Shah's dismal human rights record also raised questions about the morality of supporting his regime. His disregard for basic American values, as reflected in SAVAK, his repressive and far-reaching secret police force, was viewed as troublesome in some U.S. quarters. Nonetheless, given U.S. fears of Soviet power and of the ambitions of regional actors such as Iraq, morality took a back seat to strategic interests. In retrospect, it seems obvious that U.S. support of the repressive Shah contributed to his downfall. It opened him up to the criticism that he was a puppet of America and, therefore, a leader less likely to preserve the interests and integrity of Iranians.[6]

While U.S. support of the Shah was problematic, it also offered Washington some strategic benefits.[7] Between 1974 and 1979 the Shah established acceptable relations with all Gulf states, and was, by and large, a mediating

---

4   Henry Kissinger, *White House Years* (Boston: Little, Brown, 1979), 1263–64.
5   James A. Bill, *The Eagle and the Lion: The Tragedy of American-Iranian Relations* (New Haven: Yale University Press, 1988).
6   On the dynamics of the revolution, see Jahangir Amuzegar, *The Dynamics of the Iranian Revolution: The Pahlavis' Triumph and Tragedy* (New York: State University of New York Press, 1991); Barry M. Rubin, *Paved with Good Intentions: The American Experience and Iran* (New York: Oxford University Press, 1980); and Nikki R. Keddie, *Roots of Revolution: An Interpretive History of Modern Iran* (New Haven: Yale University Press, 1981).
7   For the views of key U.S. officials on Iran's role, see Cyrus Vance, *Hard Choices: Critical Years in America's Foreign Policy* (New York: Simon and Schuster, 1983), chaps. 14 and 15.

influence. Although the Arab Gulf states were uneasy with the Shah's imperialist designs and were irritated with his arrogance they also perceived Iran
during his reign to be a stabilizing force in the region. We can debate the
extent to which Iran played this role, but it is fair to say that, in a region
somewhat remote from the Gulf itself, it served as a conduit for improved
U.S.-Egyptian relations in the 1970s. Between 1971 and 1979, Iran and the
Saudis helped lure North Yemen and Somalia away from the USSR, and
Iran's troops also played some role in defeating a communist-backed tribal
revolt in Pakistan's Baluchistan province. In the Gulf, the Shah's troops were
useful in helping Oman suppress the Dhofar rebellion in 1975 and maintain
order thereafter. This was viewed by other Gulf states as important to their
strategic interests, since Oman's stability had implications for the rest of the
Gulf nations. Iran also served as an indirect check on Iraq and South Yemen,
which, due to their links to Moscow and their own regional ambitions, were
also viewed as threats to regional stability. And although Iran was more
hawkish on oil prices than Saudi Arabia, it served as a reliable supplier of a
high volume of oil.

Furthermore, despite the rigors of the modernization process and the
usual instability associated with state-building and Arab politics, Saudi Arabia
was more or less stable, and U.S.-Saudi relations were at least cooperative,
if not strong. In the region, moreover, the balance of power between Iran
and Iraq was fairly even. This helped deter either side from attacking the
other or smaller Gulf states.

Phase III: Vulnerability and Preparation

Little did the United States know that its reliance on Iran and Saudi Arabia
would leave it highly vulnerable in 1979, a crucial year in the history of the
Middle East.[8] The Iranian Revolution seriously weakened the U.S. position.
It undermined relations between Iran and most of the Arab Gulf states. Iran
withdrew its forces from Oman, where it had played an important security
role, and threatened to revive its historical claims to Bahrain, which the Shah
had renounced. The unsteady but beneficial U.S. relationship with the Shah
was replaced by hostile U.S.-Iranian relations. Moreover, the revolution
imperiled Saudi stability and undid the twin pillar policy by transforming
U.S.-Iranian relations from cooperation to confrontation. The collapse of
Iranian oil production in the postrevolutionary period led to a tripling of oil
prices, which damaged U.S. interests and made a U.S. strategy for regional
stability even more vital.

---

[8]   David W. Lesch, *1979: The Year that Shaped the Modern Middle East* (Boulder, CO: Westview
Press, 2001).

To make matters worse, the joint occurrence of Iran's revolution and the Afghanistan intervention raised the specter of a decline of U.S. influence in the region. The great game of the twentieth century was quite unlike that of the nineteenth century, which was fought through force by great empires seeking to expand territory and protect colonial possessions. However, it was reminiscent of it in some ways especially after the Afghanistan invasion, which heightened fears in Washington about Russian intentions. The U.S. strategic position had fallen apart from within the Gulf and now was also threatened by external forces. And its reliance on proxy foreign policy in the 1970s left it unable to respond militarily. The rapid development force (RDF), which would play a critical role during the 1990–91 Gulf crisis, had not been developed, the regional military facilities which hosted the forces of Operations Desert Shield and Storm in 1990 and 1991 had not been built to any notable extent, and regional actors were not disposed to provide logistics or political support for U.S. military efforts. In late 1979 Defense officials informed President Jimmy Carter that Washington was virtually powerless to release the fifty-two hostages seized by Islamic zealots and held in Iran for 444 days, an event that helped doom his presidency.[9]

In phase three, covering 1979 to 1990, the United States was forced for the first time to develop substantial military capability and regional support to protect its own interests in the Gulf. Whereas the Iranian Revolution had threatened regional stability from within the Gulf, the December 1979 Soviet invasion of Afghanistan threatened to do so externally. In part as a result of this dichotomy of threats, as well as the Iran-Iraq War from 1980 to 1988, between 1980 and 1991 the United States developed its military capability and gained access to military facilities that enhanced U.S. ability to project force. The regional threat to U.S. interests created by the Iran-Iraq War compounded the perceived threat of the Afghanistan invasion at the global level. It was the Iran-Iraq War, however, that altered regional perceptions of the value of an over-the-horizon U.S. force. Partly in response to the war, the RDF's role was expanded after 1982 with the explicit goal of deterring Moscow. Washington sought the capability to deter an outside threat, to respond appropriately to friendly requests for assistance, and to counteract its physical remoteness from the Gulf.[10] High-level plans for the development of the RDF had been initiated by late 1979.[11] But while its conception was sparked by the Iranian Revolution, it was budgeted, developed, and

---

9   Ibid., 9. On the hostage crisis, see Gary Sick, *All Fall Down: America's Tragic Encounter with Iran* (Boulder, CO: Westview Press, 1985).

10   This paragraph is based on Steve A. Yetiv, *America and the Persian Gulf: The Third Party Dimension in World Politics* (New York: Praeger, 1995).

11   See statements by former Undersecretary of Defense Robert Komer cited in Maxwell Orme Johnson, *The Military as an Instrument of U.S. Policy in Southwest Asia* (Boulder, CO: Westview, 1983), 15.

implemented primarily after and as a result of the Afghanistan intervention, and was configured to deter a Soviet invasion of Iran.[12]

The improvements in U.S. force projection in the 1980s were significant in convincing regional leaders of U.S. capability and resolve, not to mention in actually enhancing U.S. capability. While in 1979 sending even minimal forces would have taken many weeks, by 1983 the United States could have had the first ground force to the Gulf in just a few days. U.S. airlift, sealift, and prepositioning capabilities continued to improve substantially throughout the 1980s. From 1980 to 1987, U.S. airlift capabilities increased from 26.9 to 39.6 million-ton-miles per day. The United States also enhanced the Military Sealift Command active fleet from 44 to 57 ships, and the Ready Reserve Force from 27 to 82 ships. Overall, the Defense Department spent over $7 billion to improve sealift capabilities in the 1980s. Key improvements included a prepositioned force of 25 ships, some of which provided the first supplies during the Gulf crisis; eight fast sealift ships especially suited to transport heavy Army unit equipment, and an additional increase in the ready reserve force to 96 ships.[13]

By 1988, the United States had reached 89 percent of its sealift goal, although its capability in this area declined in the post–cease-fire period following the Iran-Iraq War.[14] In addition, the Maritime Prepositioning Ships program that had been put into effect in 1980 became an active capability, enabling forces to reach critical contingency areas within seven days,[15] which proved critical in the first weeks of Operation Desert Shield. RDF capability was also enhanced by U.S. efforts to upgrade facilities to which it was allowed access. In 1980, improvements were also made at Masirah island in Oman, Diego Garcia, and bases in Turkey, and negotiations were under way for improvements at Somalia.[16] These efforts were particularly important considering that Washington's only permanent facility in the Gulf itself had been a Defense Fuel Supply Station in Bahrain. Monies devoted to these efforts were minor prior to 1980, increased greatly from 1980 to 1982, partly in response to Afghanistan and to the Iran-Iraq War, and then decreased in 1985. This decrease suggests that the Afghanistan invasion, more than the Iran-Iraq War, was what motivated these particular efforts. Otherwise, we

---

[12] On the RDF as a response to Afghanistan, see U.S. Congress, *Rapid Deployment Forces: Policy and Budgetary Implications* (Washington, D.C.: Congressional Budget Office, 1983), 11–15.

[13] Ibid. For more details, see *Strategic Sealift, Report to Congressional Requesters* (U.S. General Accounting Office, October 1991), 14–15.

[14] *Department of Defense Appropriations for 1989*, Hearing before a Subcommittee of the Committee on Appropriations (Washington, D.C.: GPO, 1988), 175; chart 8, 184. Schwarzkopf Statement, 58.

[15] *Department of Defense Appropriations for 1989*, 914.

[16] Address by Secretary of Defense Harold Brown, in *Department of State Bulletin* 80 (May 1980), 66.

would expect that such efforts would have increased as the Iran-Iraq War dragged on, particularly after 1986 when Iran scored strategic gains at the Faw Peninsula. However, we find a precipitous decline in expenditures during this period.

On the whole, these U.S. defense efforts improved U.S. force projection capability considerably between 1980 and 1991.[17] These enhancements proved crucial for Operations Desert Shield and Desert Storm in 1990 and 1991, and to the task of projecting American capability in the region thereafter.

Concerned with global and regional threats to Gulf stability, Washington was determined not only to improve its capability to deter outside pressure on the Gulf but also to deal with pressures arising within the Gulf. In that spirit, in October 1981 President Reagan stated that there was "no way" the United States could "stand by" and see Saudi Arabia threatened to the point that the flow of oil could be shut down.[18] This statement and others of a similar kind later became known as the Reagan Doctrine, which was widely perceived as a U.S. commitment to protect Saudi Arabia against not only external threats but also internal ones. In this sense, it was a departure from the Carter Doctrine issued on January 23, 1980, in response to the invasion of Afghanistan. It committed the United States to deter or respond to "outside" as opposed to internal threats to Gulf security.[19]

To be sure, the U.S. military build-up for Gulf contingencies came at great cost and was not without its inadequacies.[20] However, if Iraq had invaded Kuwait instead of Iran in 1980, Washington would not have had an effective conventional response. The fact that President Carter considered using nuclear weapons against a possible Soviet invasion of the Gulf from Afghanistan in 1980 underscores how limited the conventional military options in the region were at that time.[21]

Phase IV: War and Containment

The fourth phase was marked by the end of the Cold War and by the Iraqi invasion of Kuwait, both of which led to further enhancements in U.S. regional capability and commitment. The end of the Cold War left Washington without a significant global rival. Thus, for the first time since the "Great Game" between Russia and Britain in the nineteenth century, the

---

17   For details, see Schwarzkopf Statement, 173–302.
18   Ronald Reagan, *Public Papers of the Presidents* (Washington, D.C.: GPO, 1981), 873; clarification of the statement, 952.
19   On the Nixon and Carter doctrines, see Palmer, *Guardians of the Gulf*, 85–111.
20   See *Rapid Deployment Forces*.
21   See *New York Times*, 27 August 1986.

Gulf region lacked major global rivalry superimposed above it. Washington's attention, which culminated in Operation Desert Storm launched on January 16, 1991, shifted from jockeying for influence against the Soviets to containing regional threats such as Iraq and Iran.

In Desert Storm, for the first time the United States fully utilized the major capabilities it had been developing in phase three. In so doing, it proved able and willing to protect regional stability, thus enhancing its credibility. But while significant steps were taken to improve U.S. rapid deployment capability in the 1980s, steps which proved critical in answering the Iraqi aggression of 1990, many weaknesses remained. This was clearly reflected in the fact that it took the United States six months to develop the forces capable of launching Desert Storm. Desert Shield was the largest movement of U.S. forces since World War II, but under more stringent time pressures, the operation would have been much more problematic, particularly if U.S. forces had been tied up in another conflict. The Gulf crisis helped the United States identify and correct some military weaknesses and gave it critical experience. Although postwar defense cuts produced some constraints on U.S. deployment capability, Washington developed its military capabilities after Desert Storm; identified key weaknesses in its ability to project, protect, and sustain a large military; and learned a number of valuable lessons which increased its ability to protect oil supplies and regional stability.[22]

First, the U.S. ability to deploy a major military force to the region improved in the 1990s. The end of the Cold War as well added to these trends. Not only did it free up immense attention that had been focused on the Soviet Union worldwide, but, as the 1991 Gulf War quite clearly showed, it also freed up military divisions that had faced the Soviet army and could now be reassigned for Gulf contingencies. That alone represented a significant development in world affairs that enabled the United States more effectively, credibly, and assiduously to protect oil stability. Absent the fall of the Soviet Union, it would have been far harder for the United States to mount operations in the Gulf, even if it had wanted to risk a confrontation with Moscow in the process.

The Desert Storm experience helped Washington identify valuable technologies and improve or downplay less valuable ones. This further enhanced U.S. capabilities for long-range deployment and fighting in a desert environment.[23] The Air Force's ability to transport materiel required to supply

22 "Desert Shield/Desert Storm: Logistics Lessons Learned," *Air Force Journal of Logistics* 15 (Fall 1991). U.S. Congress, House of Representatives, Committee on Armed Services, *Defense for a New Era: Lessons of the Persian Gulf War* (Washington, D.C.: GPO, 1992).
23 Thomas A. Keaney and Eliot O. Cohen, *Gulf War Air Power Survey: Summary Report* (Washington, D.C.: GPO, 1993), chap. 9.

Desert Shield troops, deployed or in route to the region, faced significant difficulties initially. But over time the Department of Defense and the Air Force devised some ways of alleviating these problems.[24] Improvements in the Civil Reserve Air Fleet program, which uses commercial aircraft to supplement the Air Force's airlift capability, made future fleet activations more effective.[25] In the 1990s, the U.S. military continued to buy more and faster ships and planes, which decreased the time that it takes to deploy a large military force to Iraq by two-thirds of what it took in 1991.

The Gulf crisis also revealed problems in the part of the U.S. mobility strategy referred to as "afloat prepositioning." This strategy was made necessary because of political problems associated with basing troops on Arab soil. It aimed to keep ships continuously loaded with combat equipment near potential conflict areas, thus increasing response time. Studies revealed that while equipment and supplies were delivered to Saudi Arabia eight days after the war began and almost two weeks before they could have been sealifted from the United States, some of the supplies most needed by the Marine Corps were not on the ships, so an expansion of sealift capabilities was needed.[26] By 1994, prepositioning for one of two shore-based brigades was underway, with a third to come, and U.S. access to regional facilities improved, as already noted.[27] Well before the Iraq War of 2003, their equipment was prepared in thirty-seven warehouses in Qatar and Kuwait, with equipment for another armored brigade from the Army and one from the Marines afloat on ships in the region.

Second, in addition to improving its ability to deploy quickly from out-of-theater areas, the United States improved its military position in theater. The total number of U.S. forces and equipment in the region substantially declined after the 1991 Gulf War. The United States, however, maintained considerable over-the-horizon capabilities, as represented by its naval strength and RDF, and prepositioned in key Arab states.[28] In addition, it enjoyed some form of military agreement or defense pact with all of the Gulf states except Iran, Iraq, and Yemen.[29] The U.S. naval presence, referred to as the Fifth Fleet, also increased substantially. It usually includes one aircraft

---

24   *Desert Shield/Storm: Air Mobility Command's Achievements and Lessons for the Future* (GAO/National Security and International Affairs Division (NSIAD)-93–40, 25 January 1993).

25   *Military Airlift: Changes Underway to Ensure Continued Success of Civil Reserve Air Fleet* (GAO/NSIAD-93–12, 31 December 1992).

26   *Military Afloat Prepositioning: Wartime Use and Issues for the Future* (GA0/NSIAD-93–39, 4 November 1992).

27   Fred Smith, Defense Department official, "Remarks at the Meridian International Center" (Washington, D.C.: 18 May 1994), 6.

28   International Institute for Strategic Studies, *The Military Balance, 1995–96* (London: Oxford University Press, 1995), 139, 144–46.

29   United States, State Department, *Treaties in Force, 1993* (Washington, D.C.: GPO, 1994).

carrier battle group in the area and, depending on the potential for crisis, a variety of other naval combatants.

On the ground, the U.S. presence also steadily improved after 1991. The U.S.-Kuwait Defense Cooperation Agreement was signed in September 1991 and provided for U.S. access to Kuwaiti military facilities, prepositioning of defense material for U.S. forces, and joint exercises and training. The agreement did not mandate automatic U.S. protection of Kuwait, but it raised strategic relations to a level unimaginable prior to Desert Storm. Washington also updated its access agreement with Oman (1990) and Bahrain (1991), a twenty-year defense cooperation agreement with Qatar on June 23, 1992 that also allowed U.S. access and prepositioning, and an agreement with the UAE (1994).[30]

Some of the details of these agreements have been classified so as not to ruffle any political feathers, but the agreements have enhanced the U.S. ability to operate in the region by assuring a forward land-based presence, prepositioned equipment in cooperative host environments and the ability to enhance joint military and intelligence cooperation. They also enhance deterrence.

In the case of Bahrain, it is obligated by treaty to provide the United States with basing and other facilities, though such arrangements have been handled quietly through backstage diplomacy, so as not to arouse popular opposition, which in fact has erupted on several occasions. Defense agreements between the two states extend back to 1949 when Bahrain became the de facto home base for U.S. forces in the region. After the relatively oil-poor emirate proved to be a key hub in the 1991 Gulf War—a turning point in U.S.-Bahraini relations—it was transformed in 1993 into the base for the Commander of U.S. Naval Forces Central Command.

In the post-9/11 period, Washington moved to develop the ability to operate out of several Gulf states, especially Qatar, in the event that it went to war with Iraq and Riyadh proved reluctant to host U.S. forces. Since Iraq's invasion of Kuwait, the Qataris have increasingly viewed their future security as a matter for the Americans to handle. Qatar allowed the United States to launch attack missions over Afghanistan from the Al Udeid air base near the Qatari capital of Doha—a 15,000-foot airstrip, which is the longest in the Middle East and where the United States stationed a group of warplanes, organized as the 379th Air Expeditionary Wing. This air base was classified as a secret facility until March 2002, but it later assumed even greater importance as Washington took public steps to develop it by adding runways, bolstering air control operations, constructing a sophisticated air operations

---

[30] *Developments in the Middle East*, U.S. Congress, House of Representatives, Committee on Foreign Affairs, 24 and 30 June 1992 (Washington, D.C.: GPO, 1992), 9.

center, strengthening and expanding hangars, and placing high-performance aircraft there. Some of these changes enhanced air operations in both the Afghanistan and Iraq military operations. In addition, the United States increased usage of a 262-acre base at As Sayliyah, which was completed in August 2000 and could house enough armored equipment for a heavy army brigade.

Moreover, Washington also moved some operations from Florida to Qatar in November 2002, indicating not only advanced planning for a war with Iraq but also what would become in 2003 a permanent shift of major elements of its Central Command (CENTCOM) headquarters into a "forward presence."[31] This move had been under consideration even before the Bush administration took office and was certainly debated during the Afghanistan military operation. However, the campaign to effect regime change in Iraq and potential differences with Saudi Arabia over the basing of U.S. forces added impetus to it. Unlike Saudi Arabia, which at the time claimed that it would not allow its territory to be used in an attack on Iraq unless backed by the UN, Qatar did not take this stance, contrary to some public pronouncements of its reluctance. Nor did Qatar impose uncomfortable conditions on the rules of engagement and social behavior of American forces.

On December 12, 2002, the United States signed a military pact with Qatar, allowing it to use Qatari bases in a war. The improvement in relations was a breakthrough for the United States, because it increased Washington's ability to operate in the region and decreased its dependence on Riyadh and other regional states.

U.S. air power was also enhanced. Washington maintains air expeditionary forces for quick response in various states near potential loci of conflict and has upgraded those facilities since the Gulf War. U.S. forces have also benefited from a manifold increase in the potential for using smart bombs to hit targets. This was demonstrated with efficacy in March 1999 during NATO's campaign against Yugoslavia, in which 70 percent smart bombs were used (compared to 9 percent in the Gulf War).[32] The greater efficacy of smart weapons, and their increased use as a percentage of overall bombs dropped, meant that Washington had far greater capability to hit key targets with less collateral damage in 2003 than in 1991—much less in 1979, when such technology was not an option. During the Iraq War, most of the munitions used were precision-guided, possibly as high as 90 percent.

Third, in addition to enhancements in deployment capability and in in-theater positioning, U.S. forces are better trained. When Iraq invaded

---

[31] Secretary of Defense Donald Rumsfeld, quoted in Senate Hearings on Iraq, 19 September 2002.

[32] See William M. Arkin, "Smart Bombs, Dumb Targeting?" *Bulletin of the Atomic Scientists* 56 (May/June 2000).

Kuwait, U.S. military officials believed that the training of U.S. ground forces had been excellent. However, experiences during the war revealed that additional training in joint operations, deployment, and logistical and other support functions was needed. In the postwar period, the scope of U.S. military exercises increased in a manner unimaginable prior to Desert Storm. In 1993 alone, the United States conducted seventy-seven Naval, eight Special Forces, six Army and six Air Force exercises.[33]

Fourth, the Cooperative Defense Initiative launched by USCENTCOM in the period following September 11 reduced the vulnerability of the GCC states to WMD coercion and to the effects of WMD use.[34] This initiative enhanced interoperability, active defenses, and medical countermeasures to protect soldiers and civilians against WMD.[35] Substantially increasing its commitment after September 11, Washington also honed its ability to eliminate Iraq's WMD threat—which at the time was viewed even by the United Nations as potentially serious and which may have been developed if left unfettered—and, if necessary, Iran's nuclear reactors and to deter WMD retaliation.[36] National Security Adviser Condoleezza Rice asserted the administration's position that the only way to deter WMD use "is to be clear that it would be met with a devastating response"—a notion reflected in the Nuclear Posture Review presented to Congress in January 2002.[37]

These four advancements in U.S. military capability were matched by a continuing commitment to maintain regional stability. This commitment was reflected in the controversial dual containment policy under the Clinton administration and then, after September 11, in a public and determined effort to eliminate Saddam Hussein's regime, which culminated in the Iraq War.

Dual containment arose from the notion that after the 1991 Gulf War, it was not possible to create a free-standing balance of power in the region. Anthony Lake, national security adviser at the time, observed that the United States rejected the past approach of building up Iran to check Iraq and vice versa; rather, it aimed to "neutralize, contain, and, through selective pressure, perhaps eventually transform these backlash states into constructive members of the international community."[38] Dual containment viewed Iran and Iraq as incorrigible in the absence of external pressure, because of their

---

33 *Operation Desert Storm: War Offers Important Insights into Army and Marine Corps Training Needs* (GAO/NSIAD, 92–240, 25 August 1992).
34 *Cooperative Defense Initiative Against Weapons of Mass Destruction in Southwest Asia* (Washington, D.C.: Department of Defense, United States Central Command, 2002).
35 Ibid.
36 Anthony H. Cordesman, *U.S. Forces In The Middle East: Resources and Capabilities* (Boulder, CO: Westview, 1997), 108–15.
37 Quoted in "Rice Warns Iraq, Iran, and N. Korea Of Nuclear Hits," *APS Diplomat Recorder* 56 (16 March 2002).
38 Anthony Lake, "Confronting Backlash States," *Foreign Affairs* 73 (March/April 1994), 46, 48.

ideology and historical background. As one official put it, the "current regime in Iraq is a criminal regime, beyond the pale of international society and, in our judgment, irredeemable."[39] Lake was more optimistic about Iran, but still asserted that:

> Iran is a revolutionary state whose leaders harbor a deep sense of grievance over the close ties between the United States and the Shah. Its revolutionary and militant messages are openly hostile to the United States and its core interests. This basic political reality will shape relations for the foreseeable future.[40]

After September 11, Washington drew on military capabilities that it had developed over the past two decades to seek Saddam's ouster. Elements of the policy of dual containment continued to characterize American behavior in the region, but another dimension was added to the approach: preemptive military engagement for purposes of dealing with the perceived WMD threat. Preemption through such strategies as air strikes fell in line with the Bush administration's national security doctrine, which underscored a U.S. commitment to strike potential adversaries and proliferators preemptively in order to protect regional allies and interests, and the U.S. mainland.[41]

President Bush's State of the Union address on January 29, 2002, foreshadowed a potential war with Iraq. In further crystallizing the national security doctrine of preemption, he identified Iran, North Korea, and Iraq as part of an "axis of evil," asserting that their behavior would not be tolerated and that his administration would make "no distinction between the terrorists who committed these acts and those who harbor them."[42] For the administration, the lesson of September 11 was that Washington must pre-empt threats before they manifest themselves, possibly in the form of terrorists wielding weapons of mass destruction.

Phase V: From Preemption to Nation-Building

Prior to the Iraq War, preemption remained a concept, an abstraction. Indeed, the Afghanistan operation reflected a response to aggression and punishment much more than it did preemption, though it certainly had a pre-emptive element in that Washington wanted to cripple Al Qaeda's ability to attack again. In the Iraq War, however, the administration proved quite

---

39   Martin Indyk, Speech to the Washington Institute for Near East Policy (18 May 1993).
40   Lake, "Confronting Backlash States," 52.
41   *The National Security Strategy of the United States*, September 2002, www.whitehouse.gov/nsc/nss.html.
42   CNN, 29 January 2002.

willing to add teeth to the notion of preemption through a commitment not only to remove Saddam Hussein's regime but also to keep U.S. troops in the region for an extended period of time in a possible nation-building phase in Iraq. Such a commitment was outright unimaginable and impossible in 1979, and not seriously considered by the administration of President George Herbert Walker Bush when it decided not to march on Baghdad at the end of the 1991 Gulf War, despite the potential for its success. After 9/11, George W. Bush was willing to do what his father's foreign policy team had rejected. The world had changed; the stakes had risen.

The Iraq War was one more watershed in the evolution of America's regional position in that it assumed the new role of rebuilding an Arab nation. Bush had campaigned for president on a foreign policy platform that was explicitly against nation-building efforts, but after September 11 he shifted direction. As a country, the United States had never taken on such a nation-building profile in the Middle East, though it had played such a role in post–World War II West Germany and Japan.

While the United States was in the process of eliminating the Taliban regime in Afghanistan and building a new government there, it started to focus greater public attention on Iraq. By the end of 2002, it had rallied global support for UN Resolution 1441, which forced Iraq to comply with previous UN resolutions or face potential force. Indeed, on December 7, 2002, in compliance with Resolution 1441, Iraq gave the UN a 12,000-plus page report and several compact discs that allegedly described the country's arms programs before and after 1990. In effect, the report held that Iraq had no WMD, confirming suspicions in Washington and elsewhere that Baghdad was obfuscating its capabilities.

Subsequently, Iraq allowed UN inspectors to search the country for weapons, and they found no "smoking gun," but were not completely satisfied with its cooperation. The United States, meanwhile, released intelligence information, including tape-recorded conversations of Iraqis indicating that Iraq had WMD and was trying to hide it from UN inspectors. Up until the war, Iraq repeatedly denied that it had WMD, treating the allegation as if it were an outright fabrication by a hawkish United States. It also treated U.S. accusations of its connection to Al Qaeda as nothing more than a pretext for war.

In the summer of 2003 following the Iraq War, it became clear that at least by the late 1990s or early twenty-first century, Saddam's threat was less, perhaps much less, than many had thought it to be. Reports by a close aide who had assisted Saddam for many years claimed that Saddam preferred to let the world believe that he had WMD in order to enhance his own notoriety and to deter potential attacks; this aide said that it was "common knowledge among the leadership" that Iraq had destroyed its chemical stocks and discontinued development of biological and nuclear weapons, though it had the ability to restart the programs [43] If accurate, Saddam's gamble backfired because the false impression he put out and his lack of cooperation with UN inspectors in the 1990s actually contributed to American motivations to remove his regime.

Nonetheless, after weeks of strained negotiations among members of the UN Security Council, the United States and Britain moved to present the eighteenth UN resolution against Iraq. In contrast to the position of France, Russia, and China, which sought a period of continued UN inspections to last a few more months, the eighteenth resolution pushed openly for using force should Iraq not immediately comply. After France threatened to veto the resolution, possibly with backing from Russia and China, and after Washington and London failed to secure the votes of the smaller countries on the Security Council, the two allies decided that Resolution 1441 provided sufficient basis for the use of force, even without an eighteenth resolution.

After providing Saddam, his sons, and key Iraqi leaders with an ultimatum to leave Iraq in forty-eight hours or face war, the United States proceeded to launch Operation Iraqi Freedom. It was supported by British forces and some Australian troops and backed by a broader "coalition of the willing," as the United States and Britain referred to it. However, unlike George H. W. Bush, his son faced harsh criticism that American foreign policy had become arrogant and unilateral, and had failed to form a highly engaged coalition.

On March 19, President Bush announced that the war had begun with a precision strike by two F-117 Stealth jets on a bunker suspected of containing Iraq's leadership, a strike that some believed had killed Saddam Hussein and could precipitate the regime's collapse. After Iraq did not surrender, and Saddam appeared to have escaped the attack, the United States launched a massive air attack. Known as "Shock and Awe"—a title that, to many, smacked of bravura—the brief air attack was followed by a large ground attack from Kuwait. Special forces had worked within Iraq to undermine Saddam's regime through subversion and psychological operations, and the U.S. Air Force continued to bomb key Iraqi targets, while American and British forces proceeded on the ground. At first, they faced unexpected resistance from Saddam's Fedayeen backed by some elements of Saddam's Republican Guards in cities such as Basra and Nasiriyah.

Three weeks after the "Shock and Awe" operation, Saddam's statues came crashing down with a thud heard around the world, and the process of ridding Iraq of all remnants of the dictator's regime commenced in earnest.

43   Slobodan Lekic, "Close Aide says Saddam Wanted World to Think he had Weapons," *Associated Press*, 3 August 2003.

Initially, an optimistic United States sought to run Iraq without significant official participation by Iraqis, and to slowly transfer administrative tasks to an Iraqi-led transitional government. However, this plan ran into a number of problems following the war, and Washington shifted to a quicker strategy of developing an Iraqi Governing Council. This council was officially put into place on July 14, 2003, and could be considered Iraq's first postwar government. The council, composed of twenty-five Iraqis reflecting Iraq's ethnic and religious mix, was vested with the power to hire and fire ministers, draft and approve a budget and send diplomats abroad. The council did not replace the U.S. role initially, but it did represent the interests of the Iraqi people to the Coalition Provisional Authority during Iraq's transition to a sovereign, democratic, and representative government, and worked jointly with the U.S.-led authority on such subjects as drafting a new Iraqi constitution.

In response to criticism that Washington had not planned well for the postwar period, in July 2003 Bush administration officials asserted that no one should have expected an easy transition from a brutal dictatorship that had abused the Iraqi people.[44] Widespread looting, a crumbling infrastructure, and a burgeoning guerrilla-like war created an impression of impending chaos. And raised the question: how long would American troops stay in Iraq in large numbers? Secretary of Defense Donald Rumsfeld pointed to the long and successful American role in Japan and Germany to emphasize the danger of making predictions and expecting quick results.[45] The general view from Washington was that U.S. forces would leave Iraq once Iraq's Governing Council had drafted a new constitution, held democratic elections, and demonstrated an ability to rule itself effectively. Iraq's Governing Council may be able to achieve these goals, but we must consider that the seeds do exist for the nation-building effort either to go awry over time or to proceed at a snail's pace.

As is well known, Iraq was not completely destroyed by war and therefore did not have to be entirely rebuilt, as was the case in Japan and Germany after World War II. The irony is that the U.S. military victory was so quick that elements of Saddam's regime (and elite forces) escaped destruction and melted into the population, although many of Iraq's top leaders, including Saddam, would slowly be captured. Moreover, U.S. forces did not invade key Sunni areas of Baghdad where Saddam had far greater support than in Shia areas. These realities, combined with anti-Americanism within Iraq and among the Muslim fighters that joined the fray from outside Iraq, motivated the guerrilla war against U.S. forces.

44 Secretary of Defense Donald Rumsfeld and Commander of U.S. Central Command Tommy Franks, Senate Armed Services Committee (C-SPAN: 9 July 2003).
45 *This Week with George Stephanopoulos*, ABC, 13 July 2003.

Overall, the Iraq War produced a number of consequences for the U.S. regional role. Some of them are still evolving and will likely evolve further over the years, depending on the course of the nation-building effort in Iraq, but the following points are worth making.

At the strategic level, the United States has enhanced its military options. As part of a broader strategy to create more flexibility in military capability, it improved its ability to base out of Qatar, Bahrain, Kuwait, and Oman. Moreover, the Pentagon has sought to create a network of smaller bases in Iraq that can enhance its ability to project force quickly. To what extent it can rely on this option may be determined partly by the course of Iraq's nation-building effort.

In addition, the Iraq War further enhanced American regional credibility in this sense. It did establish quite clearly that Washington would use massive force (and expense) to protect security—as it perceived it—even in the thankless task of nation-building. The days of 1979, when U.S. credibility was widely doubted, or even 1990, when the Saudis wondered if the United States would in fact stay the course against Saddam—these days were history. Future troubles in Iraq could re-ignite questions about the U.S. commitment to Iraq, but that remains to be seen.

Furthermore, the fall of Saddam's regime, as well as alternative basing options, has decreased U.S. dependence on Saudi military facilities. This effect became clear when Washington announced the withdrawal of U.S. forces from Saudi Arabia in July 2003, leaving only a small contingent behind, albeit with the option of a major entry in the event of a crisis.

Global oil stability cannot be divorced from political and military realities. Over the period of 1979 to 2003, the United States became substantially more able and willing to protect regional oil supplies against a broad range of threats. As we shall see later in the book, that strategic development also enhanced U.S. leverage in affecting oil markets directly. On balance, we would be hard-pressed to argue that oil stability was more assured in the 1970s or 1980s, when this development had not yet taken place in full. All other things being equal, it was much better to have a capable global gendarme on patrol, controversial as that could be, than to leave aggressive and potentially aggressive actors within and outside the region with greater room to pursue their agendas.

Chapter 5

THE UNITED STATES IN THE MIDDLE EAST
BEFORE AND AFTER SEPTEMBER 11

American foreign policy in the Middle East has been very controversial. Promoters of democracy have bemoaned the autocratic nature of regimes in the Persian Gulf, which some view as being propped up by a power-hungry United States. Others have assailed the oil connection between Washington and Gulf states, and resent what they have perceived as neo-colonial U.S. encroachment in the domestic and international affairs of the region. Meanwhile, Islamic extremists and their sympathizers have seen close Arab military relations with foreigners as an affront to their version of Islam.

U.S. relations with GCC states in particular have fluctuated over time and have been marked by difficult periods. However, with the partial exception of Saudi Arabia, they have improved, providing we examine them over the entirety of the past two decades. The Saudi case is more complex because of the ongoing effects of 9/11. U.S.-Saudi relations have gyrated but they had generally improved from 1980 until the attacks. The attacks definitely damaged bilateral relations, which were not wholly torn asunder because of the mutual dependencies that were built up over the past twenty-five years.

Overall, GCC states have come to depend on and trust the United States much more than they did, for instance, in 1979. They lack a serious security alternative to Washington and need its support to achieve the goals of joining the global economy in earnest and moving away from being one-good economies. The fact that these states increasingly need the United States is important to the question of oil stability. It enhances the ability of the United States to operate in the region and adds yet another reason for these states to pursue market-friendly policies.

U.S.-SAUDI RELATIONS: THE LONG VIEW

The trajectory of U.S.-Saudi relations has been influenced by many factors, but the goal here is limited to providing insight into their relevance for oil stability only. Although the United States has increasingly been able to count on other Arab states to play important security and economic roles—a good sign for oil stability—the Saudi relationship remains important.

Over time, U.S.-Saudi relations have been a composite of unspoken agreements, cautiously cooperative interactions, and hidden resentments, enmeshed in mutual dependencies that are sometimes obfuscated for political reasons. Deciphering them can be a little like breaking a secret code. If we analyzed this nexus of relationships and commitments right before and after September 11, we might well conclude that they had deteriorated. This would not be mistaken, but it would be just a short-term snapshot and only part of a more complex story. It is more useful to take the longer view, which allows us to discern some key propensities in these relations, and to put particular events such as September 11 and the Iraq War of 2003 into clearer perspective.

Israel represents one area of major difference in bilateral relations. The Saudi position on Israel has fluctuated from maximum hostility to the notion that Israel has a right to exist—*if* it meets certain conditions that Israel has largely viewed as unreasonable. Within these parameters, the Saudis have seen Israel as an occupier, a foreign entity in the land of Islam. As the caretakers of Mecca and Medina, they have felt obligated to promote Muslim causes like the plight of the Palestinians. Obviously, assailing Israel has also served local political goals. The Saudi position, of course, has contrasted starkly with that of the United States, which has deep religious, political, and strategic ties to the Jewish state. It sees Israel as an important democracy in a region hostile to democracy, and views Arab hatred of Israel as counterproductive and unacceptable. Behind a generally pro-Israel public, it has been willing, certainly since the Six Day War of 1967, to countenance tensions with Arab states that arise from its support of Israel.[1]

U.S.-Saudi differences over Israel began to develop when Israel became a state in 1948, but clearly expanded only after the 1967 Six Day War when Israel, in what the United Nations determined to be an act of self-defense, attacked Arab states that appeared poised to launch war. Israel gained control of key territories, including the West Bank and Gaza Strip, and the U.S.-Israeli relationship began to blossom in earnest.

On June 6, the second day of that war, the Saudi regime, partly in response to popular demonstrations, asserted that it would cut off oil supplies

---

[1]   William B. Quandt, *Peace Process: American Diplomacy and the Arab-Israeli Conflict since 1967* (Washington, D.C.: Brookings Institution, 2001).

to any state that aided Israel. The Saudis stopped oil shipments to the United States and Britain, but an existing market glut undermined the boycott, which was abandoned by early September when it became too burdensome on oil producers. Thereafter, the United States and Saudi Arabia managed their differences over Israel fairly well, until the 1973 oil embargo, which is covered in chapter 8. While relations were mended in the mid- to late 1970s, the embargo left an unpleasant residue in its wake, and, in any event, problems in bilateral relations recurred in 1978 and 1979.

The important point here is that the Soviet intervention in Afghanistan and the Iran-Iraq War helped strengthen those relations. The 1981 U.S. sale of AWACs aircraft to Saudi Arabia was one of several developments during the war that developed U.S.-Saudi mutual trust. While U.S. interest in the AWACs sale, as implied by several U.S. officials, was related more to the Soviet threat, the Saudi interest in cooperating with America was motivated more by the Iranian threat, although both Riyadh and Washington were concerned with threats at the regional and global level.[2] The AWACs sale also improved Saudi security and U.S. intelligence and reconnaissance reach, and set a pattern for mutual cooperation.

The AWACs sale was related to the Saudi agreement to build huge underground strategic facilities, which were intended to support a massive U.S. deployment in the event of a major Iranian or Soviet threat.[3] Oddly enough, they were used not against Iran or Moscow, but rather against Iraq in 1990. Such forces were a *sine qua non* for mounting Operations Desert Shield and Storm in 1990 and 1991.[4] For its part, Washington also reacted favorably to Saudi requests for U.S. arms and military backup support to alleviate concern about threats from Iran. While the AWACs package improved U.S.-Saudi security relations to some extent, the RDF, which in 1983 was transformed into CENTCOM, enhanced U.S. regional credibility. Although its development contributed to suspicions in the Gulf of U.S. strategic intentions, it represented one of a string of U.S. defense efforts which allayed some fears in the region that Washington was incapable of protecting Gulf security—that it, as Saudi Prince Sultan feared, "would leave the arena exclusively for the Soviets to intervene."[5] RDF joint exercises with Egypt and Gulf states improved intercountry military coordination, and the RDF

[2] For an example of U.S. interest in the AWACs sale, see Secretary of State Alexander Haig, "Saudi Security, Middle East Peace, and U.S. Interests," *Current Policy* 323 (1 October 1981), 1–3.
[3] Scott Armstrong, "Saudis' AWACs Just a Beginning of a New Strategy," *Washington Post*, November 1, 1981. Armstrong broke this story.
[4] For details on this infrastructure, see *Conduct of the Persian Gulf War: Final Report to Congress* (Washington, D.C.: GPO, April 1992), Appendix F.
[5] Quoted in *Kuwait KUNA* in Foreign Broadcast Information Service (FBIS): Middle East and Africa, 17 May 1982, C-5.

also served an important backup role for U.S. reflagging forces during the Gulf tanker war.

As is well known, the United States agreed to reflag eleven Kuwaiti tankers in June 1987. In so doing, it wished in part to defeat what former Assistant Secretary of State Richard Murphy asserted was "Iran's hegemonistic plans for the Gulf," and also to re-establish credibility with Arab Gulf states after the Iran-Contra debacle.[6] These states were disturbed by the arms-for-hostages fiasco in which the administration sought to secretly sell U.S. arms to Khomeini's radical regime in exchange for its support in saving U.S. hostages in Lebanon. Although the arms were not militarily significant, they suggested that Washington would accommodate Iran, with which it publicly had no relations, at the expense of closer U.S. relations with members of the Saudi-led GCC.

Gulf officials were initially ambivalent about the reflagging mission because it was high profile, threatened to increase superpower regional intervention, and openly challenged (and could seriously provoke) Iran.[7] But by deterring Iran's ability to prosecute the war through its attacks on shipping and on the interests of the GCC states that supported Iraq, the U.S. reflagging mission clearly benefited GCC states, especially Saudi Arabia and, of course, Kuwait. The reflagging policy also helped ensure Gulf stability, and denied Moscow a foothold in reflagging Kuwaiti tankers, which Kuwait appeared willing to allow until the United States agreed to the task itself. The reflagging mission also helped dispel beliefs that the United States was uninterested in stopping the Iran-Iraq War, and created the perception in some quarters that Washington helped constrain Iran. Overall, U.S. credibility increased significantly and its ties to Arab states improved. Only Washington proved capable enough to take action to contain Iran. The USSR, while initially invited to reflag Kuwait tankers and interested in enhancing its regional role, lacked the regional military capability and support to do so, and, in any event, was actively wooing Iran. By 1989, U.S.-GCC relations had warmed to the point that one U.S. diplomat referred to them as achieving "honeymoon" status.[8]

On the whole, however, U.S. defense efforts such as the RDF did not receive enthusiastic support in the Gulf—until Iraq's invasion of Kuwait. In part, this is because most Gulf states viewed the USSR as less of a threat than Washington portrayed it to be. In general, U.S. efforts to convince the GCC states of the impending Soviet threat failed, as had Britain's attempt to coerce Persia in the nineteenth century that tsarist Russia was the real

6   Interview with Richard Murphy.
7   *War in the Persian Gulf: The U.S. Takes Sides*, Staff Report to the Committee on Foreign Relations, United States Senate, November 1987 (Washington, D.C.: GPO, 1987), 29–30.
8   Joseph Twinam, quoted in the *Christian Science Monitor*, 9 February 1989, 8.

enemy. While Iraq's invasion of Kuwait made the importance of U.S. force projection abundantly clear—even if Moscow wasn't the raison d'être—Arab leaders would continue to debate the proper size and role of U.S. forces in the region throughout the 1990s.

Problems in U.S.-Saudi relations did not disappear, but the cooperation catalyzed by the Iran-Iraq conflict contrasted starkly with the less than cooperative relations that existed prior to it. The 1990–91 Gulf crisis motivated the highest level of U.S.-Saudi cooperation to that point. Even during the U.S. reflagging of Kuwaiti tankers in 1987, Riyadh was concerned about identifying with Washington, lest it curtail the mission if events went awry. In 1990, Riyadh was initially nervous about requesting U.S. support after Iraq's invasion, but the crisis spurred unprecedented U.S.-Saudi cooperation, gave both states invaluable political and military experience, and represented a significant break with the past.

In 1994 and 1995, the United States pursued a dual political and military strategy in the region. On the political front, it sought to assure the GCC of what Secretary of State Warren Christopher referred to as an enduring American "ironclad commitment" to their defense.[9] At the same time, by the spring of 1995, Washington stepped up its push for enhanced prepositioning capabilities in Saudi Arabia, which a number of regional observers, citing leaks from the Department of Defense, mistakenly interpreted as a U.S. effort to establish a "permanent base" in the kingdom.[10] Dual political and military approaches enhanced inter-state reciprocity and further strengthened relations. While divisive issues remained, both sides recognized their common interests in checking a revisionist Iraq and a potentially ascendant Iran, though Riyadh was more inclined to play a dual game of maintaining positive relations with both states.

By and large, Saudi leaders have managed the competitive pressures of preserving tradition amid change reasonably well—leaning pro-American while not seriously alienating domestic constituents. They have realized that they need the United States to ensure against any major future threat to their survival. As Abdallah asserted in 1998, U.S.-Saudi ties were "deep and strategic and in the long term, this fact will only increase in importance."[11] Of course, the fall of Saddam's regime makes Washington less critical to Riyadh, but far from irrelevant, as the future is inherently unpredictable. In the broader scope of time, no Saudi leader is likely to forget that of the three

9   Quoted in John M. Goshko, "Christopher Reassures Gulf States on Iraq," *Washington Post*, 28 April 1994, A21.

10 See, for instance, *Kuwait Radio Kuwait* in FBIS: NES, 13 March 1995, 17 and *Paris AL-MUHARRIR* in FBIS: NES, 20 March 1995, 14.

11 At a meeting with U.S. oil executives, one of whom reported this remark. Quoted in Nawaf E. Obaid, *The Oil Kingdom at 100: Petroleum Policymaking in Saudi Arabia* (Washington, D.C.: The Washington Institute for Near East Policy, 2000), 8.

Saudi states that have existed since 1744, the first two collapsed not as a result of internal developments but chiefly from external invasion.[12]

The Al Saud also depend on the United States to help them negotiate and benefit from globalization. The monarchy has moved slowly in the direction of globalizing its economy, beginning with the oil sector. Thus, the regime moved to open up its oil operations more significantly to participation by foreign oil companies, an endeavor in which U.S. firms have been crucial. More importantly, the Saudis also decided to accelerate efforts, launched in less earnest form after the 1973–74 oil boom, to diversify the economy away from a strict reliance on oil as an export good.[13] Despite the tensions of 9/11, an underlying dimension in U.S.-Saudi relations remains intact: Riyadh has increasingly depended on U.S. influence in the global economy for such diversification because Washington plays a central role in many international organizations and effectively plays gatekeeper to the global economy.[14]

For its part, Saudi Arabia also depends more on the United States because U.S. consumption of Saudi oil has increased significantly over the past decade, in ways that no other economy rivals. As a result, Saudi Arabia, as Edward Morse and James Richard put it, is "uniquely dependent on growth in U.S. demand."[15] Of course, economic dependence is not a one-way street. The United States benefits from Saudi investment and needs Riyadh to provide oil and to increase its production when crises or global demand require it, and also to play a cooperative role in providing for regional stability.

Dependence on the United States obviously does not allow the United States to dictate terms to Riyadh, but, as in the case of Kuwait, it does suggest that ignoring U.S. interests beyond a certain point may bring about some unacceptable or at least unpleasant risks and costs.[16] This is as true of security as it is of oil issues.

Indeed, American pressure has been applied to influence Saudi and OPEC policy. While later chapters cover these issues more closely, it is worth

[12] Mamoun Fandy, *Saudi Arabia and the Politics of Dissent* (New York: St. Martin's Press, 1999), 248.
[13] Robert E. Looney, "Saudi Arabia: Measures of Transition from a Rentier State," in *Iran, Iraq, and the Arab Gulf States*, ed. Joseph A. Kechichian (New York: Palgrave, 2001), chap. 9.
[14] The diversification plan appears to be initially successful, though not without potential pitfalls. See ibid.
[15] Edward L. Morse and James Richard, "The Battle for Energy Dominance," *Foreign Affairs* 81 (2002), 22.
[16] Interview with Abdullah Bishara. On the Saudi approach, see the statement by Ali I. Naimi, Saudi Minister of Petroleum and Mineral Resources, in *OPEC Bulletin* 31 (March 2000), 4–6. See also "Iran: The OPEC Factor and Price Prospects," *APS Review* 56 (9 April 2001) and "Naimi, Richardson Agree on Need for Stability in Global Oil Markets," *OPEC Bulletin* 31 (March 2000), 15.

sketching one important case here. In the spring of 2000, U.S. Energy Secretary Bill Richardson exerted perhaps unprecedented U.S. pressure during quota negotiations to convince OPEC officials that supply restrictions increase inflation, contribute to a deteriorating investment environment, and hurt the United States and global economies. Richardson described such "quiet diplomacy" as effective pressure on OPEC to boost production.[17]

Some members of Congress, however, were more impatient. Senator Frank Murkowski asked why OPEC could not move more quickly to take action and questioned whether it respected U.S. wishes. Other members of Congress were motivated to undo the assistance measures that the United States put in place in Kuwait, Saudi Arabia, and other GCC states after Iraq's invasion of Kuwait due to the perceived absence of reciprocity.[18] On the same day of Richardson's testimony in the Senate, the Oil Price Reduction Act of 2000, otherwise known as H.R. 3822, was introduced. It aimed to "reduce, suspend or terminate any assistance under the Foreign Assistance Act of 1961 and the Arms Export Control Act to each country determined by the President to be engaged in oil price fixing to the detriment of the United States economy."[19] After some amendments that downplayed linkage and emphasized diplomacy, the bill passed the House 382–38 on March 22, 2000, a moment when the reports indicated that the Federal Trade Commission was considering whether to file a lawsuit against OPEC.[20] Theorists might point to such congressional action as signaling U.S resolve in facing OPEC and underscoring that the administration, beset with domestic pressures, would have to take a tougher bargaining position.[21]

Subsequent events seemed to support Richardson's contention that U.S. diplomacy was related to an immediate OPEC production increase of 1.8 mb/d.[22] OPEC ministers had some difficulty arriving at a final agreement, in part because Iran was offended by U.S. "intrusion" into its deliberations, although Iran subsequently signed on.[23] Reflecting Iran's general position on the U.S. role, the Foreign Ministry spokesman Hamid Reza Asefi asserted that the "use of political and military levers and forcing other countries to secure one's own economic interests are among hegemonic methods which

---

17 Quoted in CRS Issue Brief RL30459, *Coping With High Oil Prices: A Summary of Options* (Washington, D.C.: CRS, 19 April 2000).
18 Ibid.
19 For the documents relevant to this legislation, see www.house.gov/international_relations/GILMAN_255.PDF.
20 See "House Takes Aim at OPEC for High Oil Prices," *Oil Daily* 50 (23 March 2000).
21 See Lisa L. Martin, *Democratic Commitments: Legislatures and International Cooperation* (Princeton: Princeton University Press, 2000).
22 "The U.S. Role with OPEC," *Oil and Gas Journal* 98 (24 April 2000), 19.
23 CRS, *Coping With High Oil Prices.*

do not go with any logic."[24] In January 2001, when OPEC decreased oil production, thereby igniting fears of rising prices, Saudi Arabia, which had sold the United States oil at a discount of $1 per barrel, assured Richardson that it was eager to stabilize oil markets and would increase production to enable world economic growth when necessary.[25]

FROM SEPTEMBER 11 TO SADDAM'S FALL

The historical opacity of U.S.-Saudi relations turned crude dark after 9/11. However, it is fair to surmise that while the attacks created the potential for a serious and irreparable rift in relations, developments over the past two decades militated against it. It is worth briefly exploring this dynamic here by first examining several problems that were generated or accelerated by September 11 and that had the effect of hurting U.S.-Saudi relations.

The view emerged in the United States that the 9/11 hijackers were at least affected by, if not deeply indoctrinated in, an extremist brand of Islam taught in Saudi religious schools. The royal family, after all, created the broad system of mosques, bureaucracies, and schools run by religious leaders, and they sustain, finance, appoint, govern, and sometimes even sanction or fire them. Over time, in fact, the regime has gained more influence over religious leaders and their activities and has bureaucratized the religious establishment.[26] It is, therefore, clear that the regime has influence over what is taught to Saudis about the West, including, most pertinently, the United States.

In addition, September 11 put a disturbing spotlight on the regime. The number of unsettling news stories flowed without end. The regime was increasingly seen as corrupt in some Washington circles, tied to terrorism by the American public, and as lagging far behind Kuwait, Qatar, and Bahrain in moving toward democratic practices, much less democracy itself.

Moreover, 9/11 forced a serious reconsideration about how public and intense U.S.-Saudi military cooperation should be. Saudis, including those in the royal family, began to question whether the security benefits of an American connection were worth the potential domestic costs of increasing opposition to the regime, as reflected in the internal threat from Al Qaeda.

---

24 Quoted in "Iran Slams U.S. Pressure on OPEC to Raise Output," *Xinhua News Agency*, 20 March 2000, www.comtexnews.com.
25 Morse and Richard, "The Battle for Energy Dominance," 21; "Saudi Prince Vows Stable Oil Market," *New York Times*, 14 January 2001.
26 Joseph A. Kechichian, *Succession in Saudi Arabia* (New York: Palgrave, 2001), chap. 3 and Ayman Al-Yassini, *Religion and State in the Kingdom of Saudi Arabia* (Boulder, CO: Westview, 1985), 70–76.

Some observers went so far as to say that public anger in Saudi Arabia at both the monarchy and the United States threatened to tear apart their strategic alliance.[27]

For their part, scores of Saudi religious scholars and academics did issue a manifesto in the spring of 2002 suggesting that Muslims might find common ground with the West, and liberal strains could be identified within the kingdom.[28] At the same time, however, more immoderate forces were at play with a bent for heavily and openly criticizing their counterparts. In one such rebuke, the unnamed critic, reflecting a certain amount of broader sentiment, praised the war on America as giving Muslims a "sense of relief" that action was being taken against the Americans who had so oppressed the Islamic world.[29] Many in Saudi Arabia saw the U.S. war on terrorism as a war to enhance American power at the expense of Muslims. Anti-Americanism was heightened by views that the United States had sought to strangle the Iraqi people with economic sanctions and then to take their oil in war; that Riyadh was too dependent for security on a manipulative and intrusive America; that it was in bed with Washington economically; and that pro-Israel Washington was either against or, at best, neglectful of the Palestinians.[30] The U.S. decision to withdraw key forces from Saudi Arabia in the summer of 2003 may well appease some discontents in the kingdom, but that remains to be seen.

What is certainly clear is that Riyadh was confronted, to a greater extent than in the past, with the following problem: even if mutual interests bolstered bilateral relations, U.S.-Saudi relations were a subset of and had to be forged within U.S.-Muslim relations in general. The regime became more intimately aware of the political cost at home and abroad of its close U.S. connection. Moreover, the diminished threat from Iran and Iraq over time allowed Riyadh to distance itself more from Washington, though only so far.[31] Perceptions that the Saudis wanted U.S. forces to leave were repeatedly dispelled by Saudi leaders, but they did reflect real concerns.[32]

American officials, for their part, were loath even to voice any concerns about U.S.-Saudi relations, and both states moved to deny reports that senior Saudi officials viewed the continued presence of 5,000 U.S. military personnel

---

27 This broader sentiment was captured in Eric Rouleau, "Trouble in the Kingdom," *Foreign Affairs* 81 (July/August 2002).

28 On these strains, see Richard Dekmejian, "The Liberal Impulse in Saudi Arabia," *Middle East Journal* 57 (Summer 2003).

29 Quoted in Neil MacFarquhar, "A Few Saudis Defy a Rigid Islam To Debate Their Own Intolerance," *New York Times*, 12 July 2002, A1, A10.

30 Mai Yamani, *Changed Identities* (London: Royal Institute of International Affairs, 2000), esp. 35, 71.

31 This paragraph is partly based on an interview with Chas W. Freeman Jr.

32 See "Iran and Saudi Arabia Are Watching in the Middle Of The Devil's Triangle," *APS Diplomat New Service*, 28 January 2002.

as a political liability.[33] Vice President Richard Cheney, perhaps seeking
Saudi support in the potential war against Iraq, went so far as to describe
U.S.-Saudi ties as "strong" and to assert that other descriptions of them were
"simply mistaken," and President Bush advanced a similar view, if in somewhat less spirited form.[34] The administration's broader approach, however,
was viewed by some key U.S. senators as timid and not effective in confronting the Saudis about transnational terrorism.[35] In fact, 9/11 elevated the
question of the proper U.S. role in Saudi Arabia to a national debate, with
a number of senior officials in Congress and the Pentagon going so far as to
assert that a U.S. military withdrawal from Saudi Arabia should be seriously
considered.[36] Some alleged that the Saudis sought a similar state of affairs
as well.[37]

Fourth, some U.S. officials were unhappy with the lack of Saudi military
support following 9/11. Though Riyadh broke diplomatic relations with the
Taliban, it refused to allow America use of its bases in the war in Afghanistan.
This raised questions about whether Riyadh felt under pressure to distance
itself from Washington after 9/11. However, the arrangement was not without reason. We can conjecture that the United States would have preferred
access but at the same time did not want to destabilize the Saudi regime,
especially if it could meet particular strategic goals in Afghanistan without
basing in Saudi Arabia. And, in fact, as former CENTCOM leader General
Anthony Zinni pointed out, Washington had been taking action even before
9/11 to develop other basing options so that it would not become "totally
dependent on one place."[38] Moreover, it could rely on many of the capabilities that it had developed over the years, as laid out in chapter 4, which did
not require basing in Saudi Arabia.

Fifth, the issue of Israel arose anew. The Saudis expressed disappoint-
ment with the generally pro-Israel U.S. position in the wake of Palestinian-
Israeli violence. This anger had developed even before 9/11 as reflected in an
August 2001 letter from Crown Prince Abdallah to President Bush alerting
the United States to the potential for a serious rupture in relations. However,

---

[33] See "Riyadh and Washington Affirm Ties," *MEED*, 25 January 2002. *APS Diplomatic
     Recorder* 57 (30 November 2002).
[34] CNN, 26 August 2002.
[35] For instance, Joseph Lieberman on CBS, *Face the Nation*, 24 November 2002. *The Future
     of U.S.-Saudi Arabian Relations*, United States, House of Representatives, Hearings before
     the Subcommittee on the Middle East and South Asia of the Committee on International
     Relations (Washington, D.C.: GPO: 22 May 2002).
[36] On this debate, see *MEED* 46 (25 January 2002), 2; *APS Diplomat News Service* 55
     (10 December 2002); *Economist*, 26 January 2002.
[37] Crown Prince Abdallah subsequently refuted these claims. See "Abdullah Speaks Out,"
     MEED (1 February 2002).
[38] Quoted in Elaine Sciolino and Eric Schmitt, "U.S. Rethinks Its Role in Saudi Arabia," *New York
     Times*, 10 March 2002, 24.

9/11 may have added to the desire of the Al Saud to shore up their Muslim credentials by advancing the Palestinian cause, just at a time Al Qaeda was trying to question them and to portray itself as the great defender of Muslims worldwide.[39]

But despite such differences and recriminations, the United States and Saudi Arabia sought to preserve relations. Like all oil producers, the Saudis must carefully weigh multiple factors in deciding the best oil pricing strategy at any given time. While they do not often challenge OPEC objectives, they do see, perhaps more than other producers, the bigger global picture in which the U.S. alliance matters greatly.[40] Within that picture, September 11 did hurt U.S.-Saudi relations, but it also may have made Saudi Arabia more inclined to assume a U.S.-friendly oil and security policy than it otherwise would have been, in an effort to mend relations with Washington or at least to put the brakes on their downward spiral. For instance, in late 2002, Saudi officials quietly permitted U.S. aircraft to operate from Saudi soil in bombing raids on targets in southern Iraq in response to Iraqi violations of the no-fly zone. These missions had earlier been flown out of Kuwait.[41]

Mutual dependencies made it easier to survive 9/11 and harder for the two sides to abandon one another, as evinced by the Iraq War of 2003. Until September 15, 2002, the Saudi public position on Iraq fell far short of what the United States sought, although it is likely that the private position was at least somewhat more in line. Riyadh refused to allow invading U.S. forces to use Saudi bases like the sophisticated Prince Sultan Air Base command center south of Riyadh, which was designed and built by the United States to house the air staff of the Central Command in wartime, arguing that the use of force was not warranted. In mid-September, however, the Saudis changed public course and indicated that the United States could use military bases in an attack on Iraq, if the UN Security Council passed a resolution backing military action. Saudi Arabia remained opposed to the use of force in principle, but this indicated an important shift, which very well may have been triggered by Bush's September 12 speech at the United Nations several days earlier, in which he called on Iraq to comply unconditionally with UN resolutions, sought multilateral UN support in the effort to pressure Iraq to allow UN inspectors back into the country, and showed significant, unilateral resolve to remove Saddam from power if he did not comply with UN resolutions.

39   "Saudi-U.S. Ties Set to Change as War on Terror Spreads across the Middle East," *APS Diplomat News Service*, 25 February 2002.

40   Interview with Muhammad Al-Tayyeb.

41   Eric Schmitt, "Saudis Are Said to Assure U.S. on Use of Bases," *New York Times*, 29 December 2002.

However, to some extent, the lagged effects of 9/11 continued to plague relations. In an unprecedented move, in late 2002 the Al Saud initiated a zealous defense of their efforts to fight terrorism and crack down on Saudi charities. They sought to convince Americans that they were important and useful allies, to counter anti-Saudi sentiment that might hurt relations, and to distance themselves from international terrorism. On December 3, 2002, Saudi Foreign Policy Adviser Adel al-Jubeir discussed with the media a summary Saudi report outlining how much it had done to fight terrorism and argued that Saudi Arabia had been "unfairly maligned" based on misunderstandings and deliberate lies about what Saudi Arabia has done on terrorism.[42]

In some measure, this was true: the regime was misunderstood. After all, most high-ranking members of the royal family—at least those who do not want to challenge the leadership for internal political reasons—do not sympathize with Al Qaeda, and see Osama bin Laden as a threat. Saudi Arabia withdrew his citizenship in 1994, after which he became an increasingly harsh critic of the regime and sought its demise, hoping to replace it with a Taliban-like government. Obviously, those who sympathize with him in Saudi Arabia are not fans of the regime.

But while at least most in the House of Saud do not support Al Qaeda, the real question has been whether the regime would aggressively fight terrorism, even at the risk of alienating influential Saudi businessmen, clergy, and elements of the public, which lend it credibility and support. A harsh response could even alienate mullahs and others who are not extremists but nonetheless resent royal family interference, especially under perceived pressure from Washington.

Riyadh has shown some recognition that changes are needed in its religious schools, and it has taken some steps to curb its own radical Islamists.[43] It has also moved to freeze suspected terrorist holdings, to police local charities and financial institutions more vigorously, and to provide some intelligence assistance to Washington.[44] Defending the Saudi role, al-Jubeir asserted that since Saudis do not pay taxes, the regime does not file returns and do audits, so it is not a question of "laxness in the system, it was just that we didn't have a mechanism that requires nonprofit organizations to perform audits. Now, we do."[45] Meanwhile, Muslims are expected to donate 2.5

---

42 The transcript appears in Adel Al-Jubeir Holds News Conference, Federal Document Clearing House (3 December 2002). Hereafter Al-Jubeir transcript.

43 See "Saudi-U.S. Relations Are Running through Lengthy Turbulence," *APS Diplomatic News Service*, 10 December 2001. Saudi foreign minister Faisal indicated at least that the regime had taken measures to remove anti-American teachings from its madrasas. Interviewed on CBS, 15 September 2002.

44 "Riyadh Cracks Down on Terrorists Assets, *APS Diplomat Recorder*, 27 October 2001. On intelligence assistance, see Maureen Lorenzetti, "U.S. Firms Say Timetable May Slip on Saudi Gas Deals," *Oil and Gas Journal* (21 January 2002).

45 Al-Jubeir transcript.

percent of their wealth each year to charity, which generates significant unregulated funds.

These efforts notwithstanding, the broad consensus was that the regime, as during such episodes as the 1996 Khobar Towers bombing case, had not done nearly enough in an issue of great salience to Washington.[46] A report by the prestigious U.S.-based Council on Foreign Relations found that Al Qaeda derived most of its financing from charities and that the regime had "turned a blind eye to this problem."[47] Canadian intelligence services had also warned that Al Qaeda continues to receive between one and two million dollars per month from Saudi-based charities; the United Nations echoed its concern that Al Qaeda continued to have access to between $30 and $300 million in funds controlled by otherwise legitimate businesses and charities around the world.[48] Since 9/11, U.S. federal officials have sent hundreds of written requests for specific information to their Saudi counterparts and expressed frustration that many of them have gone unanswered.[49]

U.S. Senate hearings also revealed that Riyadh had much work to do on its unregulated and seldom-audited Islamic charities. And a nearly 900-page congressional report on 9/11 released in late July 2003 involved a 28-page censored section that dealt with the Saudi role in the attacks. Needless to say, the evaluation contained in that section was not positive. The editing appeared to underscore the administration's sensitivity about complicating relations. The Saudis were reportedly furious over the report, and Saudi Foreign Minister Saud al-Faisal met with Bush and asked that Washington declassify the report so that Riyadh could properly defend itself. President Bush refused, claiming that it would "help the enemy" by revealing intelligence sources and methods, a point that some on the House Intelligence Committee publicly doubted.[50] One day after meeting al-Faisal, Bush asserted the need to spread representative government in the Middle East as a way to battle terrorism and transform those societies from which terrorism gains recruits, in what could have easily been interpreted as a reference to Saudi Arabia.[51] Ten days later, National Security Adviser Condoleezza Rice publicly discussed the development of freedom in the Middle East as the

---

46   For the view of two former Clinton officials who worked in the National Security Council, see Daniel Benjamin and Steven Simon, *The Age of Sacred Terror* (New York: Random House, 2002). See also Robert Baer, *Sleeping with the Devil* (New York: Crown, 2003), chap. 2.

47   *Terrorist Financing: Report of an Independent Task Force Sponsored by the Council on Foreign Relations* (New York, October 2002).

48   For a good, brief analysis, see Edward Alden, "The Money Trail," *Financial Times*, 18 October 2002.

49   David E. Sanger, "Bush Officials Praise Saudis for Aiding Terror Fight," *New York Times*, 27 November 2002.

50   CNBC, 30 July 2003.

51   Ibid.

"moral mission of our time."[52] The administration's growing emphasis on democratization may have been aimed partly at shifting public attention away from the failure to locate weapons of mass destruction and the virtually daily deaths of American soldiers in Iraq, but as a genuine and broader strategic goal on the Middle East it must have unnerved the Al Saud. Needless to say, if Saudi Arabia became more democratic, royal family power might well be threatened or undermined.

Events in the kingdom appeared to make the regime more serious about confronting its own profound and, to some extent, self-inflicted problems of extremism. This shift began with the May 12, 2003, Al Qaeda bombings on western residential compounds in Riyadh that killed 35 people, as well as with a plot to attack Mecca. These events pushed Saudi authorities to crack down on militants and to increase their cooperation with Washington.[53] They more zealously sought a dozen prominent Saudis suspected of giving Al Qaeda millions of dollars. For his part, FBI Director Robert Mueller praised Riyadh for a swift-moving investigation that resulted in over twenty arrests, calling it "exceptionally significant" in the fight against terrorism.[54] While this reflected typical official efforts to downplay problems in U.S.-Saudi relations, the crackdown on terrorists continued in July and August. Authorities arrested sixteen Al Qaeda–linked suspects and uncovered a network of Islamic extremists so large that it surprised Saudi officials.[55] These efforts, which pleased U.S. officials, were further energized when investigations revealed that Al Qaeda was effectively organized within Saudi Arabia, that it clearly sought to overthrow the regime, and that it even targeted senior Saudi officials, including Interior Minister Prince Nayef.[56] The Al Saud agreed to a permanent presence of fifteen FBI and IRS investigators in Saudi Arabia, an important concession to Washington.[57]

Despite the crackdown, profound questions remained about just how much the Saudis have done and can do in the war on terrorism. For their part, the Al Saud understood full well the serious damage done to their reputation with the American public and Congress. As far as they know, U.S. officials can praise them for their cooperation post-9/11 or at least refrain from criticizing them, but they cannot be sure of America's agenda. Even if

52 Quoted in Peter Slevin, "U.S. Promises Democracy in Middle East," *Washington Post*, 8 August 2003, A1.
53 Interview with Guy Caruso.
54 Quoted in Dave Montgomery, "FBI Chief Links Al-Qaeda to Deadly Blast, Praises Saudis," *Knight Ridder News Service* (2 June 2003).
55 Faiza Saleh Ambah, "Saudi Raids Uncover Network of Extremists' Sleeper Cells," *Associated Press*, 14 August 2003.
56 See Faiza Saleh Ambah, "Saudis Hint Al-Qaida Presence," *Associated Press*, 30 July 2003; "Bush Denies Saudi Request to Release 9/11 Information," *Knight Ridder New Service*, 30 July 2003.
57 CNN, 28 August 2003.

they strike an understanding behind closed doors, the public and Congress can turn against them at any moment, especially if terrorist acts continue, ones that appear to be connected to Saudi Arabia. Meanwhile, the regime has had to take into account its own Arab street. Had the U.S. and Saudi people voted on the subject after 9/11, they may very well have chosen a divorce based on irreconcilable differences.[58]

The 9/11 attacks, of course, cannot be separated from the Iraq War of 2003. This is because the war was treated by the Bush administration as part of the broader assault on terrorism sparked by 9/11. Indeed, 9/11 was simultaneously an excuse to try to eliminate Saddam Hussein and a genuine motivation, inasmuch as the administration feared that Iraq could marry up with transnational terrorists and provide them with WMD for massive terrorist attacks.

The Iraq War has had a mixed effect on U.S.-Saudi relations. As noted briefly in chapter 4, it decreased mutual dependence in the security arena by diminishing the threat from Iraq and forcing Washington to develop further alternative basing operations. But while security relations have become less crucial, the removal of Iraq as a threat also removes a key source of inter-state tension. No longer will allied raids against Iraqi air defense sites provoke Saudi political and religious sensitivities.

While the two states need each other less for security than they did in the past, U.S. dependence on Saudi oil may also decrease if Iraq proves capable of ramping up its oil production. Of course, nation-building in Iraq could prove quite difficult and take many different turns. And, in any event, we should also note that even if the United States and global economy can count on increased Iraqi oil exports in the future, Saudi Arabia will remain vital because it has the largest idle capacity of any oil producer and can bring it to market in a cost-efficient manner.

THE UNITED STATES AND KUWAIT

As with Saudi Arabia, except even more strongly, U.S.-Kuwaiti relations improved notably. This matters for energy stability because Kuwait became more inclined to pursue market-friendly oil policies. While the U.S.-Kuwaiti relationship is not without its problems and anti-Americanism has grown in Kuwait since the 1991 Gulf War, these relations have clearly improved in the past two decades.[59]

Prior to the Iraqi invasion, Kuwait supported Iraq against Iran in the Iran-Iraq War. Moreover, of the six GCC states, Kuwait was the most critical of the

[58]   On polls showing anti-Americanism, see the results of a survey of nine Muslim countries. The USA Today/Gallup poll was released on February 27, 2002. See www.usatoday.com/news/attack/2002/02/27/usat-pollside.htm.
[59]   Ibid. Eighteen percent of Kuwaitis surveyed viewed the September 11 attacks as justifiable.

U.S. regional role and the most sympathetic toward Moscow for most of the 1980s. The Gulf War, however, made Washington indispensable to Kuwait.

The Kuwaiti leadership understands that its security depends on the United States for the foreseeable future. Saddam's regime is defunct and the insurgency may eventually be broken or seriously diminished. But that is not clear. Nor can Kuwait predict how a new Iraqi regime would view it over time. Thus Iraq may again threaten next-door Kuwait or Iran may seek to flex its regional muscles. Kuwait no doubt recognizes that the United States has longstanding interests in the region and is unlikely to withdraw anytime soon. But world politics is dangerous and American foreign policy is transient. Kuwait must consider that in the future, the U.S. president, Congress, and public may not support another massive intervention to save Kuwait or its royal family from a future regional threat.[60]

In fact, after Iraq invaded Kuwait, many American leaders argued that U.S. troops should not be jeopardized to protect a monarchy, an oil outpost run by a wealthy family. That sentiment permeated elite decision-making circles in the first days of the crisis and influenced the first National Security Council meeting on August 2, 1990, involving President Bush and his closest advisers.[61] That the U.S. Senate finally did support the war vote in a 52–47 vote, and that the United States finally went to war against Iraq on January 16, 1991, possibly obfuscates the profound difficulty of selling such wars to the public, a difficulty exacerbated by Kuwait's lack of democratic status.[62] Some members of Congress who supported the move toward war even called for a new democratically elected regime in Kuwait. As President George H. W. Bush put it, members of Congress argued that the United States had "no real national interest in restoring Kuwait's rulers" and that since they are "not democratic," Washington should call for UN-sponsored elections in Kuwait in lieu of restoring the royal family.[63]

To guard against a worst case scenario of losing American support, Kuwait is generally strongly inclined in favor of actions that can help ensure U.S. support. This may explain why, during the crisis, it hired several U.S. public relations firms, spending more than $11 million. Such efforts were clearly aimed at altering Kuwait's image as a state that lacked democracy and treated women as second-class citizens.[64] Since the Gulf War, Kuwait has remained concerned about its image. As former GCC Secretary General Abdullah

---

60 Even the Saudis had doubts about whether Washington would take a strong stand on their behalf against Iraq in 1990. Interview with Prince Bandar.

61 Interviews with Brent Scowcroft and Richard Haass.

62 Arab Gulf leaders are fully aware that the U.S. public and Congress were reluctant to go to war against Iraq. Interview with Abdullah Bishara.

63 George Bush and Brent Scowcroft, A World Transformed (New York: Simon and Schuster, 1999), 358.

64 Interview with Thomas Pickering.

Bishara put it, Kuwait needs "to be worth saving and respecting"—becoming more democratic is one way to accomplish this goal.[65]

Of course, Kuwait's security problem has been connected to its oil policy as well. It has been committed to a market-friendly oil policy, which serves both its market and security interests, partly because it seeks to ensure international and American support against worst-case, future security threats. As the CEO of the Kuwait Petroleum Corporation Nader Sultan points out, after the Gulf War, Kuwait "definitely" became "more sensitive" to international and American needs and concerns.[66] That is an important shift because it underscores how U.S.-Kuwaiti security relations have created positive spillover into the oil market arena.

As with the U.S.-Saudi relationship, the U.S.-Kuwaiti relationship has also been tested by September 11. The majority of the bombers were Saudis, but several Kuwaitis played prominent roles in Al Qaeda. Moreover, questions later arose about the extent to which Kuwait was supporting the war on terrorism. Shaikh Saud Nasser Al Sabah, Kuwait's Ambassador to the United States during the Gulf War, criticized Kuwait in mid-October 2001 for being "hesitant and timid" in the U.S.-led campaign against Osama bin Laden and Al Qaeda, blaming Kuwait's Islamists and their charities for the tepid response.[67] While this criticism was probably fair, it is also important to note that Kuwait claimed in mid-October that it had shut down 127 unlicensed charities and the cash flow to potential terrorist organizations, and by January 2001, U.S.-Kuwaiti cooperation was well underway for preventing the criminal misuse of Kuwait's financial system and charities.[68] Kuwait also launched a public relations campaign to underscore its support of the United States. Clearly, the regime understands the importance of the United States on a strategic, political, and economic level, and despite domestic pressures to distance itself from Washington, will be reluctant to take any actions that jeopardize the U.S. connection.

THE AMERICAN ALTERNATIVE: NO REAL SUBSTITUTE

Whatever the impact of September 11 and the Iraq War, one thing remains fairly clear: an overview of two decades of regional politics and security reveals clearly that there is no real substitute for the U.S. regional role. While other outcomes might be preferable in theory, other actors lack one or more of the following attributes for serving that role: the military capability and demonstrated will to use it, the trust of Arab Gulf states, the strategic access

65 Interview with Abdullah Bishara.
66 Interview with Nader Sultan.
67 "Shaikh Saud Hits Govt's Support for U.S. War on Terrorism," *APS Diplomatic Recorder*, 20 October 2001.
68 *Kuwait Times*, 27 January 2002, 5.

to regional facilities, the global contacts and allies, and the influence in key
international institutions

No state or combination of states can currently assume the responsibil-
ities the United States has taken on following Britain's withdrawal east of
Suez in 1971. It should be said that Asian and European states in fact are
increasingly interested in playing a larger regional role, and European
navies did play a supportive role during the reflagging mission and 1990–91
Gulf crisis, but they lack the unity, the capability, the interoperability of
forces, the ability to deter and contain significant threats, and the similar-
ity of preferences to take a lead role or even a significantly increased role.

International organizations and alliances such as the United Nations or
NATO can play important roles in cooperation with the United States but
they cannot replace Washington. As for the EU states and Japan, they lack
the combination of military capability, access to regional facilities, and the
political and military coordination and will to play a major role.

Another partial alternative to a U.S.-dominated role worth examining is a
larger role for the GCC. The GCC has developed considerably from its
inception in 1981, and after the Gulf War showed a desire to become a more
legitimate security organization. However, the GCC remains incapable of
deterring or even significantly impeding a major attack on one of its members, chiefly because it lacks the manpower and combat training, but also
because it is not effectively unified. Indeed, all of the weapons bought by
GCC states over the years were not enough to deter the Iraqi invasion and
occupation of Kuwait. Repeated attempts by GCC states in the post-crisis
period to develop a more effective military arm have fallen short, despite
hopeful plans to do so initiated as early as 1981.

Moreover, in the postwar period, Arab states sought to develop a form of
collective security under the Damascus Declaration issued on March 6,
1991, which called for strategic collaboration between the GCC states Egypt
and Syria.[69] In exchange for security support in the form of Egyptian and
Syrian military contingents permanently stationed in the Gulf region, the
GCC states would provide much-needed capital for the Syrian and Egyptian
economies. Egyptian and Syrian troops would be stationed in Kuwait, Saudi
Arabia, and other Gulf states in order to back a smaller GCC military force
against Iraq, Iran, or other threats to Gulf security.

Collective security, while initially successful, faced several obstacles.
While the Gulf states thought that Egypt and Syria were seeking maximum
remuneration for minimal military support, Egypt and Syria believed that Gulf
states wanted maximum security for minimal money. After initially supporting

---

[69] For the text of the Damascus Declaration, see *Damascus Domestic Service* in FBIS: NES,
       7 March 1991, 1.

the security plan, the Saudis questioned the logic of hosting foreign forces on their soil. The last time the Egyptians were involved on the peninsula, the Saudis called on U.S. forces to deter them from challenging Saudi interests. The Saudis also feared that Arab states might become involved in royal family politics, thus undermining the regime, and that added financial burdens would strain an already stretched budget. Egypt increasingly became annoyed with Saudi procrastination in implementing the accord and, by early May 1991, decided to follow in Syria's footsteps by withdrawing its 40,000 troops from Saudi Arabia and Kuwait. Gulf states, uncomfortable with entrusting their security to Egypt and Syria, did not find the security arrangement economically feasible. They preferred to rely on the U.S. security umbrella and independent military efforts. Thus, while GCC states continued to interact with Egypt and Syria in the political and economic arenas, they downplayed the military side of the Damascus Declaration.

One more alternative faces even more significant obstacles than the others and could not conceivably be implemented until major changes take place in Iran. This alternative is to include Iran in a regional security framework based on cooperation between the GCC and Tehran. The logic here is that Iran would be less inclined to challenge regional stability because it would feel itself part of the security structure. Through the politics of inclusion, Iranian foreign policy would become more moderate and responsible. In addition, with the United States playing a less important role, Iran would feel less threatened and challenged by U.S. power and thus would become less aggressive toward western interests. That Iran's revolution has clearly waned and the forces of moderation are afoot further adds some ballast to this alternative.

While this plan is not without reason, it remains unclear to what extent Iran would try to co-opt other Gulf states, seek regional hegemony, and slowly decrease the ability of the United States to protect regional stability in the event that Iran (or possibly Iraq) were to seriously challenge U.S. interests sometime in the future. Iran, in fact, has espoused such notions since the Iranian Revolution. Witness Rafsanjani's assertion that Iran is "very concerned about the presence of infidel forces on Islamic territories. If one day we feel that these infidel forces intend to stay in the region, then it would become our duty to expel them from the area."[70]

For a security plan including Iran to have even partial success, forces of moderation in Tehran would have to prevail decisively, and Iran and the United States would have to initiate a meaningful and seemingly irreversible rapprochement. It is possible, albeit unlikely, that in the coming years, the risks of increasingly including Iran in such a security arrangement will

[70] See text of the Rafsanjani interview and speech in *Tehran International Service*, FBIS: NES, 15 October 1990, 63.

decrease enough to make the potential benefits of such a move exceed the potential costs. But Iran is unlikely, even in that event, to replace the United States as the central anchor of regional stability.

As U.S. capability for protecting oil stability increased and as it became clearer that U.S. capability, as laid out in chapter 4, was indispensable for that role, outside states and GCC states became more dependent on Washington. This was a dynamic that was well understood even by 1990 in Baghdad, although exaggerated, whether intentionally or not. Thus, Saddam would assert in a speech on July 16, 1990, that the United States:

> maintains its presence in the Gulf because, in view of the developments of world politics, the high prospects of the oil market and the increasing need for this oil by the Americans, Europeans, Japanese, and Eastern European countries, and perhaps the Soviet Union, the Gulf is the most important spot in the region, and perhaps the world. The country that will have the greater influence in the region through the Arab Gulf and its oil will maintain its supe-riority as an undisputed superpower . . . . And it [the United States] may seek to determine the price of oil in accordance with a certain vision that serves the interests of the United States and ignores the interests of others.[71]

Of course, Saddam painted a quite cynical view of U.S. motivations, which greatly oversimplifies them. But it is true that power in the Persian Gulf region can translate into broader global influence, if managed with an adroit foreign policy.

U.S. relations with Arab Gulf states are not unproblematic, but they have largely improved with respect to activities salient to oil stability. These rela-tions may suffer major setbacks but are not likely to fail altogether in the foreseeable future, barring a major unforeseen global development. Depen-dence does not always translate into American influence by any means, but it is added incentive for regional states to take direct and indirect actions that protect global oil stability, be it through military, economic, or political actions. Of course, a better outcome for both the United States and the region would be to create an indigenous security system that allowed the United States to play a secondary and over-the-horizon role in the region. But while that may be possible someday, it does not appear likely in the near term.

---

[71] Foreign Minister Tariq Aziz providing excerpts of Saddam's 16 July 1990 speech, in *Baghdad AL-THAWRAH*, FBIS: NES, 12 September 1990, 30.

Chapter 6

THE COLD WAR AND GLOBAL INTERDEPENDENCE

At the same time that the Middle East was being rocked by Iraq's invasion and occupation of Kuwait, the world was facing another seismic event: the last chapter of the Cold War and the subsequent fall of the Soviet Union in 1991. Not only did this development alter the trajectory of world history and force us to rethink what seemed to have become the eternal verities of superpower confrontation, it also produced many ripple effects that altered the evolution of oil stability.

The fall of the Soviet Union in 1991 changed Moscow's military and political role in the Middle East. It became less likely, willing, and able to engage in activity that could directly or indirectly challenge regional stability. Moreover, the end of the Cold War laid the road for greater economic dependence on Washington, which has made Moscow more pliable on issues relevant to oil stability. Important elements in Russia's foreign policy establishment have continued to view U.S.-Russian interaction as a power struggle, but Moscow's tendency to rival the United States has been tempered, and its inclination to cooperate increased, by the fact that it has needed Washington far more in the post–Cold War era than during the Cold War itself. Russia's economic needs have been driven by fundamental changes in the global economy and in the post–Cold War nature of world affairs, which are unlikely to be reversed.

The balance of this chapter begins by discussing the immediate effects of the end of the Cold War on Moscow's role in the region. It then shows how U.S.-Russian cooperation on most issues salient to oil stability has largely increased over time—despite going through different phases, some of which were much less cooperative than others, especially on the issue of Iran's nuclear aspirations.

THE END OF THE COLD WAR

Oil stability depends on stability in the Gulf region, both real and perceived. The Soviet dimension in 1979 and 1980 added instability to the
region. While we can debate the extent to which Moscow was wedded to
Marxist-Leninist ideology and prone to serious risk-taking, it was certainly
more threatening in 1979 than in 1990 or 2003. As laid out in chapter 2,
by 1979 Moscow had appeared to make significant gains in the global
balance of power and in the Middle East, while Washington had lost credibility in important quarters. The 1972 Soviet-Iraqi Treaty of Friendship
and Cooperation, for instance, provided for the qualified Soviet use of the
Iraqi base at Umm Qasr and increased Soviet-Iraqi cooperation in other
ways. Moscow became Iraq's top arms supplier and helped create the Iraqi
army that invaded Iran in 1980 and Kuwait in 1990. By the late 1970s, Iraq
began to moderate its policies and to turn to the West for economic assistance and for arms, and Soviet-Iraqi relations faced serious pressures in
the 1980s, well before Iraq's invasion of Kuwait.[1] Nonetheless, Moscow
maintained strong ties to Baghdad, which were viewed as useful in prose-
cuting its rivalry with the United States both in and outside the region.
Beyond the Arab Middle East, Moscow also had its sights on revolutionary Iran. It felt strong enough about its interests and prospects regarding
Tehran that it invoked the 1921 Soviet-Iranian Treaty, which allowed it
to intervene in Iran if Soviet security were threatened. In November 1978,
it even warned Washington not to intervene in Iran on the behalf of
the Shah, a bold move because at the time oil-rich Iran was after all
an American ally that helped Washington protect regional oil supplies.[2]
In Washington, Russia's warning was viewed—correctly, it turned out—as
the opening salvo of a more developed effort to gain a foothold in Iran.[3]
When the Shah abdicated his throne in January 1979, Moscow seriously
tried to lure Iran out of the U.S. orbit, only to discover that the Ayatollah
Khomeini's contempt for the United States did not translate into an affinity
for Moscow.[4]

---

1 Steve A. Yetiv, "The Evolution of U.S.-Russian Rivalry and Cooperation in the Persian Gulf,"
   Journal of South Asian and Middle Eastern Studies 21 (Spring 1998).
2 Shahram Chubin, "Soviet Policy toward Iran and the Gulf," *Adelphi Papers* 157 (Spring
   1980), 11.
3 Gary Sick, *All Fall Down: America's Tragic Encounter with Iran* (Boulder, CO: Westview
   Press, 1985), 95–97.
4 Nonetheless, the USSR continued to woo Iran, to Washington's chagrin. Thus, great U.S.
   attention, reflected in the Iran-Contra fiasco in 1986–87, focused on severing Moscow's relations with Iran, for fear that these two states could undermine U.S. regional interests. For
   instance, see declassified memo "Towards a Policy on Iran," from Graham Fuller to the
   director of the CIA, 17 May 1985.

The foregoing developments were related to oil stability. Doubts about the U.S. regional role unnerved oil-rich Arab states concerned about Moscow's profile and Washington's credibility. The rejectionist states and Iran, while not united, had some potential to radicalize regional politics, to challenge the domestic stability and foreign policy position of key oil producers, and to prosecute more forcefully the Arab-Israeli conflict, thus also enhancing the chances that oil could be used as a weapon.

The period of 1979 contrasted starkly with the post–Cold War period. The Soviet military presence was removed from the periphery of the region, including thousands of military advisers in Syria, Iraq, Libya, South Yemen, and Ethiopia. Political ties to these states either were downgraded in importance or changed significantly, as in the case of Iraq, where Moscow transformed itself from Iraq's top arms supplier to one of the actors that grudgingly agreed to contain it in the 1990s. The rejectionist front no longer obtained arms, aid, and political succor from Moscow.

To be sure, Russia promoted global multipolarity and global action under UN auspices, which in effect was intended as a check on U.S. unilateralism and capability where possible. A multipolar world, as the Russian Minister of Foreign Affairs Igor Ivanov put it, would be an "alternative" to the logic of unipolarity.[5] However, while Russia officially promoted the notion of multipolarity, it has been less likely to engage in counterbalancing and more likely to see world affairs in the off-setting terms of globalization and interdependence.[6]

Of course, some might argue that Moscow also controlled Iraq during the Cold War, thus increasing regional stability, but, in fact, it failed to stop Iraq's invasion of Iran in 1980 and Kuwait in 1990, which threatened global oil supplies. Although the Cold War was winding down at the time, Russia's military and foreign policy establishment still supported Iraq. Meanwhile, the superpowers, rather than engaging in sporadic and cautious cooperation, were heavily focused rivals, seeking to undermine each other wherever possible. That the USSR did not succeed in doing so should not detract from the fact that the rivalry was real, produced negative effects, and could have ended differently.

While the fall of the Soviet Union altered Moscow's position in the region, the end of the Cold War also laid the foundation for another effect: it increased Russian dependence on the United States and enhanced U.S.-Russian cooperation, about which the balance of this chapter focuses.

[5] Igor Ivanov, "Russia and the World at the Boundary of the Millenniums," *International Affairs* 46 (2000), 3.
[6] On the foreign policy concept statement of the Russian Federation, see the General Provisions, in *International Affairs* 46 (2000), esp. 1–7.

GORBACHEV AND "NEW THINKING," 1985–1991

Even under Soviet leader Mikhail Gorbachev, the superpowers had begun to cooperate on a series of issues ranging from resolving regional conflicts to economic reform.[7] Russia's growing need for U.S. economic support enhanced its proclivity to cooperate on issues directly and indirectly salient to oil stability.

As early as 1989, President George H. W. Bush moved ahead in presenting Gorbachev with a list of potential economic benefits. They included granting most favored nation (MFN) status, extending technological support, asking Congress to remove prohibitions against offers of credit to Moscow, and offering greater cooperation at the UN. That Moscow's regional behavior was linked to its view of U.S.-Russian relations at the global level was best demonstrated in the Gulf crisis. The Soviet Union had longstanding relations with Iraq and was very reluctant to see it attacked by U.S.-led forces, but Gorbachev believed, as one high-level insider noted, that cooperating with the United States was of paramount importance.[8] This could never have occurred during the pre-Gorbachev era, when Moscow viewed Baghdad as crucial to global rivalry and regional influence.

Even with superpower relations warming, Moscow was still split on how to approach Iraq. Foreign minister until January 1991, Eduard Shevardnadze represented one group as the sole spokesperson for closer cooperation with the United States, while the Arabists, led by Yevgeny Primakov, promoted a more traditional role in the Middle East.[9] Primakov, who was close to Iraq's elites, including Saddam Hussein, was quite reluctant to see Iraq's political and military position undermined.[10] The internal power struggle in Moscow remained intense, and in retrospect it seems likely that the United States was largely unaware of the profound opposition that Shevardnadze and Gorbachev faced from the military, Arabists, and others who resented U.S. power in the Middle East and globally, opposition that in fact did influence Gorbachev to turn to the right in the political spectrum.[11]

---

[7]   James A. Baker III with Thomas M. DeFrank, *The Politics of Diplomacy: Revolution, War and Peace, 1989–1992* (New York: Putnam, 1995), 71–72, 151–56.

[8]   Pavel Palazchenko, *My Years with Gorbachev and Shevardnadze: The Memoir of a Soviet Interpreter* (University Park, PA: Pennsylvania State University Press, 1997), esp. 215. George H. W. Bush, *The Public Papers of the President, 1990*, Vol. 2. (Washington, D.C.: GPO, 1991), 1206.

[9]   For a good biography of Primakov, see Roy Medvedev, *Post-Soviet Russia: A Journey through the Yeltsin Era* (New York: Columbia University Press, 2000).

[10] Secretary of State James A. Baker III, interviewed on *Frontline*, PBS, broadcast 9 and 10 January 1996.

[11] Palazchenko, *My Years with Gorbachev*, 215. Robert O. Freedman, "Moscow and the Iraqi Invasion of Kuwait," in *The Middle East after Iraq's Invasion of Kuwait*, ed. Robert O. Freedman (Gainesville: University Press of Florida, 1993), 81–82.

In September 1990 the two superpowers met in Helsinki. In talks between Bush and Gorbachev, the pro-Iraqi bureaucracy pressured Gorbachev to seek linkage between Saddam's withdrawal from Kuwait and a post-crisis international conference to be convened on Middle East peace. Gorbachev argued for this linkage, but when the United States asserted that it would allow Saddam a potential political victory, he shifted his position and agreed to a more active U.S.-Soviet stance, although he still did not agree to the use of military force.[12] To entice Gorbachev into further cooperation against Iraq at Helsinki, Bush offered significant economic incentives. Gorbachev denied a quid pro quo, but it is safe to surmise that one existed. Indeed, Bush even asserted that Moscow's "convincing cooperation . . . gets me inclined to recommend as close cooperation in the economic field as possible."[13]

Despite its bureaucratic fights over Middle East policy, Moscow desperately needed western technology and economic support to transform its economy away from communism and toward hybrid capitalism, and it needed U.S. political support to integrate itself into the world economy. U.S. Secretary of State James Baker, who went to Moscow a few days after the Helsinki summit, was told as much in a private meeting with Gorbachev on September 12, 1990. In that encounter, Gorbachev noted bluntly, in the context of a broader discussion on the Gulf crisis: "We need help. We're in the middle of the transition right now. As we move toward implementing these reforms, there's going to be great dissatisfaction. It's very difficult for us now. The domestic situation is getting much worse."[14] Among other things, Washington arranged for the Saudis to extend a generous $4 billion line of credit through the winter, which Baker viewed as "instrumental in solidifying Soviet support for the use-of-force resolution and keeping them firmly in the coalition throughout the crisis."[15]

Moscow supported U.S.-led sanctions against Baghdad during the conflict and UN Resolution 687 at the end of it. Debates continued in Moscow about how to approach relations with Iraq, with some calling for their termination and others calling for them to be nurtured, but Moscow was not reluctant to take a tough line against Baghdad. Thus, it condemned Iraq when it was revealed that it was hiding nuclear weapons research material in June 1992 and later that year when it endorsed a U.S.-led resolution calling on

---

[12] George Bush and Brent Scowcroft, *A World Transformed* (New York: Alfred A. Knopf, 1998), 366–68.

[13] See Freedman, "Moscow and the Iraqi Invasion of Kuwait," 88–89, 95.

[14] Quoted in Baker, *The Politics of Diplomacy*, 294. For another participant's analysis, see Palazchenko, *My Years with Gorbachev*, esp. 214–15.

[15] Baker, *The Politics of Diplomacy*, 295.

Iraq to meet all of its obligations under UN Resolution 687.[16] In this time period, Gorbachev continued to seek to integrate the USSR into the world economy and to seek "a new level of cooperation" with the United States, although some traditional thinkers like Primakov continued to strive for a more independent policy.[17] This took place despite Russia's desire to penetrate Iraq's postwar reconstruction market, obtain payment for outstanding loans to Baghdad, and reconnect politically with a potentially rehabilitated former ally. Moscow's actions were important for oil stability. Keeping Iraq in a political and military box reassured global markets psychologically, possibly deterred renewed adventurism on Saddam's part, and prevented him from using the mere existence of military strength as political leverage on various oil issues, including the potential to use oil as a weapon or to increase oil prices through production cuts. Clearly, U.S.-Russian cooperation was preferable to rivalry for achieving that goal.

THE RISE OF YELTSIN, 1991–1993

In the early 1990s, Russia continued to prove willing to comply with U.S. demands in order to maintain good relations and obtain U.S. economic and other support.[18] The foreign policy of Boris Yeltsin, who succeeded Gorbachev in a messy transition, was dominated by liberal-democratic idealism. It was based on the notion that interdependence made sense; that the United States, Western Europe, and the major international economic institutions that it dominated would be crucial and effective for what ailed Russia; and that compromise and restrained behavior on the part of Russia was in order, including on issues like arms proliferation and relations in the Middle East.[19]

Yeltsin's pro-American foreign minister, Andrei Kozyrev, laid out a foreign policy strategy in 1991 that could support Yeltsin's chief goal of economic revitalization. Russia would abandon hostility toward the United States and instead embark on a road of increasing cooperation, which involved distancing itself further from previous clients such as Iraq, Libya,

---

[16] On this period, see Robert O. Freedman, "The Soviet Union, the Gulf War, and Its Aftermath: A Case Study in Limited Superpower Cooperation," in *The Middle East and the United States: A Historical and Political Assessment*, ed. David W. Lesch (Boulder, CO: Westview, 1999), 374–76.

[17] Quotation in Palazchenko, *My Years With Gorbachev*, 295.

[18] Peter Dombrowski, "German and American Assistance to the Post-Soviet Transition," in *The International Dimension of Post-Communist Transitions in Russia and the New States of Eurasia*, ed. Karen Dawisha (New York: M. E. Sharpe, 1997), 228–32.

[19] Peter Reddaway and Dmitri Glinski, *The Tragedy of Russia's Reforms: Market Bolshevism against Democracy* (Washington, D.C.: United States Institute of Peace, 2001), 294–95.

and Syria.[20] Such a shift would make it harder for these states to take a range of actions, such as war with Israel or politically motivated oil policies, that could hurt oil stability.

Russia was formally inducted into the IMF on April 27, 1992, which gave it the right to apply for multibillion-dollar IMF loans, although it of course had to meet IMF conditions in order for this to happen. Subsequently, the United States and its allies used the IMF as an instrument to gain Russian compliance on a range of western policies, banking on the fact that Russia would not want to forgo crucial foreign investment.[21] During the first half of 1993 alone, the Group of Seven countries (G-7)—the United States, Japan, Germany, France, Britain, Italy, and Canada—assumed a multilateral assistance program to Russia totaling some $30 billion, including a $6 billion ruble stabilization fund and $4 billion in immediate debt relief. Washington tried to work multilaterally and through multiple institutions to raise and dispense aid to Russia, and Russia understood—some might even say exaggerated—U.S. influence. Thus, as former Finance Minister Boris Fyodorov put it, "everybody understands that IMF and G-7 is [the] United States government."[22]

Under Yeltsin, Russia counted on a "partnership for economic progress" understanding between the two states to yield it crucial trade, economic, and investment opportunities. The Russian-American intergovernmental commission on economic and technical cooperation benefited Russia by facilitating trade and U.S. loan guarantees and multibillion dollar credits for a variety of Russian projects. By 1999, the United States became Russia's third-largest trading partner, behind the Ukraine and Germany, and enjoyed a favorable balance of trade of $3.7 billion, as well as the singular status, as of January 1, 2000, of leading all others with 35.6 percent of all foreign investments.[23]

U.S. support of Russia vis-à-vis other major industrialized states became critical. Gorbachev was invited to join the then G-7 club on an informal basis; under Yeltsin and then Vladimir Putin, Russia achieved membership. However, Russian influence in the group remained fairly limited and subject partly to Washington's wishes. That is also true of the World Trade Organization (WTO), which came into being in 1995 as the successor to the

[20] Ibid. Roland Danreuther, "Russia, Central Asia, and the Persian Gulf," *Survival* 35 (Winter 1993–94), 95–97. Richard K. Herrmann, "Russian Policy in the Middle East: Strategic Change and Tactical Contradictions," *Middle East Journal* 48 (Summer 1994), 456–67.

[21] Anatol Lieven, "Ham-Fisted Hegemon: The Clinton Administration and Russia," *Current History* 98 (October 1999), 311.

[22] *Frontline* interview with Fyodorov, www.pbs.org/wgbh/pages/frontline/shows/interviews/fyodorov.html.

[23] V. Chkhikvishvili, "Areas of Differences and Agreement," *International Affairs* 46 (2000), 12.

General Agreement on Tariffs and Trade (GATT), formed in the wake of World War II. The United States did extend support for Russia to join the WTO, membership which Russia recognizes as crucial to its global economic growth, but this enterprise did not advance until Clinton and Putin stepped up the dialogue in July 2000.[24]

REALITY SETS IN: YELTSIN AND PRIMAKOV, 1993–1998

After the fall of empire, the Gulf crisis, and the August 1991 coup attempt in Russia, Moscow appeared to accept that it no longer would be influential in the Gulf region. But by late 1992 and 1993, it reversed course and sought to enhance its regional position, though not nearly in the scope that characterized Cold War competition.[25] Since then, some elements in Russia's foreign policy establishment have taken actions to realize that objective. They have referred to Russia's interest in checking U.S. power, in wooing Iran, and in using the region for global influence.[26]

As suggested earlier, in the immediate aftermath of the fall of the USSR, Yeltsin adopted an anti-Iraq policy which lasted at least through 1992, and even Kozyrev initially supported the U.S. bombing of Iraq in 1993. However, Yeltsin, under fire from conservatives at home who thought that Russia should have supported Iraq much more, sought to break with the Anglo-American sanctions policy toward Iraq as early as 1993, when Moscow dispatched an emissary to Baghdad to work toward Iraqi compliance with international demands.[27] From 1994 until virtually the 2003 war in Iraq, Russia attempted to deter U.S. military strikes on Iraq when it failed to cooperate with UN inspection teams or threatened Kuwait. Moscow did signal in August 1944 that it would consider selling Iraq arms if it met UN conditions for lifting sanctions, but Iraq failed to do so.[28]

Part of the shift in view away from an anti-Iraq position in 1993–94 had to do with the fact that relations with Washington had become strained over the pace and nature of economic reform, arms control, the situation in the Balkans, and especially NATO expansion and the future of security arrangements for

24 Ibid., 13.
25 Danreuther, "Russia, Central Asia, and the Persian Gulf," 105–8.
26 For one view of Russia's regional motives, see Stephen J. Blank, "Russia's Return to Mideast Diplomacy," *Orbis* 40 (Fall 1996).
27 On the conservative view, see Herrmann, "Russian Policy in the Middle East," 466–70. Aleksandr Shumilin, "Russian Foreign Ministry's Baghdad Nights: What Was I, Melikov, Doing in Iraq Last Week?" *Current Digest of the Post-Soviet Press* (hereafter *CDPP*) 45 (March 1993), 14.
28 Robert O. Freedman, "Russian Policy toward the Middle East: The Yeltsin Legacy and the Putin Challenge," *Middle East Journal* 55 (Winter 2001), 74.

post–Cold War Europe. But it was also related to internal dynamics in Russia, including the earlier victory in 1993 of nationalists, Communists, and other hardliners in Duma elections. The idea of liberal-democratic idealism held sway in Yeltsin's first years of power, but that changed in 1993 when the more traditional view of foreign policy eclipsed it.[29] The Duma elections, as one U.S. official in Moscow put it, "indicated doubts within the public about the value of both democratic and economic reform."[30] Yeltsin and Kozyrev had been very interested in good relations with Washington but faced increasing opposition in Russia's Duma from 1993 to 1995. Reforms started to go off track soon after the events of October 1993 in the Duma and other internal political factors became important, concomitant with a growing view that the West was seeking to undermine Russian power.[31]

In January 1995, Moscow agreed to supply Iran with a 1,200 megawatt and an 800 megawatt power reactor and to sell research and scientific data intended for Iran's universities for $800 million. Despite U.S. intelligence data, which indicated that Iran was already engaged in a nuclear weapons program and that these reactors would quicken its pace, and despite intense pressure from President Clinton during the Moscow Summit of May 1995, Yeltsin adamantly refused to halt the sale. Russia maintained that Iran was complying with all of the provisions of the International Atomic Energy Agency (IAEA) and the Nuclear Non-Proliferation Treaty (NPT) and that all spent fuel would be open to IAEA inspection. While Russia was willing to push its interests to the brink, it remained concerned about how its action in the Gulf would affect U.S. relations at the global level.

In some measure, Moscow sought to assure Washington that it would limit its military cooperation with Iran—while pursuing aspects of it nonetheless. In a confidential June 1995 deal signed in Moscow between Vice President Albert Gore and incumbent Prime Minister Viktor Chernomyrdin, Russia promised not to sell tanks and battlefield weapons to Iran after December 31, 1999, as long as it was permitted to do so until then. In May 1995, President Clinton strongly insinuated that this nuclear cooperation could jeopardize the "future" of U.S.-Russian relations. By July 1995, Russia sought to identify a list of equipment that it could sell to Iran without arousing any objections by the United States.[32]

---

29 Reddaway and Glinksi, *The Tragedy of Russia's Reforms*, 78, 294–95.

30 *Frontline* interview with Thomas Graham, Chief Political Analyst at the U.S. Embassy (1994–97), www.pbs.org/wgbh/pages/frontline/shows/interviews/graham.html.

31 *Frontline* Interview with Donald Jensen, Second Secretary at the U.S. Embassy in Moscow (1993–95), www.pbs.org/wgbh/pages/frontline/shows/interviews/graham.html. Leon Aron, "Foreign Policy of Postcommunist Russia," in *The New Russian Foreign Policy*, ed. Michael Mandelbaum (New York: Council on Foreign Relations, 1998), esp. 25–26.

32 *Moscow INTEFFAX* in FBIS: SOV, 24 July 1995, 5.

At the global level, economic issues still remained important in Russia's hierarchy of issues, and Kozyrev was not reluctant to note in 1995, perhaps too optimistically, that cooperation in U.S.-Russian relations existed on "almost every big issue in the world."[33] At the same time, however, opposition to U.S.-sponsored reforms and to U.S. intervention in Russia's economic affairs was mounting in the Duma and in the broader public.[34]

Yeltsin had taken an anti-Iraq approach in 1995, favored close relations with Washington, and opposed an overwhelming vote on April 25, 1995, in the Duma to lift the sanctions on Iraq. But in January 1996 he fired Kozyrev, replacing him with the hard-line Primakov, who was highly respected in the Duma.[35] The rise of Primakov as foreign minister (January 1996 to January 1997) and continuing pressure in the Duma contributed to a change of approach. A Russian news correspondent asked why Primakov, who would become Prime Minister in August 1998 only to be dismissed by Yeltsin on May 12, 1999, why Russia is so interested in the Middle East. He responded that under peaceful conditions, the region would be "one of the strongest economic poles" and that Russia's general power would increase if it obtained "a far-flung base of support."[36] That is, global policy could be aided by a strong regional position. The Primakov doctrine, as it would come to be known in some circles, sought to counterbalance the United States, pull Europe away from its transatlantic partner, and allow Russia to compete more confrontationally at the global level.

However, the world had changed, something that Primakov understood fairly well. Indeed, he still viewed good relations with the West as important, and he sporadically supported the United States and its allies in the Middle East.[37] In the spring and summer of 1998, his speeches repeatedly emphasized that Russia must smoothly make its way into the world economy.[38] For his part, Yeltsin underscored throughout his tenure the importance of trade with the West and entry into such institutions as the WTO.[39] If Kozyrev placed greater emphasis on engagement with the West and, in turn, on compliance rather than on counter-balancing strategies, Primakov

[33] Opening remarks at a press conference (18 January 1995) in *U.S. Department of State Dispatch* 6 (23 January 1995), 48.
[34] For polling information, see Janine R. Wedel, *Collision and Collusion: The Strange Case of Western Aid to Eastern Europe* (New York: Palgrave, 2001), 172.
[35] See Freedman, "Russian Policy toward the Middle East," 60–61, 72–75. Also, see *Tehran Abrar* in FBIS: NES, 20 September 2000.
[36] Interview with Primakov by Vladimir Abarinov, in *Sevodnya*, 5 November 1996 in *CDPP* 44.
[37] See Aron, "Foreign Policy of Postcommunist Russia," 30–31.
[38] Medvedev, *Post-Soviet Russia*, 334.
[39] See Boris Yeltsin, *Midnight Diaries* (New York: Public Affairs, 2000), 138–39.

leaned much more the other way. But this neither broke entirely with the past nor represented a clear-cut change of tactics. He understood full well, despite his domestic rhetoric to the contrary, that only the United States, its allies, and U.S.-led institutions could help Russia through an uneasy economic transition. At the same time, he saw balancing approaches as useful in enhancing economic leverage with the West and in checking U.S. hegemony.[40] In line with that approach, Russia sought stronger ties to China and Iran.[41] Russia sometimes sold Iran arms over serious U.S. objections in order to jockey for regional influence, to check U.S. power, and to gain bargaining leverage with the West.[42] Such sales did not go far enough to rupture relations, and they did strengthen Russian links to Iran, which Moscow has seen as an actor that can help Moscow balance the United States.[43]

Yet even under Primakov's tenure as foreign minister, Russia appeared to be constrained in important instances, such as when the United States fired forty-four cruise missiles at Iraq in September 1996 to punish Saddam for attacking the Kurds in Northern Iraq. The Russian leadership did not support this action at the UN, which allowed the government to appease internal pro-Iraqi military and political factions. But more importantly, Russia also did not veto or condemn the U.S. action. Many analysts expected a tough Russian stance, but Moscow assured Washington that it preferred cooperation.[44] Positive U.S.-Russian relations at the global level were a major factor. Yeltsin noted in May 1998 that economic prowess was what mattered in world affairs and that for Russia to address its weakness is "both a domestic and foreign policy task."[45] As Strobe Talbott, deputy secretary of state under Clinton, recalls, Yeltsin would typically state through 1998 in his discussions with Bill Clinton that there was "no problem" that they could not resolve.[46]

40 On changes wrought by the rise of Primakov, see Blank, "Russia's Return to Mideast Diplomacy." Also, text of interview with Primakov in *FBIS: CEURA* (21 March 1996), 15.
41 Coit D. Blacker, "Russia and the West," in *The New Russian Foreign Policy*, ed. Mandelbaum, esp. 182–87.
42 See Leszek Buszynski, "Russia and the West: Towards Renewed Geopolitical Rivalry," *Survival* 37 (Autumn 1995), esp. 120. On Russia's renewed interest in and policy toward the Gulf, see Stephen Foye, "A Hardened Stance On Foreign Policy," *Transition* 9 (9 June 1995), 36–40.
43 For instance, see *Tehran IRNA*, in FBIS: NES (8 March 1995), 51. Also, *Tehran ABRAR*, in FBIS: NES (17 March 1995), 71.
44 Vladimir Abarinov in *Sevodnya*, September 20, 1996 in *CDPP* 38. Interview with Victor Posuvaljuk, Vice-minister of Foreign Affairs of the Russian Federation, in *Argumenty i Facty* 37 (September 1996).
45 Quoted in *Rossiskaya Gazeta*, cited in Freedman, "Russian Policy toward the Middle East," 65.
46 *Frontline* Interview with Talbott, at www.pbs.org/wgbh/pages/frontline/shows/interviews/talbott.html.

The United States, however, has been much more willing than the French, British, and Russians to subject its own defense and commerce sectors to serious restrictions with respect to what they can sell Iran or Iraq.[47] It has put in place sanctions to enforce its position against companies and countries that support Iran militarily and strongly opposed Russian nuclear cooperation with Iran.[48]

After being repeatedly accused of selling arms to Iran, Moscow asserted in September 1997 that the key arms transfers in question, as well as training by Russian scientists, were being made by Russian companies without government consent. While partly true, many in the Russian government push the view that such sales benefit Russia's economy and its relations with the Muslim world.[49] Moreover, as one Russian diplomat put it, the "sales of weapons are occurring because of reforms that have pushed scientists out of work and companies that need to make money."[50]

Nonetheless, Russia, as well as China, certainly could do more to stop the sales made by their companies. The United States exercised some sporadic but not much lasting leverage. After a G-8 (expanded from the G-7 to include Russia) meeting where the economic importance of the United States to Russia was no doubt evidenced, Yeltsin made a pledge to Clinton that Russia would stop exports to Iran and would even create a new government commission to tackle that task. Later, in July 1998, Russia announced a criminal investigation into the potential violation of laws governing the export of dual-use technologies, promised more stringent oversight, and arrested citizens believed to be involved in the transfer of nuclear technology. While this trade has continued, allowing Iran to improve its ability to produce medium-range ballistic missiles indigenously, it has been periodically curtailed, especially when the United States or Israel have provided the Kremlin with evidence that private and state-owned firms have been selling Iran dangerous technologies.[51] The Duma passed a new export control law in July 1999 that provided the government with greater authority to investigate and punish such firms; in May 2002, Putin reorganized the oversight capability of the government to strengthen its enforcement abilities. These actions, however, still left a broad gray area of potential sales and transfers that could benefit Iran's programs.

47 Interview with Robert Pelletreau.
48 See Warren Christopher, "Presidential Executive Order Expands U.S. Sanctions against Iran," *U.S. Department of State Dispatch* 6 (8 May 1995), 387–88.
49 Off-the-record interviews with various current officials. Interview with Chris Kessler.
50 Off-the-record interview.
51 Interview with Chris Kessler.

In the effort to stem proliferation, it was not uncommon for the United States to ask the Russians at lower levels of government: "Where are your priorities? If you want to be part of the world community and integrated into the global economy, then you need to watch your arms exports."[52] At higher levels of government, Washington also conducted strong negotiations with the Russians, which were led by Gore. In those negotiations in 1995, mentioned earlier, the United States linked assistance to Russia to arms sales to Iran. Russia, in turn, agreed to process energy rods back in Russia rather than in Iran, which helped ensure that Iran would not obtain fissile materials, and stopped the type of high-level technological assistance that the United States viewed as particularly dangerous. Washington also put Russian companies on notice, asserting that bilateral relations and business prospects would suffer if they continued cooperating with Iran. While Congress also wanted to cut all U.S. assistance to Russia, enhancing the government's ability to pressure Moscow, much of it was aimed at denuclearizing Russia's forces.[53]

In line with placing intense pressure on Russia not to sell Iran fissile materials or the technology to produce them, Washington persuaded Russia not to sell Iran centrifuge technology as part of the reactor deal when President Clinton met Boris Yeltsin in May 1995, and assigned their deputies, Vice President Gore and Chernomyrdin to work out the details. Russia subsequently denied that it had ever planned to sell centrifuge and advanced enrichment technology to Iran, and Iran denied having had interest in this technology or in keeping the spent fuel from the plant in the Persian Gulf city of Bushehr.[54] The reactor deal proceeded and remained an irritant in U.S.-Russian relations thereafter, but it appeared to be scaled back in effect in this time period.

THE REFORMS DEBACLE AND THE RISE OF PUTIN, 1998–SEPTEMBER 11, 2001

Leadership changes in Russia notably affected U.S.-Russian relations. Yeltsin, for instance, was far more inclined toward cooperation than Putin, though September 11 changed Putin's approach.[55] Prior to 9/11, Putin sought positive relations but focused more on avoiding confrontation than establishing close ties. Even so, his foreign policy behavior was shaped in part by the state of

---

52 Off-the-record interview with State Department official.
53 Paragraph based on interview with Robert Pelletreau.
54 Anthony H. Cordesman, *Iran and Nuclear Weapons,* working draft paper (Washington, D.C.: Center for Strategic and International Studies, February 7, 2000), 18.
55 See A. Bogaturov, "A Quasi-Alliance between the United States and Russia," *International Affairs* 46 (2000), 115–25.

Russia's economy. U.S.-Russian relations, for instance, eroded toward the later 1990s as views solidified, certainly by 1998, that the intervention of the United States in Russia's political and economic realms was less the solution than the problem.[56] U.S. support for Russian reformers also alienated other Russian constituencies, further fueling anti-Americanism.[57] Under Putin, the notion of a U.S.-Russian strategic "partnership" was even struck from Russia's revised national security doctrine and replaced with more traditional descriptions of U.S.-Russian rivalry.[58]

The first few years of the Yeltsin era were based on the notion that interdependence and U.S.-driven economic reforms were useful, but that notion lost its luster as the Russian economy faltered. Myriad problems accompanied the increased Russian reliance on U.S. or U.S.-led support through institutions like the IMF. International aid was given with strings attached, and it was often hijacked by corrupt, misguided, or ineffective officials. Moreover, it raised questions about whether Russian leaders were American puppets and strengthened anti-liberals in the Russian body politic waiting for the failure of reforms so that they could pin it on the West-leaning liberals. In addition, it did not appear to have a positive effect on the Russian economy, unless one wants to argue counterfactually that the economy would have been even worse without western intervention.[59] Russian engagement with and dependence on the United States became unpopular, and the Kremlin gained from blaming the West for its economic problems.[60] Unlike Yeltsin, Putin and his foreign policy establishment were not averse to underscoring concerns about predominant U.S. power, be it in the Gulf, the Middle East peace process, or at the global level.[61] Nor was Putin reluctant to try to rebuild Russia's relations with traditional client states of the Soviet era.

---

[56]   For an analysis of the reforms by U.S. and Russian officials, see www.pbs.org/wgbh/pages/frontline/shows/interviews. Also, see Lawrence R. Klein and Marshall Pomer, eds., *The New Russia: Transition Gone Awry* (Stanford: Stanford University Press, 2001).

[57]   See Oleg Stepanenko, "Money Elected Chubais," *Pravda* 234 (17 April 1997).

[58]   Stephen Cohen, *Failed Crusade: America and the Tragedy of Post-Communist Russia* (New York: W. W. Norton, 2000), 176, 191–93.

[59]   Ibid. Serguey Braguinsky and Grigory Yavlinsky, *Incentives and Institutions: The Transition to a Market Economy in Russia* (Princeton: Princeton University Press, 2000). While much doubt exists about whether that strategy made sense or was implemented effectively, IMF and other loans have been and will continue to be important to Russia's growth prospects. See Reddaway and Glinski, *The Tragedy of Russia's Reforms*, 292–96. Also, see www.pbs.org/wgbh/pages/frontline/shows/interviews/graham.html.

[60]   Reddaway and Glinksi, *The Tragedy of Russia's Reforms*, 633. See interview with Pavel Voschanov, Yeltsin's press secretary from 1991 to 1993, at www.pbs.org/wgbh/pages/frontline/shows/interviews/voschanov.html.

[61]   Vladimir Lapsky, "The Middle East: A Draw Or A Common Defeat?" in *CDPP* 52 (2000), 6.

THE CASE OF IRAN

The erosion of U.S.-Russian relations at the global level had consequences for Russian behavior in the Gulf. Not coincidentally, by November 2000 Russia had retracted the pledge it had made to Gore in 1995 about limiting arms sales to Iran, on the pretext that the deal was supposed to remain confidential but was made public by Gore during the U.S. presidential campaign in 2000.[62] A better explanation is that Moscow was not happy with the level of economic support it had been receiving from Washington, needed the money from arms sales to Iran, and that Chernomyrdin had lost political influence over the plan he brokered, as he had been dismissed by Yeltsin in March 1998. That he was replaced by Primakov simply emphasizes the slow erosion of relations during that period, certainly by the latter 1990s. While Washington was making progress with Chernomyrdin, Primakov appeared to believe that Russia could purchase strategic goodwill from Iran on a range of issues if it continued nuclear cooperation with it. Thus, earlier advances made in U.S.-Russian cooperation on Iran were reversed, though Primakov acted as if Russia was still cooperating.[63] The United States was forced to take a tougher line. It imposed sanctions on Russian companies and used a carrot-stick approach with more stick than carrot, an approach it felt generated Russian compliance.[64] But the success did not last.

U.S.-Russian relations began to sour in 1998 partly as a result of Russian opposition to U.S. policy toward Serbia, Iran, and Iraq. When UN inspectors withdrew from Iraq in November 1998, the ensuing U.S.-British air strikes were condemned by Russia, though not backed by any serious action inside or outside the UN. Russia also took a strong stand on NATO expansion in part so that it could relax its opposition in exchange for benefits from the West, including probable participation in the Paris Credit Club and an invitation to join the WTO.[65] However, NATO expansion was also a bona fide sticking point.

Given Russia's dire economic situation in the summer of 1998, it could not easily resist U.S. pressure. It thus promised to do its utmost to prevent the transmission of missile technology to Iran. But perhaps to hedge its concern over a possible U.S.-Iranian rapprochement, by November 1998 Moscow had reverted to securing a contract to build the Bushehr nuclear

---

62 John Broder, "Russia Ending Deal on Arms Negotiated by Gore," *New York Times*, 23 November 2000, A1, A18.

63 Interview with Strobe Talbott; Strobe Talbott, *The Russia Hand: A Memoir of Presidential Diplomacy* (New York: Random House, 2002), 295–96.

64 Vann Van Diepen, Deputy Assistant Secretary of State, C-SPAN, 2 August 2002.

65 Vladimir Naedin in *Izvestiya*, 16 May 1997.

reactor.[66] Such cooperation continued through 2003, but with a twist. Iran revealed in early 2003 that it was nearly ready to start up a gas centrifuge uranium enrichment pilot at Natanz in central Iran, and satellite photos revealed construction large enough to house tens of thousands of centrifuges, far in excess of what IAEA inspectors had found in Baghdad after the Gulf War.[67] In February, Mohamad El Baradei, the head of IAEA, confirmed that Iran had joined an exclusive club of only ten countries that could build gas centrifuges. This was an important revelation, which at once made Russian-Iranian cooperation less important and embarrassed Russia. It made it less important because the Natanz site was much more threatening than Bushehr, and it embarrassed Moscow because Russian officials had long defended their nuclear dealings with Iran on the basis that Iran would never be able to build centrifuges. If fully operational, these centrifuges could provide Iran with three nuclear weapons per year.[68] As for the Bushehr project, which is set to be launched in 2005 instead of the original target date of 2004, Moscow has argued that the reactors would be used to provide electric power from nuclear generators. Russia's reactor design can produce only limited amounts of plutonium. Moreover, President Mohammad Khatami of Iran, in contrast to earlier muscle-flexing statements by Rafsanjani, has asserted that Tehran seeks nuclear capability for power generation only and that it has no desire for nuclear weapons, because "we cannot use such weapons based on our Islamic and moral teachings."[69] But Washington and many in the world community mistrust Tehran's intentions, partly because it has vast supplies of natural gas (15 percent of world supply) that can produce electricity much more cheaply than nuclear power can and because it has obfuscated the existence of its program, even from Moscow.

Reports emerged from various intelligence agencies in the summer of 2003 that Iran was farther along in developing a nuclear weapon than previously believed, receiving help from North Korea, Pakistan, and China, as well as from Russian scientists, some traveling to Iran with false identities and working without government approval.[70] For its part, Russia promised on June 3, 2003, that it would not deliver nuclear fuel to Iran unless it sign an agreement to return the spent fuel, which can be used to make nuclear

---

66 Freedman, "Russian Policy toward the Middle East," 69.
67 Douglas Frantz, "Iran Appears To Be Zeroing in on Building Nuclear Bomb," *Los Angeles Times*, 4 August 2003.
68 David Albright and Corey Hinderstein, "Furor over Iran," *Bulletin of the Atomic Scientists* (May-June 2003).
69 Quoted in Ali Akbar Dareini, "Iran Says It Won't Give Up Its Nuclear Technology Program," *Associated Press*, 7 August 2003.
70 A three-month analysis by the *Los Angeles Times* is summarized in Frantz, "Iran Appears To Be Zeroing in on Building Nuclear Bomb."

weapons, to Russia, and the IAEA is given control over this process. While it appeared to waffle on this promise by June 5, by late August the Russian cabinet did approve a draft agreement on this point, which pleased Washington.[71] Moreover, Moscow continued to insist along with the E.U. and the United States that Iran submit to nuclear inspections. Meanwhile, the IAEA charged Iran on June 6 with failing to honor commitments to safeguard nuclear material.

While U.S.-Russian progress on the nuclear front was developing—though still lacking—it appeared that Russia was willing to accept some limitations on conventional arms sales to Iran. Despite scrapping the Gore-Chernomyrdin agreement by the time of the June 2000 summit in Moscow, Russia assured the United States that it would sell only defensive weapons to Iran. Russia has been prevented by other agreements from selling nuclear, biological, or chemical arms and technology to Iran, but the United States has been concerned that Moscow or Russian companies might help Iran improve the Sahab-3 missile, which has a range of about 1,000 miles, or help Iran obtain other missile or nuclear technology. Russia has responded that most of the arms sales would be "to service and maintain old Soviet equipment," and that Moscow would stick to its international obligations on transfers to Iran.[72] To that effect, Putin has attempted to reinforce federal government controls over Russian institutions and companies, some of which the United States had sanctioned in 1998 based on intelligence reports that they were training Iranian scientists.[73] Many observers in Russia's foreign policy establishment were concerned that such arms could be used against Russian interests in Central Asia in the future, and could also harm U.S. relations. Reflecting some of this concern, Andrei Kozyrev asserted in March 2001 that he would be "extremely cautious in doing any weapons business with Iran since that would put Russia on particularly thin ice."[74]

THE CASE OF IRAQ

Russia's efforts to reintegrate Iraq into the international community gained some speed from 1993 to 1996, and accelerated even more during Putin's first few months. Russia sought not only to develop Iraqi oil fields but also to get paid back nearly $8 billion in loans.

71 *Xinhua News Agency* (3 and 5 June 2003).
72 Quoted in "Russia Says No Arms for Tehran," *New York Times*, 7 December 2000, A16.
73 See Oksana Antonenko, "Russia's Military Involvement in the Middle East," *Middle East Review of International Affairs* 5 (December 2000), meria.biu.ac.il.
74 Quoted in Patrick E. Tyler, "Russians Question Wisdom of Their Coziness with Iran, *New York Times*, 16 March 2001.

In 1994, Saddam evidently launched a program, while under UN inspections, that was intended to train 1,000 scientists for Iraq's nuclear program, and, in reality, turn the "whole country into a factory for WMD," capable of producing possibly a nuclear weapon by 2004 and two or three a year by 2005.[75] While it became clear after the Iraq War that Saddam was less capable than had been believed, at a minimum he did retain in the 1990s the intellectual infrastructure to build WMD and the proclivity to use oil as a weapon.

In the 1990s, Saddam sought to split the UN Security Council members in order to achieve an end to sanctions, without relinquishing the biological and chemical weapons that the UN believed Iraq possessed in massive quantities. In doing so, he also sought to pre-empt a massive U.S.-led attack. Russia was his best bet for realizing these goals.[76] Iraq remained an important state in Moscow's Middle East strategy, albeit one diminished by its own travails associated with the failed invasion of Kuwait. Russia, however, did not push efforts to lift sanctions on Iraq to the point of damaging U.S.-Russian relations. It did not exercise its UN Security Council veto, nor did it formally argue that the U.S. position on Iraq was untenable.

Ultimately, in December 1999 the Security Council adopted Resolution 1284, which reorganized the inspections program. It called on Iraq to allow the re-entry of the UN inspection teams, which it had earlier ejected from the country, and it reinforced the system of monitoring, inspection, and verification. The resolution gave inspectors six months to reach preliminary conclusions about whether Iraq was developing prohibited weapons, and it held out the prospect that economic sanctions might be lifted if inspection teams believed that Iraq had fully cooperated. The United States wanted an even tougher resolution, but, as Ambassador Pickering recalls, after difficult negotiations with other Security Council members, all parties ultimately achieved Resolution 1284 with language that leaned toward the United States position.[77]

Russia had wanted to veto the resolution, but it sought to avoid a confrontation in the Security Council, chiefly with the United States, so the most it was willing to do, along with France and China, was abstain.[78] It is important to note that in February 2001 the Russian Duma pressured the government to withdraw unilaterally from the UN sanctions regime against Iraq. However, the government, looking for opportunities to cooperate with Washington for economic and other reasons, rejected these pressures. This

[75] Testimony of a senior Iraqi nuclear scientist and defector, Dr. Khidir Hamza, U.S. Congress (C-SPAN, 19 September 2002).
[76] Charles Tripp, *A History Of Iraq*, 2nd ed. (Cambridge, U.K.; Cambridge University Press, 2002), 259–264, 278–84.
[77] Interview with Thomas Pickering.
[78] Alexei Vassiliev, "Russia and Iraq," *Middle East Policy* 7 (October 2000), 127–28.

was not a minor matter, because Russia was important to containing Saddam Hussein. In the post–September 11 atmosphere, Russia decided to shift course on Iraq. It joined the United States in tightening sanctions in the summer of 2002, despite the fact that Russian companies, which had by far the largest share of Iraqi trade under the United Nations oil-for-food program, wanted to keep Saddam's favor. Moscow's former position had been that Iraq needs to know when sanctions will be lifted, but it now emphasized that Iraq must be careful to comply in eliminating its WMD. For its part, Iraq did not even recognize Resolution 1284, nor did it heed subsequent resolutions. Rather, it made it abundantly clear at the time that it was not ready to accept the re-entry of the UN inspection teams.

Meanwhile, Russia and Iraq signed a new five-year economic cooperation agreement in the fall of 2002 worth $40 billion over a ten-year period. The agreement was problematic and angered Bush administration officials, chiefly because it signaled Moscow's intent to nurture or improve relations with a state that Washington had very publicly labeled as one-third of the "axis of evil," in the same period that it was trying to garner international support for a potential war against Iraq. However, the agreement was less problematic than it might have seemed. Russia, which had complained that it lost more than $30 billion due to the sanctions on Iraq, emphasized that the agreement did not violate UN resolutions against Iraq and did not involve arms sales.[79] Moreover, the agreement dealt with exploiting hypothetical opportunities in Iraq's oil sector, which a U.S.-led invasion could dash; represented Russia's ongoing contract deals with Iraq during the embargo period; and partly resulted from internal political pressures that Putin either sought to appease or did not fully control. In response to the agreement, Washington emphasized the potential economic costs to Russia in terms of lost deals with the West of doing business with Iraq. Secretary Donald Rumsfeld, the first official to address the deal, asserted that the "Russian administration is fairly pragmatic at this stage and their interest in the United States is greater than their interest in Iraq" and that even a U.S. attack on Iraq would not damage relations because of Russia's view of the longer-term benefits of economic ties to the West.[80]

It is important to note that while France, Russia, and China preferred to avoid a war in Iraq, and certainly opposed one on Washington's terms and timetable, none of them threatened to veto the U.S.-favored Resolution 1441, which allowed for inspections and possibly war. Rather, chiefly France

[79] "Iraq, Russia Discuss Ways to Enhance Oil Sector Cooperation," *Xinhua News Agency*, 31 January 2001.
[80] Quoted in Thom Shanker, "Rumsfeld Warns that Iraq Ties Will Hurt Russian Pocketbooks," *New York Times*, 22 August 2002, A8.

but also Russia sought to change some of the resolution's language in order to put brakes on a quick move toward war, leaving such authorization until after the arms inspectors reported violations by Baghdad.[01] Ultimately, France and China signed Resolution 1441, which allowed the United States to interpret any "material breach" by Iraq as a casus belli. Russia did threaten to veto the eighteenth UN resolution against Iraq calling more explicitly for war, though Moscow avoided an open breach with Washington. While Putin supported earlier efforts to contain and defang Iraq and possibly to go to war on a much slower timetable, he could not do so for a war that was viewed worldwide, and in Russia as well, as rushed or outright ill-advised. U.S.-Russian relations, while chilled, did get back on track after the war. On April 3, Putin underscored that Russia was directly dependent on the American dollar, technology, and investment.[82] Asymmetrical interdependence proved to be a stronger factor than the rift over Iraq, though it had failed in the Iraq War to push Russia into Washington's camp, underscoring that it was just one among many factors that affected U.S.-Russian relations.

SEPTEMBER 11, 2001

The altered global economic context was a major factor in affecting the trajectory of U.S.-Russian relations, although the 9/11 attacks also played an important role. They pushed Putin into closer cooperation with Washington, despite pressure from domestic opponents to do otherwise. Russia supported the U.S. right, under the UN Charter, to take military action against the Taliban; was understanding when NATO invoked Article 5 indicating that an attack against one of its members was an attack against them all; and demonstrated resolve against terrorism.[83] That resolve was important because terrorism was aimed at such things as overthrowing the Saudi government and replacing it with a Taliban-like, anti-western regime; evicting U.S. forces from the Gulf region; fueling a civilizational divide; and contributing to serious tensions between Israel and the Muslim world.

Secretary of State Colin Powell asserted in mid-November 2001 that Russia had given the United States "unprecedented cooperation" since September 11 and that, in turn, Washington can bring Russia into the global economy and institutions.[84] Putin, who had already established a good

---

[81] On this jockeying and for the draft of the resolution at this time, see *New York Times*, 23 October 2002.

[82] Thane Gustafson, *Changing Course? Iraq and the "New" U.S.-Russian Relationship* (Cambridge, MA: Cambridge Energy research Associates, 2003), 2–3.

[83] Talbott, *The Russia Hand*, 411–16.

[84] Colin Powell, Speech on U.S. Middle East Policy, CNBC, 18 November 2001.

rapport with President Bush, was the first leader to contact him after 9/11.[85] Russia offered political support in fighting terrorism as well as action in stabilizing global oil markets, something that is addressed in chapter 9. Moreover, at the military level, Putin gave the green light to autocratic leaders in Central Asia to allow U.S. special and conventional forces on their soil, an act that would have been inconceivable during the Cold War. The two states also agreed to enhance intelligence cooperation in the fight against terrorism, a relationship that developed effectively, as indicated by the joint U.S.-Russian operation that arrested a Briton and various accomplices in August 2003 who were involved in attempting to sell Al Qaeda shoulder-fired Russian missiles capable of downing commercial airliners.

In exchange for Russian cooperation in fighting terrorism, the United States invited Russia to play a more important role with the (at the time) G-7 nations in dealing with the terrorist threat to the global economy. In November 2001, Bush asserted that "great progress" had been made at the Bush-Putin summit on the issue of counterproliferation so that weapons "don't fall into the wrong hands" and suggested that such progress was made against the backdrop of U.S.-Russian economic relations.[86]

In supporting U.S. efforts, Russia had much to gain from Washington, economically and strategically. President Bush talked more seriously of bringing Russia closer to Europe, which turned into a reality in May 2002 when Russia joined NATO's nineteen permanent members as a non-voting member. Of course, Russia was also fighting its own nasty war against Muslim rebels in Chechnya and feared radical Muslim movements in most of the Central Asian republics on its borders. As Strobe Talbott put it, Russians knew that "if bin Laden had his way, the entire North Caucasus—Chechnya and several surrounding republics—along with other Islamic areas of the Russian Federation" would be part of "a new caliphate."[87] In supporting the U.S. war on terrorism, Russia was empowering the United States to help do some of Russia's dirty work in its own backyard, including eliminating the Taliban leadership and Al Qaeda, which helped train the same Muslim rebels and radicals that Russia itself feared, while assuring that the United States would depart from its backyard when the job was done. Meanwhile, the United States became more tolerant of Russia's use of military force in Chechnya.

The end of the Cold War and 9/11 enhanced U.S.-Russian relations but did not preclude serious differences. As former U.S. Ambassador to the United Nations Thomas Pickering describes China and Russia's common

---

85 Bob Woodward, *Bush At War* (New York: Simon and Schuster, 2002), 119–20.
86 President George W. Bush and President Vladimir Putin News Conference, 15 November 2001, CNBC.
87 Talbott, *The Russia Hand*, 412.

attitude, the "stronger a state felt about an issue, the more willing it was to take a whack."[88] On that score, President Bush repeatedly sought to convince Putin that the benefits of stopping support for Iran's nuclear program, which included more American aid and economic support, far outweighed the costs.[89] Yet, in late July 2002, Russian officials disclosed a draft of a ten-year program to expand economic, industrial, and scientific cooperation with Iran, including proposals to build as many as five more nuclear-powered reactors in Iran such as Bushehr. It is true that under U.S. pressure, Russia backed off from the proposals and appeared more willing to scrap them and that the minister of Russia's nuclear agency Aleksandr Y. Rumyantsev suggested for the first time that Moscow would take into account "political factors" in fashioning its relations with Iran.[90] It is also true that Putin gave Bush assurances of special safeguards for these reactors, and perhaps more importantly, that he moved to replace Yevgeny Adamov, head of the Ministry of Atomic Energy, who showed a proclivity to make nuclear deals with Iran that were not approved by the Kremlin.[91] This indicated an increasing interest on Putin's part to at least lay the foundation for potential cooperation with Washington. However, it was not clear if Russia could control how Iran would use the Bushehr reactor in the future; in any event, Russia was also providing Iran with nuclear assistance outside of the Bushehr project.

Some debate exists on the extent to which Russia will try to reassert its power in the Republics of the former Soviet Union.[92] However, barring shocking changes in world politics, the end of the Cold War has irreversibly altered Moscow's role in the Middle East and ability to shape world politics. During the Cold War, Moscow sought to jockey for military position in and on the periphery of the Gulf region. In 2003, that motivation is scarcely at play. On the whole, the areas where Russia was willing to take major risks in the region have decreased, and the areas of cooperation have expanded. In the past, Moscow sought to undermine U.S. relations with Saudi Arabia. It no longer does so, although it has aimed to improve its own Saudi relations. As one measure of change, Moscow had been Iraq's top arms supplier prior to the Gulf War, but afterwards it both abided by the UN arms embargo and supported U.S.-led force in that war.

[88]   Interview with Thomas Pickering.

[89]   Michael Wines, "U.S. Expects Russian Help to Stem Nuclear Weapons," *New York Times*, 15 May 2002, A8.

[90]   Quoted in Steven Lee Myers and Michael Wines, "Russia's Overtures to 'Axis of Evil' Nations Strain Its Ties with U.S.," *New York Times*, 1 September 2002, 10.

[91]   Interview with Strobe Talbott. See also Robert O. Freedman, "Putin and the Middle East," *MERIA* 6 (June 2002).

[92]   See David W. Rivera, "Engagement, Containment, and the International Politics of Eurasia," *Political Science Quarterly* 118 (Spring 2003).

While Russia's propensity to accommodate the United States in the Gulf fluctuated throughout the 1990s, it did not cross several key red lines in that period. It did not violate the UN economic embargo by engaging in trade with Iraq or motivating others to do so; initiate official airline flights or any provocative high-level visits to Baghdad, with some minor exceptions; or sell arms to Iraq or seriously move in that direction either directly or through third parties. While it did sell Iran dual-use capabilities and missiles, a very serious problem, it did not sell fissile materials or sophisticated technologies for producing such materials. Moreover, Russia responded to some American efforts to curb arms exports to Iran and to develop export controls to constrain its own arms companies.

The end of the Cold War marked a fundamental departure from the past. Coupled with rising interdependence, it transformed the context of world affairs and left Russia far more engaged with the United States and U.S.-led institutions than before. For the first time since World War II, Moscow found itself increasingly dependent on the United States and the West. That enhanced Russia's proclivity to accommodate U.S. interests in the Gulf, in the war on terrorism, and directly in oil markets, as we shall see later in the book.

While Russians have preferred to think that they do not need the United States much, and although their level of need and perception of it has fluctuated greatly, the United States can still provide "a lot to Russia in positive terms and could do a lot of negative things to it as well," as one seasoned diplomat aptly put it.[93] Over time, Russia's leaders, including Putin, have increasingly understood that Russia's future lies with the West and that relations with states such as Iran cannot supplant Russia's dependence on the West, and especially on the United States, for investment, trade, technology, and political support in key international institutions. Putin has noted repeatedly that what Russia needs "above all" is absolutely nondiscriminatory access to world markets and U.S. markets.[94] And Russia has continued to seek increased western economic support, trade, and entry into the WTO on positive terms. As one Russian leader put it, Moscow has no choice but to "constantly look for a necessary balance between our economic needs and the need to obstruct such shifts in the rest of the world that could only aggravate our position as a dependent and weak great power."[95] Even the most vocal critics of the U.S. role in Russia's economic debacle have argued that with a more sensible approach like an updated Marshall Plan, U.S.-led aid efforts could be crucial to Russia's rehabilitation, which one respected

---

93   Interview with Robert Pelletreau.
94   For instance, quoted in *New York Times*, 26 May 2002, A10.
95   A. Pushkov, "Russia and the New World Order," *International Affairs* 46 (2000), 16.

Russian economist has estimated would require $500 billion over a ten-year period.[96]

The realities of global change, however, do not mean that the United States can obtain Russian compliance on any issue germane to oil stability, but they do offer greater leverage than Washington had in 1980 or 1990. Putin's challenge, and presumably that of any Russian leader, is to preserve Russian autonomy and independence of action within the constraints of at least near-term asymmetrical interdependence. No matter how much Putin may want to rebuild Moscow's former position with client states or to balance the United States, he will labor, like future Russian leaders, under these constraints.[97] In that sense, while the leader in Russia will certainly matter, the context of action will impose its own will as well.

[96] See Cohen, *Failed Crusade*, 220–25.
[97] On competing pressures in Russian foreign policy, see the account of the Russian Foreign Minister in Igor S. Ivanov in *The New Russian Diplomacy* (Washington, D.C.: Brookings Institution, 2002).

Chapter 7

THE CHINA FACTOR

Of all countries, the People's Republic of China is perhaps the one most concerned about assuring global oil. It became a net importer of oil during 1993 for the first time since the early 1960s, and its oil demand has grown 80 percent over the last ten years.[1] By 1998, the import value of oil accounted for 61 percent of total Chinese imports.[2] Some projections suggest that it will be six to ten times more dependent on imported oil by 2030 than it was in 2002, and, according to the International Energy Agency, China's oil imports from the Gulf in particular are expected to rise to nearly 80 percent of its total oil imports by the year 2020.[3] While China's undersea oil exploration may prove lucrative, its production at Daqing, Shengli, and Liaohe is almost fully exploited, and the oil reserves-to-production ratio has decreased since the early 1980s.[4] In the early 1990s China had thought that its own oil production would be major. However, as time passed, it became clear that the infrastructure needed for drilling and producing its own oil would be too complex and prohibitively expensive, and that output from its own fields had not grown at the expected rate.[5]

As a result, China has understood that it cannot escape high dependence on Gulf oil, which has raised concerns about whether it can assure its supply.[6]

[1] See www.eia.doe.gov/emeu/cabs/china/eglance.html. State Economic and Trace Commission, "Tenth Five Year Plan for Developing the Oil Industry" (Beijing: SETC), www.setc.gov.cn

[2] For a good table illustrating this, see Xiaojie Xu, "China and the Middle East: Cross-Investment in the Energy Sector," *Middle East Policy* 7 (June 2000), esp. 125–27.

[3] For some useful graphs on this subject, see www.iea.org/about/nmcchina.htm.

[4] Xu, "China and the Middle East," esp. 125–27.

[5] Interview with Edward Kagan. On the rate of output, see Xiaojie Xu, "The Oil and Gas Links between Central Asia and China: A Geopolitical Perspective," *OPEC Review* 23 (March 1999), 41.

[6] See, for instance, FBIS-CHI, 30 October 1997. Also, see Xu, "China and the Middle East," esp. 124–25.

That has been and will remain its dominant regional interest, and one that affects its broader foreign policy agenda. Indeed, the PRC has become so concerned about adequate oil supplies that it is increasingly interested in trying to protect its own oil lifeline from the Gulf, though it does not have the capability to do so and will not for the foreseeable future.

Unlike Moscow, Beijing has never had a significant military position in or near the Persian Gulf, nor has it ever had highly developed relations with regional states. However, China's foreign policy toward the Middle East and issues that relate to the story of oil stability is important. In particular, the PRC can affect the stability of the Gulf region through arms sales to states such as Iran; through its role in the United Nations, where aspects of global behavior toward the region are fashioned; through its broader role in the war on terrorism; and possibly in the future through pressure on oil-producing states to maintain adequate supplies.

China has been concerned about American global power, about its own rising dependence on Gulf oil, and about the U.S. ability to affect its oil supply line. It has been especially concerned about long-haul shipping from the Middle East, in case of Sino-American crises, such as over Taiwan. As a result, the PRC would like to see U.S. influence in the Middle East clipped, and to act as a counterweight, possibly with other states, against U.S. capability. And it would certainly like to enhance its own ability to protect and ensure the flow of oil to its growing economy. However, China has been less willing to push this agenda to the point of jeopardizing a wide array of economic benefits that accrue from positive relations with the United States. Indeed, the PRC has faced growing dependence on the United States economically at the global level and on its role in protecting global oil in the Gulf against any major military threats. This dependence has made it less likely to challenge the United States in areas salient to regional stability. This is not to say that the two states do not and will not rival each other on key questions, but rather that changes in economic relations influence how China approaches regional-level issues, as they have with Russia.

CHINA AND ASYMMETRICAL INTERDEPENDENCE

Like Russia, China clearly prefers a multipolar world to one dominated by the United States.[7] And, like most European states except Britain, China

---

[7] See Beijing Xinhua in FBIS-CHI, 27 March 1997; *Beijing Xinhua* in FBIS-CHI, 13 October 1999; *Beijing China Radio International*, in FBIS-CHI, 5 December 1999; *Hong Kong AFP* in FBIS-CHI, 22 June 2000. For the full text of the China's white paper published by the Office of the State Council in China, see *Beijing Xinhua Domestic Service*, in FBIS-CHI: 16 October 2000. See Ezra F. Vogel, ed., *Living with China: U.S.-China Relations in the Twenty-First Century* (New York: W. W. Norton, 1997), 27. Robert G. Sutter, *Chinese Policy Priorities and their Implications for the United States* (New York: Rowman and Littlefield, 2000), 48.

views the key threats to regional oil stability differently than Washington
does. It does not see Iran as a "rogue state" per se—it also didn't see Iraq
in those terms—but has treated both states largely in economic terms: they
provide significant business opportunities and are key oil producers. China
has wanted them to refrain from destabilizing the region, but it has also preferred to avoid U.S.-led military solutions to regional problems. Beijing's concern about a unipolar world and its differences with the United States over
policy in the Gulf have not, by and large, produced serious tensions or prevented some important forms of cooperation. Rather, Chinese officials have
repeatedly made it clear that they must try to get along with the United
States, whether they like it or not.[8] That is largely, but not solely, a function
of increasing Chinese dependence on the United States for a variety of purposes. The following sections trace the evolution of this dimension of Sino-
American relations and what it means for oil stability.

THE OPEN DOOR POLICY

Historically, the PRC has not viewed interdependence favorably and has preferred self-reliance. Like the United States, it has sought to avoid engage-
ments with foreign powers, but was not drawn into world affairs by World
War II to nearly the extent that the United States was. Other nations have
been eager, especially in the 1990s, to pull the PRC into interdependent
relations, but China was far more reluctant to oblige and certainly did not
include such a goal in its policies, whether implied or enacted.[9] However, as
the 1990s progressed, it began to downplay its independent role in world
affairs as the complexity of the post–Cold War world became apparent.[10]
Starting in 1991, its leaders increasingly favored the idea of interdependence, underscoring that it was a fact of international life, important to China's
development, and a contributing factor to peace, security, and cooperation.[11]
Indeed, by 1997, the PRC became the second-largest recipient of foreign
direct investment in the world, after the United States.[12] In 1987, Beijing
remained aloof to global economic crises, but by 1998 a "totally different

8   See Sutter, *Chinese Policy Priorities*, esp. 41–43.
9   See Thomas W. Robinson, "[In][ter]dependence in China's Post-Cold War Foreign Rela-
    tions," in Samuel S. Kim, ed., *China and the World: Chinese Foreign Policy Faces the New
    Millennium* (Boulder, CO: Westview, 1998), 200.
10 See James C. Hsiung, ed., *Beyond China's Independent Foreign Policy* (New York: Praeger,
    1985).
11 See Robinson, "[In][ter]dependence," esp. 202–3.
12 Kevin G. Cai, "Outward FDI: A Novel Dimension of China's Integration into the Regional
    and Global Economy," *China Quarterly* 160 (December 1999), 856–80.

mentality" in China had emerged, based on an inchoate but developing appreciation for global interdependence.[13]

Over the past two decades, China has increasingly focused on how to benefit from participation in world trade.[14] From 1978 well into the 1990s, its foreign trade dependence nearly quadrupled, as measured by both exports and imports as a percentage of gross national product.[15] Beijing has viewed the United States, by far its biggest trade partner, as critical to the approach of benefiting from participation in the global economy.[16] While Washington maintained a trade surplus with China until 1983, the U.S. trade deficit with China increased steadily in the 1990s, to levels that can only be described as staggering.[17] The United States no doubt wants greater access to China's 1.3 billion citizens, but by any measure the PRC is far more dependent on Sino-American trade than vice versa.[18] This is the most profound and important form of asymmetrical interdependence in their relations.

While China's orientation was shifting, so was the U.S. global role and position. The United States had always been influential in the global economy and in the international economic institutions that China zealously joined in the 1990s.[19] However, the end of the Cold War and increasing globalization made it even more influential.[20] These developments, in addition to the PRC's shift toward a trade- and market-oriented national strategy, made Beijing even more dependent on the United States, thus making it vital, as one Chinese official put it, to keep U.S. relations "moving in the right direction."[21] Avoiding Sino-American tensions, in fact, was a key goal driving Deng Xiaoping's formulation of foreign policy after the fall of the Soviet Union, and the PRC's approach thereafter.[22] Beijing remains highly concerned about a range of bilateral issues, including the U.S. strategic role in Asia and its position on Taiwan and Tibet. But the

13 Shanghai Foreign Affairs Office official quoted in David M. Lampton, *Same Bed, Different Dreams* (Berkeley: University of California Press, 2001), 159.

14 Barry Naughton, "The Foreign Policy Implications of China's Economic Development Strategy," *Chinese Foreign Policy: Theory and Practice*, ed. Thomas W. Robinson and David Shambaugh (New York: Oxford University Press, 1994).

15 For data, see Robinson, "[In][ter]dependence," esp. 205.

16 Off-the-record interview with a Chinese diplomat.

17 *International Trade Statistics Yearbook* (various issues).

18 U.S. Department of Commerce, International Trade Administration (various years). Also, see Robinson, "[In][ter]dependence," esp. 210–12.

19 Lampton, *Same Bed*, esp. 159–203.

20 See Michael Yahuda, "China's Foreign Relations: The Long March, Future Uncertain," *China Quarterly* 159 (September 1999), 658–59.

21 Off-the-record interview.

22 Quansheng Zhao, *Interpreting Chinese Foreign Policy: The Micro-Macro Linkage Approach* (New York: Oxford University Press, 1996), 221; Michael D. Swaine and Ashley J. Tellis, *Interpreting China's Grand Strategy* (Santa Monica, CA: Rand, 2000).

U.S. market offers Washington the most leverage, because China's rapid growth is tied to that market.[23] Its economy is a fraction of the U.S. economy, its per capita income is below $1,000 dollars per year, and its transportation and telecommunications infrastructure is several decades behind that of the United States.[24]

THE INFLUENCE OF INTERNATIONAL ORGANIZATIONS

The United States and its allies are also crucial to China's strategy in key institutions such as the IMF and the World Bank.[25] They can affect Beijing's ability to seek favorable outcomes on issues ranging from trade to human rights issues to commercial space cooperation. China became the world's top recipient of multilateral assistance from these institutions by the late 1980s.[26] The benefits of joining the WTO are equally immense. Many mid- and lower-level Chinese foreign policy officials have been ambivalent about participation in the WTO, but the top leadership has seen it as crucial to the PRC's future. China's entrance into the WTO has also benefited Washington by lowering trade barriers for U.S. goods and opening the Chinese market in key sectors such as finance, telecommunications, and agriculture. But for China the WTO and other international economic institutions are crucial to economic growth and integration in the global economy.[27]

As the most influential state in the WTO and the lead negotiator among the organization's contracting parties, the United States, more than any state, can affect the terms and conditions that govern China's role in the WTO. In private diplomacy, it has repeatedly linked Chinese behavior on a range of issues to WTO issues.[28] Not only is the United States crucial in ongoing WTO working negotiations, it will continue to be. WTO membership has ensured China's access to the global trading system on reasonable terms, but it comes with strings attached. That access will occur under a system of rules, agreed to and monitored by the international community and enforced through WTO dispute settlement procedures and WTO-authorized sanctions in the event of non-compliance.

23 Interview with Edward Kagan.
24 See Vogel, ed., *Living with China*, introduction.
25 On E.U. influence, see Daniel Arthur Lapres, "The E.U.-China WTO Deal Compared," *China Business Review* 27 (July-August 2000).
26 On China's role in international institutions, see David Lampton, "A Growing China in a Shrinking World: Beijing and the Global Order," in Vogel, ed., *Living with China*, 124–29.
27 William R. Feeney, "China and the Multilateral Economic Institutions," in Kim, ed., *China and the World*.
28 Interview with Thomas Pickering.

This process, of course, is subject to the interpretation of member states. If the United States is unsatisfied with the extent to which China has cut tariffs, eliminated quotas, dropped import-licensing restrictions, and published heretofore secretive trade laws, statutes, and regulations, it can move to challenge its interests within the WTO. Or it can threaten to withdraw support from China's attempts to pass the WTO's review process by its member states. U.S. support is especially important to Beijing because it is already suspicious that it may be accorded perpetual secondary status within the WTO. The United States can also support Chinese economic and technological efforts in bilateral relations and its ability to abide by and avoid tension on accords dealing with issues ranging from textiles to intellectual property rights to high-technology.

AMERICAN EFFORTS AT LINKAGE POLITICS

China's asymmetrical interdependence is important. Even more so than Russia, the PRC has been careful to eschew too strong an anti-U.S. regional strategy. It might want to do so, but its behavior is circumscribed because it needs the United States outside the Gulf in several key ways. As one State Department official involved in PRC negotiations put it, "If China challenged the United States too much in the Gulf, that could muddy broader bilateral relations which are the centerpiece of China's foreign policy, and that's not worth it to China."[29]

The President has used trade for purposes of linkage, as has Congress. In this effort, most favored nation (MFN) status has been an important carrot. It was later called normal trade relations (NTR) and then permanent normal trade relations (PNTR) status. PNTR status is conferred by the United States on 133 states and removes the conditional one-year review associated with NTR. Until China received PNTR status, Congress voted on MFN annually based on certain criteria that China was expected to meet and which it has passed yearly since 1980. Many of the opponents of engagement with China have vigorously opposed PNTR for China.

Trade status has been linked to Chinese human rights practices (although Clinton delinked these issues in May 1994) and, less overtly, to Gulf-related issues, including arms proliferation.[30] For example, in mid-

---

[29] Off-the-record interview with State Department official.

[30] On this delinking, see *U.S. Department of State Dispatch* 5 (30 May 1994), 345–46. The proliferation connection is clear, for instance, in *Additional Requirements on the Extension of China's Most-Favored-Nation Trade Status in 1993*, Hearing Before the Subcommittee On Trade of the Committee On Ways And Means, House of Representatives, 29 June 1992 (Washington, D.C.: GPO, 1992), esp. 5, 18, 21.

1987 the United States, annoyed by the threat that Chinese missiles in Iran's possession posed to U.S. ships in the Gulf, asserted that it would withhold technology transfers to China if it did not change its policy on arms sales.[31] In 1990, members of Congress proposed to lift China's MFN status after reports indicated that it was resuming the sale of short-range ballistic missiles to Iran. In 1996, it was revealed that Beijing was providing Iran with the technology for advanced chemical weapons factories. Under U.S. law, these sales, if proven, could trigger economic sanctions unless the president waives them for reasons of national interest or national security requirements. The sanctions could include a ban on economic and military aid, a cessation of international loans or loan guarantees, suspension of certain sensitive U.S. commercial exports to China, or any combination of these. Clinton ordered the suspension of $10 billion in Export-Import Bank financing of U.S. business deals in China, pending further investigation of the sales.[32]

Beginning with China's Open Door policy, Beijing began to join the main arms control treaties and multilateral organizations that it had spurned in the 1970s, a trend that was clearly related to an interest in improving relations with the West.[33] By 1997, China's Foreign Ministry Arms Control and Disarmament Department was tasked with the job, in conjunction with the development of an export control structure, of ensuring that China's arms and technology transfers did not damage its foreign relations.[34] International and especially U.S. pressure on China to adhere to global non-proliferation arms control norms and agreements increasingly influenced Beijing's policies in the 1980s and especially the 1990s, despite pressure from elements of China's military not to sign the Non-Proliferation Treaty and Comprehensive Nuclear Test Ban Treaty in 1996.[35] As U.S. officials saw it, Beijing agreed in 1992 to the guidelines of the Missile Technology Control Regime and in March 1992 to accede to the NPT, partly because MFN had been preserved the year before. Indeed, the United States combined high-level discussions with targeted sanctions, and Beijing sought to pre-empt any efforts in Congress in 1992 to link MFN status to concessions on security issues that it considered too onerous.[36] President George H. W. Bush cited China's participation in the NPT when

31 Lillian Craig Harris, *China Considers the Middle East* (New York: IB Tauris, 1993), 222.
32 Julia Chang Bloch, "Commercial Diplomacy," in Vogel, ed., *Living with China*, 203.
33 Lampton, *Same Bed*, 163–64.
34 Ibid., 170.
35 For evidence of Beijing's policy changes, see Bates Gill and Evan S. Medeiros, "Foreign and Domestic Influences on China's Arms Control and Nonproliferation Policies," *China Quarterly* 161 (March 2000). On pressure from the military, see Yahuda, "China's Foreign Relations," 654.
36 See *Additional Requirements*, esp. 18, 30.

he recommended normal trade status in June 1992 and vetoed legislation to place conditions on MFN status in September 1992.[37] That China agreed to forgo the sale of a 20-megawatt nuclear research reactor to Iran in the autumn of 1992 was also widely believed to be related to its concern about losing MFN status.[38] Even more important, after a firestorm of U.S. protests, China agreed not to provide Iran with a 300-megawatt power reactor.[39]

Thereafter, the PRC's proclivity to sell to Iran fluctuated with the quality of Sino-American relations, and with the will and ability of the United States to pressure China with carrots and sticks. Thus, the implementation of the Sino-American nuclear cooperation agreement signed in Beijing in 1995, which was meant to give China access to U.S. civilian nuclear technology as a carrot, depended on China's compliance on nuclear trade with Iran.[40] And, in December 1996, Beijing agreed to cancel the construction of a facility that could produce uranium hexafluoride—a gas that is key to Iran's efforts to enrich fissile uranium—at least partly because it did want to hurt Sino-American relations.[41] The Chinese Foreign Ministry issued a statement on October 21, 1997, asserting that its "peaceful use of nuclear energy with Iran has not been carried out because of some disputes over the contract."[42] Unlike in the case of Russia, the Clinton administration succeeded in convincing Beijing to forgo significant nuclear assistance to Iran as part of a broader Sino-American agreement on peaceful nuclear cooperation.[43]

Regarding conventional weapons, China's record remained sketchy. With respect to the Gulf, reports emerged as early as 1992 and continued throughout the 1990s that Beijing was attempting to sell Iran prohibited capabilities.[44] The State Department formally notified Congress in early June 1997 that China had sold cruise missiles to Iran, which could be used to challenge U.S. forces in the region. By 1997, Washington warned Beijing that such sales could have a "damaging political effect" on U.S. relations, and China

37   White House Statement, Letter to Congress, and Report to Congress on Extension of MFN Status to China, *Department of State Dispatch* 3 (8 June 1992), 452.

38   See Steve Coll, "U.S. Halted Nuclear Bid by Iran," *Washington Post*, 17 November 1992, A1.

39   On the protests, see Robert Shuey and Shirley A. Kan, *Chinese Missile and Nuclear Proliferation* (CRS Report IB92056, 4 October 1994); *Nucleonics Week*, 24 September 1992.

40   Thomas W. Lippman, "Stepped-Up Nuclear Effort Renews Alarm about Iran," *Washington Post*, A1.

41   Gill and Medeiros, "Arms Control," citing interviews conducted with Chinese officials in Beijing, 81.

42   Anthony H. Cordesman, *Iran and Nuclear Weapons*, working draft paper (Washington, D.C.: Center for Strategic and International Studies, February 7, 2000), 10.

43   See Robert J. Einhorn and Gary Samore, "Ending Russian Assistance to Iran's Nuclear Bomb," *Survival* 44 (Summer 2002), 52–53.

44   See *Additional Requirements*, 89–90.

assured Washington in the fall of 1997 and thereafter that it would not export anti-ship cruise missiles, other missile-related technology, or nuclear technology to Iran.[45] U.S. officials believe that China's acquiescence, which was reconfirmed by Jiang Zemin in January 1998, resulted in part from the recognition, impressed on Beijing by Washington, that Iran could destabilize the region and disrupt oil supplies on which China's economic growth depends.[46] But it was also related to the benefits that the PRC did not want to forgo or thought it could attain from such cooperation. Thus, in spite of protests by its own National Nuclear Corporation, Beijing agreed to halt nuclear assistance to Iran during President Zemin's visit to the United States in October 1997 in return for a U.S. agreement to allow U.S. firms to sell China the technology it needed for nuclear power plants.[47]

By the late 1980s, China agreed not to sell more Silkworm missiles to Iran after the United States repeatedly complained that such sales make it harder to protect Gulf shipping and assured China that it would lift the freeze that had been placed on technology sales in 1987 in response to such sales to Iran.[48] While China has subsequently inquired about possible buyers without actually signing contracts, thus testing this agreement, it has largely cooperated with it.[49] The issue of arms sales arose again in 1996, this time with respect to shipments to Iran of the C-802, China's most advanced sea-skimming cruise missile at the time. Once again, a set of threats from the United States, as well as the potential that Congress would impose sanctions, was related to China's promise in September 1997 to stop such shipments.[50]

However, it was not until November 2000 that the PRC appeared to firm its commitment not to sell components and technology that could be used to produce such missiles and other dual-use items. For the first time, China promised to publish a list of restricted missile-related and dual-use items and to scrutinize the export of other technologies that could have dual uses. This promise represented China's heretofore most significant and sweeping commitment not to sell nuclear missile technology abroad. China made it partly in exchange for a pledge by the United States to forgo implementing sanctions, to expand commercial space cooperation, and to allow the launching of U.S. satellites by China, although China also considered the negative impact of arms sales to Iran on relations with Arab states such as Saudi Arabia and Kuwait, where it has steadily improved relations from

45   Robert Burns, "U.S. Warns China on Iran Trade," *Associated Press*, 19 January 1998.
46   Daniel L. Byman and Roger Cliff, *China's Arms Sales: Motivations and Implications* (Washington, D.C.: Rand, 1999), 10–12.
47   Cordesman, *Iran and Nuclear Weapons*, 10.
48   Gill and Medeiros, "Arms Control," 75.
49   State department officials cited in Zhao, *Interpreting Chinese Foreign Policy*, 96.
50   Gill and Medeiros, "Arms Control," 76.

1980 to 2000.[51] It was not, however, until August 2002 that Beijing in fact announced and signed into effect the long-awaited regulations that it promised. The new regulations created a system of licensing and registration for companies that export missile-related items or any dual-use technology that could be used to launch such weapons. The move was positive, if committed to in earnest, in that it denied important capabilities to states such as North Korea and Iran.[52]

On that score, while the United States has sought to use linkage in Sino-American relations to its advantage, China has also tried to use arms sales as a bargaining chip on issues such as trade, technology transfer, and Taiwan.[53] Thus, Chinese Premier Li Peng agreed to limits on arms sales to Iran and Iraq in July and October 1991 but ceased cooperation when President George H. W. Bush decided to sell 150 F-16 aircraft to Taiwan.[54] In January 1992, China asserted that it would agree to provisions of a 1987 international agreement restricting the export of missiles and missile technology if U.S. sanctions preventing the sale of U.S. satellite parts and high-speed computers to China were lifted. In June 1995, it delivered important missile component parts to Iran and Pakistan, at a time when Washington, in a change of sixteen years of official policy, allowed an unofficial visit by Taiwan's President, Lee Deng Hui, only to agree five months later not to sell Iran two nuclear reactors.[55] That decision was related to China's concern that the deal might fail due to Iran's economic problems, and to Iran's nuclear cooperation with Russia to complete a much larger nuclear reactor at Bushehr on the Gulf coast.[56]

CHINA AND THE UNITED NATIONS

China's proclivity to at once act as a counterweight against Washington, precisely as balance of power theory would predict, and yet also pay respect to the reality of dependence explains why its actions are sometimes split.[57] In

51 Christopher Bodeen, "China Commits to not Selling Technology of Missiles Abroad," *Associated Press*, 23 November 2000.
52 See Paul Mann, "No Breakthrough on Chinese Proliferation," *Aviation Week and Space Technology* (11 March 2002), 57.
53 Jonathan Rynhold, "China's Cautious New Pragmatism in the Middle East," *Survival* 38 (Autumn 1996), esp. 106–9.
54 Steinberg, "Chinese Policies on Arms Control," 13.
55 Elaine Sciolino, "C.I.A. Report Says Chinese Sent Iran Arms Components," *New York Times*, 22 June 1995, A1.
56 Elaine Sciolino, "China Cancels a Sale to Iran, Pleasing U.S.," *New York Times*, 28 September 1995, A1, A5.
57 See Alastair Ian Johnston, "International Structures and Chinese Foreign Policy," in Kim, ed., *China and the World*, esp. 60.

line with Beijing's concern about U.S. global power, it sought to hamstring U.S. efforts to use force in the Gulf, as the 1990–91 Gulf crisis revealed, although it was very careful not to push the United States too far. When Washington sought to enforce UN sanctions against Iraq in August 1990 as two Iraqi ships challenged the UN embargo, China, France and Russia preferred that it be done fully under UN auspices, whereas Washington wanted greater autonomy in stopping Iraqi ships. The United States had to consider seriously the potential for a Chinese or Soviet veto in the UN Security Council.[58] Throughout the crisis, Beijing pressed for an Arab solution to the crisis and against the U.S. position, which precluded any compromise with Iraq.

However, while China sought to place a check on the United States in the Gulf crisis, it also supported the first eleven UN Security Council resolutions pertaining to the Iraqi invasion. It also abstained on Resolution 68, which permitted U.S.-led forces to use force to evict Iraq from Kuwait. That was not produced by magic or altruism. China, in fact, as one diplomat put it, had a hard time "understanding how the United States and the Security Council can intrude on Iraq's sovereignty, which China considers a cardinal value, a principle that they stick to very strongly."[59] Rather, the United States agreed not to oppose expanded World Bank loans to Beijing in exchange for support in the Gulf.[60] Moreover, China's cooperation was intended, in part, to lead to an easing of U.S. sanctions imposed after the 1989 prodemocracy movement was crushed in Tiananmen Square, which included suspension of loans and a ban on high-level official contacts. As one western diplomat put it, it is "very much in their minds that good things are expected to accrue to them from taking these correct positions."[61] Obversely, in 1990, when China resumed ballistic missile arms sales to Iran, it was at a time when Sino-American relations were highly strained by the facts that China had crushed the pro-democracy movement and that Washington had responded with sanctions. As one diplomat put it, "the Chinese feel that the relationship with the U.S. is so bad that they can take the risk of selling these missiles—for the next two or three years."[62]

China's abstention from Resolution 687 was a useful concession to the United States. The resolution, as noted earlier in the book, gave U.S.-led states license to weaken Iraq, and in 2002 and 2003, they used it, along with

---

58   On this episode, see Lawrence Freedman and Efraim Karsh, *The Gulf Conflict, 1990–1991: Diplomacy and War in the New World Order* (Princeton: Princeton University Press, 1993), 145–48. Various author interviews.

59   Interview with Chris Kessler.

60   Lampton, "A Growing China," in Vogel, ed., *Living with China*, 126.

61   Quoted in Lena H. Sun, "China Hopes Its Cooperation Will Yield Benefits," *Washington Post*, 7 August 1990, A14.

62   Quoted in Daniel Southerland, "China Said to Sell Missiles," *Washington Post*, 29 March 1990, A5.

Resolution 1441, as a justification to launch war. For his part, Secretary of State James Baker had an evidently successful discussion with Chinese officials before the vote in which he talked about MFN status for China, potentially suggesting that Washington would respond negatively if Beijing voted against U.S. wishes.[63] As one U.S. official put it, the Chinese "may wrap themselves up in their flag and get defensive when we pressure them on arms sales and such issues, but they are pragmatic and will weigh the costs and benefits of their actions which linkage affects.[64]

Improvements in Sino-American relations after 1996 and especially after the summit meetings of 1997 and 1998 convinced some in China that there was more to be gained by cooperating with the United States, even half-heartedly, than by supporting regional states hostile to Washington. At those summits, China agreed to stop cooperation with Iran on nuclear matters, to halt sales of anti-ship missiles to Iran, and to halt its support of Iran's ballistic missile development. In the mid-1998 summit, Beijing further moderated its anti-U.S. position in the Middle East.[65] It is no coincidence that it needed U.S. support to deal with the Asian financial crisis, which threatened to undermine its economy. Its economic dependence on the United States at the global level affected its policy in the Gulf. China was careful not to take the lead role from Russia and France in challenging the U.S. interest in maintaining tough UN sanctions on Iraq. This caution was related to its concern about maintaining good relations overall with Washington.[66] In fact, Beijing signaled even ahead of France and Russia that it would not oppose a tough UN resolution to force weapons inspections in Iraq, thus helping America reach its goal in striking UN resolution 1441.

In some cases, U.S. diplomats have linked economic benefits to China's position on Gulf issues.[67] In other cases, it is clear that U.S. economic incentives have spurred cooperation. Thus, for instance, in June 1991, the United States and Britain sought to change the rules of permissible trade with Iraq. Russia threatened to veto this effort, but China in fact agreed to it in exchange for the release by the United States of $80 million in frozen Chinese business deals with Iraq. Beijing in particular agreed to an important provision that requires Security Council approval of a long list of potential military items. As

63   Interview with Steven Grummond.
64   Interview with Chris Kessler. Thus, Japan's cutoff of foreign aid to China in connection with its nuclear testing appeared to motivate China's decision to stop nuclear testing and to sign the Comprehensive Test Ban Treaty, after which Japan reinstated the support. Gill and Medeiros, "Arms Control," 69.
65   Sutter, Chinese Political Priorities, 157–58.
66   Interview with Edward Kagan.
67   Interview with Robert Pelletreau.

China's Guofang put it, the "U.S. has promised to take care of some of our concerns."[68]

THE PRC AND NUCLEAR PROLIFERATION

In addition to being increasingly dependent on the United States economically, China recognized toward the end of the 1990s that the U.S. role in protecting Gulf stability cannot be replaced.[69] And as President Zemin has repeatedly stated and other Chinese officials have echoed, Beijing views the stability of the region to be in the fundamental interest of regional states, the world, and the PRC.[70] Thus, while the Chinese want to challenge the United States where they can and make sure that it does not altogether dominate the region, they do not want to weaken it too much.

Beijing has provided technical assistance and equipment to Iran's nuclear weapons program under IAEA safeguards, but the United States persuaded it by 1997 to end all new nuclear cooperation with Iran. That near-term and possibly longer-run success was related to China's growing recognition that, as one NSC official put it, if anything "disrupted the supply lines, China would be very vulnerable."[71] That realization, however, has not eliminated serious conflicts of interest. In March 1998, the United States discovered that the China Nuclear Energy Corporation was negotiating to sell Iran several hundred tons of anhydrous fluoride. This material can be used to separate plutonium and help refine yellow cake into uranium hexafluoride to produce U-235, both of which are on nuclear control lists. Under pressure, China agreed to halt the sale.[72] In January 2001, the United States claimed that Chinese enterprises and corporations may very well have assisted Iraq in building the fiber-optic cable project used for air defense. After conducting an internal investigation, China denied the charge and warned the United States, through a statement by Foreign Minister Tang Jiaxuan, that any arms sales to Taiwan could do "severe harm" to Sino-American relations, as if the United States wanted to use the Iraq issue for cover to sell arms to Taiwan.[73]

68 Quoted in Colum Lynch, "Trade Deal Won Chinese Support of U.S. Policy on Iraq," *New York Times*, 6 July 2001, A17.
69 Interview with Edward Kagan.
70 "Chinese President Meets GCC Secretary General," *Xinhua News Agency* (1 November 1999). "China Promises Cooperation with Kuwait for a Peaceful Gulf," Xinhua News Agency, 21 February 2000. "China Supports Efforts to Restore Normal Situation in Gulf Region," *Xinhua News Agency*, 22 May 2000. See www.comtexnews.com.
71 Quoted in Joseph Fitchett, "A New China Embracing Nuclear Nonproliferation," *International Herald Tribune*, 11 December 1997, 1.
72 Cordesman, *Iran and Nuclear Weapons*, 53.
73 See *Hong Kong Wen Wei Po*, in FBIS-CHI, 26 February 2001.

Interestingly, one week after the fiber optic activity was discovered, Washington said that it would seek a UN condemnation of Chinese human rights behavior. This appeared to be linked to the fiber optic episode. Moreover, in 2003, China admitted to supplying Iran's crucial Natanz nuclear facility with uranium hexafluoride—a clear provocation to Washington.

Overall, the United States remained unsatisfied because China has not fulfilled some of its promises, or done so only after excessive pressure from Washington, but Beijing has made improvements on various questions such as arms transfers to the Gulf.[74] That is related to broader changes in its global orientation and to asymmetrical interdependence between the two states. Otherwise, China would be less restrained in its behavior on many fronts. As U.S. Secretary of Defense William Perry put it as early as 1996, China is "pushing the envelope with nuclear help to Pakistan. But at least there is an envelope, which did not exist 10 or 15 years ago on proliferation. Their actions could be much worse."[75] A similar dynamic was reflected when Chinese pilot Wang Wei collided with the U.S. Navy EP-3E surveillance plane over the South China Sea in April 2000. Beijing initially refused to return the plane or the twenty-four crew members who were forced to execute an emergency landing in China. But eventually the matter was resolved. It is more than speculation to believe that Beijing recognized that, despite domestic pressure to stand firm against Washington, it had too much to lose economically by holding the U.S. crew. Indeed, threats emerged across the U.S. political spectrum that China could lose MFN status or, as President Bush asserted, that relations could be "damaged" if the crisis were not resolved. Later in May, despite differences over whether the United States could fly the plane back home or use a less overt way to bring it back, as China preferred, Foreign Minister Li Zhaoxing asserted that the PRC sought cooperation and friendship with the United States for the "sake of our common interests."[76]

FROM OSAMA BIN LADEN TO SADDAM HUSSEIN

The September 11 attacks enhanced Sino-American relations. Transnational terrorism concerns both states, and both states want to see it defeated. As an example of their cooperation, the United States announced in August 2002 that it was adding the Eastern Turkistan Islamic Movement, a Chinese separatist group, to its list of terrorist organizations, for which China had strongly lobbied. Meanwhile, China issued new regulations intended to

---

74 Interview with Chris Kessler.
75 Quoted in Lampton, *Same Bed*, 159.
76 Quoted in Elaine Kurtenbach, "China Urges Understanding on Spy Plane Return," *Associated Press*, 10 May 2001.

restrict the export of missile technology to the countries of America's declared "Axis of Evil"—North Korea, Iran, and Iraq. Libya and Syria were added for good measure. In Secretary Powell's view, 9/11 helped "speed up an improvement" in Sino-American relations.[77] Beijing is also concerned about combating Central Asian extremism and undermining the Uighur separatists in Xinjiang, an oil-rich region which, if not controlled effectively, could not only pose economic problems for China but potentially also trigger or embolden other separatist efforts. The role of the United States in Afghanistan and against Central Asian extremism, while discomfiting to China from a strategic standpoint of bringing greater U.S. influence into the region, is quite positive from the perspective of fighting terrorism.

However, while the 9/11 attacks enhanced bilateral relations, several issues remained problematic, especially Taiwan. Many Chinese military and intelligence officials view U.S. strategic relations with Taiwan as impeding the potential provided by September 11 to strengthen Sino-American relations. The heir apparent to China's presidency at the time, Hu Jintao, declared that "selling sophisticated weapons to Taiwan or upgrading U.S.-Taiwan relations is inconsistent" with U.S. commitments to Beijing.[78]

Beijing has feared that in any crisis over Taiwan, the United States might cut off its Persian Gulf oil lifeline. While China has begun to take modest steps to secure its own access to regional oil, including significant investment and improved diplomatic relations in the Gulf, it faces a number of obstacles.[79] It is a latecomer to the game of rivalry in the Middle East and has no military position there. Nor does it have developed political relations with regional states and the carrots and sticks to develop or maintain new ones at a level necessary to start playing a military role. On that score, Beijing lacks force projection capability for and basing potential in the region. Furthermore, Saddam's Iraq may have offered China a door into the regional security framework, but Saddam has since fallen, and Iran, while interested in playing great powers off each other, has also moderated its foreign policy stance and may eventually move in Washington's direction, if domestic pressures for moderate reform continue to mount apace. It would take China a decade or more and significant financial expenditure to create even a moderate capability for protecting its oil lifeline from the Gulf, and even then

---

[77] Quoted in James Dao, "Closer Ties with China Help U.S. on Iraq," *New York Times*, 4 October 2002, A16.

[78] Quoted in Peter Slevin and John Pomfret, "U.S. Meets with Key Chinese Leader," *Washington Post*, 2 May 2002, A1.

[79] On access to regional oil, see Ed Blanche, "China's Mid-East Oil Diplomacy," *The Middle East* (January 2003). On investment, see Amy Myers Jaffe and Steven W. Lewis, "Beijing's Oil Diplomacy," *Survival* 44 (Spring 2002), 122–25. On improved relations, see Mohamed Bin Huwaidan, *China's Relations with Arabia and the Gulf, 1949–1999* (London: Routledge, 2002).

such an effort would likely generate tensions with a far stronger United States.

As the foregoing discussion may suggest, China's position preceding and during the Iraq War was largely to be expected. On the one hand, Beijing did not want to see the United States flex its muscles in the region unfettered and to enhance its regional and global power. This sentiment fell in line with its concern about U.S. hegemonic and unilateral power and with its preference for a multipolar world. The PRC saw benefits in following the lead of France, Russia, and Germany—states that would be useful insofar as they sought to balance the United States. Beijing was also concerned that war could set a precedent for American pre-emptive action against other weak states whose sovereignty it could violate without consequences. The PRC believed, too, that war could destabilize the Middle East in a manner that could threaten global oil supplies, and that providing UN inspectors with more time to complete their mission was preferable to the unpredictability of war.

At the same time, the PRC did not want to alienate the United States on Iraq's behalf. Saddam, after all, was hardly a paragon of virtue and had established himself as an aggressor in a region increasingly critical to China. And the United States, while viewed as adventuresome and muscle-bound, was vital to Beijing for reasons discussed earlier in this chapter

These competing motivations pushed China to take a moderate stance relative to France, Germany, and Russia. China was not sharply critical of American war preparations against Iraq in late 2002, as it had been in the past, and Bush administration officials believed that they might be able to gain China's support for military action against Iraq. Beijing supported UN Resolution 1441 but it opposed going to war on Washington's timetable and largely played the role of quiet dissenter. Unlike France and, to a lesser extent, Russia, China did not threaten to veto the American-led effort to adopt a second UN Security Council war resolution, nor was it ever likely to do so. Nor did China play an obstructionist role to lobby against the U.S.-led effort, as France did. Rather, Beijing voiced its opposition to the second resolution, asserting unwaveringly—though, compared to others, delicately—that the UN Security Council and not the United States should issue the final decision on whether to invade Iraq.

Of course, the United States became even more entrenched in the Gulf after the Iraq War of 2003. That has made it even harder for Beijing to fathom trying to develop the ability to secure its own access to regional oil while not competing too openly with the United States in that endeavor. Such a bold effort would require much political and eventually strategic jockeying in and outside the Middle East, and China prefers to try to ensure oil supplies by seeking a stronger commercial position in exploration and production abroad.[80] In any case, asymmetrical interdependence will provide it with an important incentive to maintain good relations with Washington as a means of assuring access rather than in trying to rival it in any serious manner.

China has sought to check the United States but has been able to go only so far in doing so. Developments in Sino-American relations at the global level have clearly affected China's behavior in areas that affect oil stability. It has become increasingly dependent economically and in various international organizations on the United States. U.S. pressures could have been ignored when China was more insular and less growth-oriented, but that became harder when its goals and emphases changed and Washington assumed an increasingly important role in the global economy.

To be sure, China's cooperation with Washington on issues related to oil stability was selective, but it was important. Regardless of Beijing's motivations, we know that it backed the UN Resolution on November 29, 1990, which authorized the U.S.-led coalition to use force against Iraq, and that it notably abstained from UN Resolution 687. These resolutions were vital to reversing and containing Iraq's threat to the region. In terms of arms sales, Beijing engaged in sporadic efforts to stem the sale of materials, components, and weapons to Iran. This was less effective on the conventional side, but Beijing took some more important measures to curtail contacts with Iran in the nuclear arena. China also instituted domestic export controls and began to impose penalties for that purpose. In addition, the regime largely did maintain economic sanctions against Iraq from 1991 through the 2003 war, and it adhered to the UN arms embargo against Iraq despite a major loss of revenue. While it was often critical of U.S. activities in the Gulf, especially when it pertained to the periodic military attacks on Iraq, it did not oppose the no-fly zone in Iraq. In addition, it chose neither to veto U.S. efforts at the UN nor to form a serious anti-American alliance or alignment against Washington with Moscow and other states. At most, it offered a calculatedly moderate feint in that direction.

It is fair to bet that China will remain concerned about its economic interaction with Washington, that it will become much more dependent on Gulf oil, and that it will increasingly want oil stability. As a result, it is likely that Washington will continue to have leverage with the PRC that can redound to the benefit of oil stability, leverage that, in the absence of asymmetrical interdependence, it would lack. This leverage is neither trivial nor all-important, but in the mix of factors that shape bilateral relations in the area of oil stability, it is substantial.

---

[80] See www.eia.doe.gov/emeu/cabs/china.html.

We can also guess that China's increasing dependence on Middle East oil will make it more likely, along with the United States and other oil importers, to try to pressure oil-producing states to adopt approaches that favor oil stability, and to otherwise help create an environment conducive to oil stability. Asymmetrical interdependence should facilitate U.S. efforts to enlist China in doing so, but rivalry in Sino-American relations regarding oil stability is also likely to remain part of the mosaic of their relations.

Chapter 8

THE OIL WEAPON

The story of oil stability is not just about longer-term political and security developments in Middle Eastern and global affairs, although they are integral parts of that story. It is also about major disruptions in oil supply that might occur as a result of the oil policies and behavior of oil-producing nations. Such disruptions can arise for a variety of reasons, but this chapter will explore a special case: the potential for the use of oil as a political weapon.

We would be remiss to argue that the potential for the use of the oil weapon is not a palpable reality. In 2000, during the second Palestinian Intifada, Crown Prince Abdallah warned that Riyadh would break relations with any country that moved its embassy in Israel to Jerusalem.[1] In April 2002, an official close to him reportedly suggested that Riyadh would use the "oil weapon" to support the Palestinian uprising against the Israelis, but the regime subsequently dismissed that possibility.[2] However, Iraq did cut off exports and Iran and Libya threatened to follow suit. Many Saudis still believe, as Gregory Gause has put it, that their "country's finest hour was when it defied the United States with the 1973 oil embargo."[3] The Saudis, as Robert Pelletreau, former U.S. deputy secretary of state, observes, would have to make a "serious calculation about using or threatening to use the oil weapon," which "cannot be discounted given the vagaries of Middle East politics."[4] A perception certainly exists among observers of the global scene that Arab oil could be used as a weapon, as it has been used that way before.[5]

1 Interview with Robert Pelletreau.
2 Quoted in Patrick E. Tyler, "Saudi to Warn Bush of Rupture over Israel Policy," *New York Times*, 25 April 2002, A1.
3 Gregory F. Gause III, *Oil Monarchies* (New York: Council on Foreign Relations, 1994), 122.
4 Interview with Robert Pelletreau.
5 Interview with Omar Farouk Ibrahim.

However, several key developments, in addition to the role of Saudi Arabia covered in the next chapter, have much decreased the potential for the use of the oil weapon over time. OPEC states have learned important lessons from the 1973 embargo and the second oil shock of 1979. Moreover, the Middle East has slowly been shorn of leaders who would use the oil weapon independently or lead others in such an effort. Furthermore, the Arab-Israeli conflict, which in the past has driven Arab states to use the oil weapon, remains heated, but the potential for it to escalate into a broader Arab-Israeli war has diminished considerably, contrary to what media coverage and disheartening violence might suggest.

THE LESSONS OF THE 1973 EMBARGO: THE OIL WEAPON BACKFIRES

Over the course of the twentieth century, Arab oil producers slowly gained the power to use oil as a political weapon. However, it didn't take many attempts for these countries to learn that they did so at their peril. In the first half of the century, the world oil market was dominated by seven major oil companies—also known as the Seven Sisters—namely, Exxon (the former Standard Oil of New Jersey), Chevron (the former Standard Oil of California), Texaco, Royal Dutch/Shell, Mobil, Gulf, and British Petroleum. In addition there existed a handful of independents, most of them American. The world's proven and exploitable reserves were either outright owned or controlled under contract by these companies, but this slowly changed. In 1938, the future Arabian American Oil Company (Aramco) first discovered oil in large quantities in Saudi Arabia, and over the following decades the Saudis slowly took control of the company from Americans.[6] Iran began to move away from this structure by nationalizing oil in 1951, after the Shah of Iran was effectively stripped of his powers by the parliament in 1950. That turned the Anglo-Iranian Oil Company (later British Petroleum) into a company without portfolio.[7] A U.S.-organized coup put the West-leaning Shah back in power in 1953, replacing the government of the popular Prime Minister Mohammed Mossadegh. Between 1945 and the 1973 Arab oil embargo, the price of oil was posted largely by the big oil companies, rather than determined by the market. The price was set based on the need to accommodate the interests of both oil-consuming and oil-producing countries.

---

[6] On this oil and security relationship, see Parker T. Hart, *Saudi Arabia and the United States: Birth of a Security Relationship* (Bloomington, IN: Indiana University Press, 1998) and Anthony Cave Brown, *Oil, God, and Gold: The Story of Aramco and the Saudi Kings* (New York: Houghton Mifflin, 1999).

[7] On the Seven Sisters and the global oil industry, see Danice Yergin, *The Prize: The Epic Quest for Oil, Money, and Power* (New York: Simon and Schuster, 1990).

By 1960, power began to shift in earnest to oil-producing nations. Decolonization and nation-building infused many of these states with the proclivity and wherewithal to assert rights over their own resources. OPEC was formed in 1960 in this context, initially by Saudi Arabia, Kuwait, Iran, Iraq, and Venezuela. Later, it expanded to include Algeria, Ecuador, Gabon, Indonesia, Libya, Nigeria, Qatar, and the United Arab Emirates. Interestingly, few of the members thought that it would last, much less become a major institution on the global stage.[8] But it proceeded to try to increase its ability to affect production and pricing in relation to the major oil companies.[9] By 1973, OPEC had wrested the price-setting role from major oil companies, thus signaling the end of an age in which the majors had played this role.[10]

And it was also not until the 1970s that the individual Arab states of OPEC demonstrated a propensity to use it for both economic and political purposes.[11] After the unsuccessful embargo during the Six Day War of 1967, Saudi Arabia, Kuwait, and Libya established the Organization of Arab Petroleum Exporting Countries (OAPEC) the following year, an organization that included exclusively Arab oil producers and aimed to increase their power. The existence of OAPEC would become crucial in 1973, because it was during the Arab-Israeli War, launched by Arab states on the Jewish high holiday of Yom Kippur of that year, that OAPEC launched its first oil embargo. The embargo chiefly targeted the United States and the Netherlands for their actions in support of Israel. It sought to support Arab states and the Palestinians in their fight against Israel, avoid isolation by those same Arab nations and by important elements of the Saudi public, and make a profit. Unlike the 1967 embargo, which was less coordinated and coincided with a global oil glut, this embargo was far more effective, and over time increased in intensity. The Saudis played an especially crucial role by manipulating their predominant spare capacity to drive prices higher.

The embargo, which represented perhaps history's biggest peaceful transfer of wealth from industrialized states to developing ones, clashed directly with a central objective of OPEC enshrined in Article 2 of the OPEC Statute drafted in 1960: the pledge to achieve order and stability in the international oil market.[12] The embargo, which some believed might bring about an Arab

8   Interview with Omar Farouk Ibrahim.
9   Indeed, the first sentence of the first resolution passed in September 1960 asserted such a goal. See *OPEC: Official Resolutions and Press Releases, 1960–1990* (Vienna, Austria: OPEC, 1990), 1–2.
10 This generated a change from a vertically integrated market structure to a de-integrated one. Nordine Ait-Laoussine, "Pricing of Oil: The Need for a New Stabilizing Mechanism," *Middle East Economic Survey (MEES)* 34 (16 September 1991).
11 On the development of OPEC, see Jahangir Amuzegar, *Managing the Oil Wealth: OPEC's Windfalls and Pitfalls* (London: I. B. Tauris, 1999), chap. 3.
12 *OPEC: Official Resolutions and Press Releases, 1960–1990*, 1–2.

Golden Age based on Black Gold firepower, remains transfixed in the collective memory of many diplomats and leaders. They had to deal with the economic dislocation it caused, and their citizens faced endless lines at gas stations and prices that went up 40 percent in a few months. No event in the post–World War II era produced effects as sudden, widespread, and negative for the global economy as the embargo, earning it the dubious distinction of being the nadir of oil stability.[13]

The longer-run consequences of the embargo taught Arab oil exporters a lesson they would not soon forget. It spiked worldwide inflation, which not only hurt the economies on which they relied but also raised the prices of goods that they themselves imported from the West. More important, the embargo seriously damaged trust in these producers worldwide. As OPEC officials observe, the major lesson that the producers learned and still remember is that "the embargo led to a situation where nation's holding oil were viewed with great suspicion by others and this suspicion pushed them to seek alternatives to oil" and that it was crucial "to commit resources to consumers in a predictable and trustworthy manner."[14]

The embargo unified western leaders in the pursuit of oil security and pushed industrialized countries to develop and exploit other sources of energy (coal, nuclear, geothermal, solar, wind). It also motivated them to invest in new technologies that could allow for non-OPEC oil exploitation, including huge improvements in offshore technologies.[15] These would become vital many years later and increase competition with OPEC. Moreover, the embargo pushed states to decrease oil consumption domestically over the longer run—a typical effect of higher oil prices, as consistently demonstrated by scholars—and to use energy more efficiently.[16] They focused great attention on changing their national approaches in order to decrease dependence on OPEC oil.[17] Many of these efforts did not endure in full, and the use of oil per unit of growth increased in developing economies (as opposed to the industrialized ones), but these efforts did serve as a whole to highlight to oil-producing states the dangers and limits of using the oil weapon.[18]

---

[13] Though economists do differ on how adverse the effects were on the global economy. Philip K. Verleger, Jr., *Adjusting to Volatile Energy Prices* (Washington, D.C.: Institute for International Economics, 1993), 29–31.

[14] Interviews with Omar Farouk Ibrahim and Muhammad Al-Tayyeb.

[15] Interview with Mohamed Hamel.

[16] Richard Pindyck, "Inter-fuel Substitution and the Industrial Demand for Energy: An International Comparison," *Review of Economics and Statistics* (May 1979).

[17] On early efforts at energy cooperation, see Verleger, *Adjusting to Volatile Energy Prices*, esp. 11–16.

[18] On developing versus industrialized economies, see Edward R. Fried and Philip H. Trezise, *Oil Security: Retrospect and Prospect* (Washington, D.C.: The Brookings Institution, 1993), 8–9, esp. Table 2–1. On the dangers of using the oil weapon, see Verleger, *Adjusting to Volatile Energy Prices*, 4.

That lesson was driven home by the fact that oil exporters lost market share over time—market share they never recovered—as non-OPEC energy sources were developed. By 1979, OPEC's market share was already seriously undermined, in part by non-OPEC exploration.[19] In 2002, OPEC market share was down significantly from its peak of 52 percent in 1973. Based on the relationship between real oil prices and supply over the past thirty years, some models project that, at $30 p/b, OPEC loses market share as non-OPEC supply grows at a strong 3 percent.[20]

Such lessons were a function of more than the 1973 episode alone. While it is hard to assess relative causal weight, the second oil shock, which started in 1979 and stretched into the next year, also played a substantial role. The fall of the Shah in January 1979 precipitated serious internal conflicts between secular and clerical factions. Oil production, which had already dropped during the chaos of the revolution, nearly halted. At the outset of the crisis, the Saudis chose not to use spare capacity to offset the shortfall and dampen the price escalation, while other OPEC producers cut production. They did not initiate the effort independent of regional events but were aided by the disruption in oil supplies caused by the revolution and the Iran-Iraq War, which erupted in September 1980.

By this time, OPEC states had already seen some of the negative effects of using oil as a political weapon, but the lessons of 1973 had not yet been absorbed fully enough to prevent this second oil shock. However, like the 1973 embargo, the second oil shock, combined with a global economic malaise, contributed to a decrease in demand from 30 mb/d in 1980 to 15 mb/d by 1985.[21] While OPEC's power peaked from 1973 to 1980, it declined in the 1980s, something that was not lost on oil leaders.[22] It is now well understood by OPEC officials and economists that excessively high prices can generate "long-term damage" that can "easily outweigh any short-term benefit."[23] Prices that go too high above $30 p/b can trigger technological investments. Over time, these investments help produce lower-cost oil and threaten the value of Arab oil assets in the ground that may not be put to market for twenty or thirty years.[24]

19   Noreng, *Crude Power*, 146–51.
20   The effect is lagged by about eighteen months due to the delay between the period of high prices, and the effects of the investment and development that they trigger. Thus, the high oil prices of 2000–2001 suggests that non-OPEC output would grow in 2002 and 2003. See *OPEC Outlook* (Deutsche Bank: 9 March 2002).
21   Ian Seymour, "What Is or Should Be OPEC's Oil Price Target," *MEES* (22 April 2002).
22   Shukri Ghanem, *OPEC: The Rise and Fall of an Exclusive Club* (London: KPI Limited, 1986), 141–62. Also, see Robert Mabro, ed., *OPEC and the World Oil Market: The Genesis of the 1986 Price Crisis* (Oxford: Oxford University Press, 1986).
23   See Statement by Dr. Ali Rodriguez Araque, The Secretary General of OPEC, www.opec.org.NewsInfo/Speeches/sp2002/spAraqueTripoliJan02.htm.
24   Interview with Omar Farouk Ibrahim.

LEADERSHIP AND INTER-STATE DYNAMICS

While the lessons of 1973 and 1979 remain fresh enough to help deter the use of the oil weapon, it is also important to understand that other changes in Middle East politics have also served this purpose. Indeed, over time, the more radical leaders in the region who might have led the charge to use oil as a weapon have either weakened or passed from the scene altogether. Moreover, as the result of inter-state dynamics, it has become less likely that a hawkish alignment, pushing for lowered supply, will be struck.

In some measure, OPEC members try to separate politics from economic decisions. OPEC decisions are influenced by advice from OPEC's board of economists, which is tasked with providing economic rather than political analyses. OPEC has even held meetings in times of dire conflict, such as during tense periods of the Iran-Iraq War, because, as one OPEC official put it, "the price of non-cooperation in OPEC was too high."[25] But OPEC is hardly immune to past history, family feuds, the whims of leaders and personalities, and the politics of inter-state tension. Moreover, while economic input is important in decision-making, it cannot bridge differences of opinion over levels of production. There is no magic economic formula to do that, even if all agree on the numbers. As former acting OPEC Secretary-General Fadhil Al-Chalabi has put it, OPEC decisions usually result from political compromise and are made by oil ministers who are "politicians."[26]

The nature of leadership has been one of the most significant political factors at play in the politics of the Middle East. Strong, charismatic, and sometimes radical leaders can affect OPEC directly or through the politics of the Middle East into taking a more hawkish stance on production or even launching a minor or major oil embargo. Such leaders were present in the 1960s and 1970s, but not at this time.

For his part, after rising to great heights in the 1970s and early 1980s, Saddam slowly lost influence in counterproductive wars and then fell from power altogether in 2003. Meanwhile, after rising to power in 1969 in a military coup, at about the time that Saddam's influence was growing in Iraq, Libya's Col. Mohammar Qaddafi played a vital role in increasing OPEC power against major oil companies and on the global scene, and he spurred other OPEC members to assume more aggressive oil policies. He has since lost significant influence. Shut out of the global economy, Syria remains an economic basket case, and the death of President Hafez Assad has deprived it of a seasoned leader and a staunch defender of pan-Arabism. Meanwhile, Egypt has, since the Camp David accords, become a force for moderation—quite

---

[25] Interview with Javad Yarjani.
[26] Quoted in Wilfrid L. Kohl, "OPEC behavior, 1998–2001," *Quarterly Review of Economics and Finance* 42 (2002), esp. 224.

different from its Nasserist pan-Arab past. Iran's politics are less conducive to autocratic rule than in the past, and Tehran has been weakened by revolution, war, and international isolation.

In addition to the leadership factor, revolution and war in the region have made it harder for a hawkish alignment to be struck within OPEC. The Iranian Revolution injected a profound dose of mistrust into Saudi-Iranian relations in the 1980s, which spilled over into the oil arena. This became especially clear when Riyadh flooded oil markets in 1986. It increased output from below 2 mb/d to almost 6 mb/d, and then by the late fall of 1985 to almost 9 mb/d, leading to a major oversupply of oil to global markets and a price collapse. Riyadh had multiple motivations for this act. Chiefly, it sought to address the growing loss of market share to non-OPEC producers and quota busting, or over-production, on the part of OPEC members.[27] But the United States also preferred lower oil prices for its economy, and secondarily to hurt the Soviet Union, which depended on oil revenue, and Riyadh appeared to oblige, due no doubt to its strategic relationship with Washington.[28] Challenging Iran was not the primary motivation, but the Iranian media and some officials understandably saw Saudi oil policy through the prism of the Saudi-Iranian political rivalry and in light of the Saudi support of Iraq against Iran in the Iran-Iraq War. They went so far as to accuse Saudi Arabia of an oil conspiracy aimed at defeating revolutionary Iran.[29]

To be sure, Saudi-Iranian relations began to improve in the late 1980s, as presented in chapter 2. However, the Saudis remained concerned about Iran's regional designs. For their part, the Mullahs in Iran have still not reconciled themselves to the Saudis' monarchical rule, despite the waning of the revolution. Even if they did, we would still note that oil stability is threatened much more when hawks align than when a hawk and a dove improve relations. This is because hawks already have market-related interests in common on which to forge joint oil policies, while the hawk and dove may still differ on oil policy significantly enough that improved political relations may not strike serious or long-lasting cooperation on oil policy.

While Saudi-Iranian relations have been fundamentally affected by developments in the past two decades, so have Iran's relations with Iraq. Even after the Shah's abdication, Iraq and Iran maintained a wary association.[30]

27 For excellent analyses of this time period, see Wilfrid L. Kohl, ed., *After the Oil Price Collapse: OPEC, the United States, and the World Oil Market* (Baltimore: Johns Hopkins University Press, 1991).

28 For evidence of this, see Peter Schweizer, *Reagan's War* (New York: Doubleday, 2002), 238–42.

29 See Henner Fürtig, *Iran's Rivalry with Saudi Arabia between the Gulf Wars* (Reading, UK: Ithaca Press, 2002), 233.

30 See R. K. Ramazani, *Revolutionary Iran: Challenge and Response in the Middle East* (Baltimore: Johns Hopkins University Press, 1986), 59, 74.

The revolution, however, created the potential for the spread of Iran's brand of Islam. This at once threatened Iraq next door and gave Iraq the opportunity to attack Iran while Iran was caught in revolutionary throes. Overall, the Iran-Iraq War engendered a legacy of profound distrust, which was attenuated only by the fact that Iran and Iraq shared the dubious distinction of having been so weakened by war and so contained by Washington as to be less concerned about each other than they otherwise would have been. Thus, even if both states preferred higher oil prices, their potential to cooperate in reaching this goal was, at the very least, highly diminished. Neither state was interested in taking any action that might strengthen the other, despite the market advantages. Had the Iran-Iraq War not taken place, it is fair to argue that Iran and Iraq would have been far more able to cooperate in creating a coalition within OPEC to push for higher oil prices. This was, in fact, the trajectory prior to the Iran-Iraq War, when both states had greater influence and capability and better relations, and sought such an outcome in oil markets.[31]

Meanwhile, the potential for Iraq to pressure Saudi Arabia and Kuwait into being more hawkish was largely dashed by Iraq's invasion of Kuwait, which left Iraq politically isolated and Saudi Arabia and especially Kuwait wary about taking any actions that could strengthen Saddam's power. Even before this crisis, Kuwait was willing to risk challenging Iraq on oil issues; after the crisis, Kuwait's proclivities in that direction received ballast from profound anger at Saddam, coupled with fear that he might re-energize and threaten Kuwait once again.[32]

The 1991 war seriously disrupted the operations of OAPEC whose members include Algeria, Bahrain, Egypt, Iraq, Kuwait, Libya, Qatar, Saudi Arabia, Syria, and the United Arab Emirates. And the negative residue of that war is still felt among some of these countries that took different positions in that war and do not fully trust one another to this day.

Even within OPEC, leadership changes at lower ranks have worked against radical oil policies. In the 1970s, OPEC was run by oil ministers with a high degree of nationalistic fervor and who had experienced OPEC's increasing power and independence. But this leadership would slowly change. By the 1980s and 1990s, OPEC was increasingly run by technocrats and driven by economic analyses.[33] Politics remained an important dimension but it became more divorced from organizational behavior than it had been.

---

[31]   See Stephen Pelletiere, *Iraq and the International Oil System: Why America Went to War in the Gulf* (Westport, CT: Praeger, 2001), 221.
[32]   Interviews with various Kuwaiti officials and citizens.
[33]   Interviews with Omar Farouk Ibrahim and Javad Yarjani.

THE ARAB-ISRAELI CONFLICT

Changes in the Arab-Israeli conflict have also made it less likely that the oil weapon will be used. To be sure, a number of developments could trigger partial or full use of the oil weapon. In one scenario, Israeli military responses to major Palestinian or other terrorist attacks on Israeli civilians, could kill many Palestinians and result in an Israeli reassertion of control over major parts of the West Bank and Gaza Strip. The Saudis, if feeling under pressure from the Arab street and especially insecure domestically, might take some action on the oil front. Provocative behavior by an Arab state such as Syria or its well-armed proxies in Lebanon could also result in an extensive Israeli military operation. A perceived or real threat by Jewish extremists to Muslim parts of Jerusalem could stimulate domestic pressures on Muslim leaders to take action. Changes in Arab leadership through coup, revolution, or regular succession could also ignite short- or longer-term extremism.

Outside of the Arab-Israeli conflict, an Israeli military strike on Iran's nuclear facilities could, under the right circumstances, possibly trigger the use of oil as a weapon, though some Saudis might privately be relieved at such a strike. While no one can rule out oil weapon politics, in reality they have become far less likely over time.

At the regional level, the connection between the Palestinian question and the policy of Gulf states has never been clear-cut. The House of Saud has struggled sporadically with the PLO, such as in the 1990–91 crisis when Yasser Arafat and the Palestinian people largely sided with Saddam Hussein, an act that Saudi and Kuwaiti leaders vividly recall.[34] It prompted them to expel thousands of Palestinians, cut aid, and reconsider their relations with Arafat. While they sympathize with the Palestinian cause in a broad sense, it is not clear that they would sacrifice anything for the PLO leadership by playing oil politics with the West.

Arab states, moreover, are fully aware that the regional power balance has shifted significantly in Israel's favor over the past twenty years. Israel has been strengthened through high-technology integration, cooperation with the United States, and improved relations with Turkey. Ultimately, its possession of nuclear weapons and ability to deliver them accurately represents a trump card, even in the event that its conventional forces are defeated. In addition, the most strident anti-Israel states have been weakened, have lost their Soviet patron, and face a stronger and more influential United States. As discussed in chapter 2, the Arab rejectionist front, which preferred war

---

[34] Ann M. Lesch, "Contrasting Reaction to the Persian Gulf Crisis: Egypt, Syria, Jordan and the Palestinians," *Middle East Journal* 50 (Winter 1991); Daoud Kattab, "Emotions Take Over," *Middle East International* (31 August 1990).

to any peace with Israel, was powerful in the 1970s.[35] The Saudis even decided to oppose strongly the Camp David accords, which Washington thought they might support, at least symbolically, partly so as not to offend this front. But the front has long since lost power.

For its part, Egypt, while involved in a cold peace with Israel, is at least more constrained by its treaty with Israel than it would have been in the absence of such a treaty. Surely that is also true of Jordan, which has had closer relations with Israel than Egypt has. And as for Iran, it was not part of the rejectionist front, which was a pan-Arab manifestation, but it was more anti-Israel and anti-American after the fall of the Shah than it would become in the 1990s. These factors are not cast in cement in the mercurial Middle East, but they do greatly decrease the proclivity of regional antagonists to engage in brinkmanship with Israel that could, as in the 1967 Six Day War, lead to a pre-emptive Israeli strike, and they certainly make war less palatable to Israel's adversaries. They also increase the probability that if war occurred, it would be over quickly, thus decreasing chances for an embargo to be launched and for any that does occur to be prolonged and debilitating. The decreased potential for an Arab-Israeli war is clearly positive for oil stability.

Economic factors are also at play. In the past, Arab states and the Palestinians could count on Moscow for support. But post–Cold War Moscow is clearly uninterested in playing such a draining role, even if it could. Meanwhile, Egypt and Jordan have become dependent on U.S. economic and military aid and trade, and most Arab states want U.S. high-technology and support for accessing the global economy. Even formerly pro-Soviet Yemen has sought better relations with Washington. Anti-American rhetoric aside, they know, as do the GCC states, that serious entry onto the potentially lucrative—albeit bumpy—globalization train requires America's imprimatur.

On that score, relations of growing economic need are not limited to the Arab Gulf. The importance of the United States to Iran has also increased, despite stormy relations and Tehran's pursuit of nuclear capability. After the Soviet Union and its satellite states fell from power, Iran had, as Shireen Hunter puts it, "no alternative to the West as a source of technology and financing for its economic reconstruction."[36] It has since expressed interest in joining the WTO, more than three-quarters of whose members are developing or undeveloped countries.[37] This has provided some further incentive for Tehran to moderate its foreign policy in the region. As Shaul Bakhash

---

35 Safran, *Saudi Arabia*, 238–39.
36 Shireen T. Hunter, "Iran from the August 1988 Cease-Fire to the April 1992 Majlis Election," in *The Middle East after Iraq's Invasion of Kuwait*, ed. Robert O. Freedman (Gainesville: University Press of Florida, 1993), 200.
37 *OPEC Bulletin* (June 2000), 7.

observes, there was "a realization among the president's advisers and certainly in the new Parliament that one of the issues that must be dealt with to attract foreign investment and expand the economy are Iran's relations with the U.S."[38] This may explain why Iran, under pressure from the United States, for the first time admitted in late July 2003 that it was holding senior Al Qaeda leaders and, more important, that it would pursue others more vigorously.[39]

A breakthrough in U.S.-Iranian relations is not likely in the next few years, but might transpire thereafter. *President* Mohammad Khatami of Iran believes that the United States would have to make some major gestures to create any potential for improved relations. Sticking points range from Iran's desire for a U.S. apology for its role in overthrowing Prime Minister Dr. Mohammad Mossadegh in 1953, with which the United States moved to comply, to resentment over U.S. economic sanctions against Iran and over the U.S. military presence in the region.[40]

But even if relations do not improve significantly, Washington has more leverage with Tehran now than in the past, just as it does with Arab Gulf states. This leverage may be used directly on issues related to oil stability or indirectly to try to persuade Iran to cast off its spoiler role in the Middle East peace process, and possibly to help restrain Hamas and Islamic Jihad behind the scenes. One Iranian editorial captured an aspect of the increasing dependence of regional states on Washington. Reflecting broader views in Iran, it asserted that a two-day Arab summit in Amman, Jordan, in April 2001 was the "Summit of the Impotent," involving states that could do little on behalf of the Palestinians partly because of their security and economic dependence on the United States.[41]

For its part, the Iraq War has further diminished prospects for an Arab-Israeli war, possibly to their lowest point since Israel was founded in 1948, and added a positive impetus for peace. Of course, achieving Middle East peace is a grand and elusive challenge—in truth, the word *quixotic* does not seem out of place—and the course of the peace process can change abruptly. But one effect that has been structural for the Middle East is that Iraq has been diminished for the foreseeable future as a military threat to Israel, as a financial supporter of Palestinians who kill Israeli civilians, and as an ally for any combination of states that might want to launch a war against Israel or, short of a war, to use the oil weapon. That is a rather important development as we look to the future. It may tend to make Israel feel more secure in making concessions to the Palestinians and others with which it lacks a

---

[38] Interview with Professor Shaul Bakhash, *Near East Report*, 6 March 2000.
[39] CNN, 23 July 2003.
[40] For an interview with Khatami, see cnn.com/world/Middle East, 7 September 2000).
[41] "Summit of the Impotent," *Iran Daily*, 10 April 2001, 4.

peace accord, and make the choice of war for Arabs even less inviting than it has been in the past two decades. That hardly guarantees success in peace-making or war-avoidance, but it may prove helpful.

The oil weapon remains a concern for global oil markets. No one can predict the course of world affairs, and it is possible under certain scenarios that it would be used either collectively or by individual oil producers. But there are sound reasons for believing that this potential has decreased significantly over time, which means that one of the most serious threats to oil stability has abated.

Chapter 9

MULTIPLE CUSHIONS FOR OIL SHOCKS

While it is vital to explore the potential for the use of the oil weapon, it is equally important to examine the ability to supply oil to global markets in the event of crises such as wars, revolutions, coups, labor strikes, and limited or collective embargoes. Indeed, a hallmark of oil stability is precisely the ability to deal with oil crises once they arise, be they driven by political, economic, or security events.

Important developments have taken place over the past two decades, which, while meaningful in their own right, have also influenced the evolution of oil stability. Since the mid-1970s, Saudi Arabia has become more committed to global oil stability. In addition, the rise of non-OPEC oil producers and the potentially evolving situation in Iraq have allowed for increased and diversified sources of oil. Moreover, the development of strategic petroleum reserves (SPRs) has added a significant cushion should oil supplies be interrupted. Considered together, these developments offer a shock absorber that did not exist to nearly such an extent in the past. They have made it more likely that the global economy can count on sources of oil to deal with the negative effects of disruptions in the supply of oil.

OPEC HAWKS AND DOVES

Before exploring the central developments laid out above, it would be worthwhile examining intra-OPEC dynamics in some detail. The terms "hawks" and "doves" are widely used to describe factions within OPEC. These terms mask the nuances in positions taken by OPEC members and, thus, are not

generally appreciated by OPEC officials,[1] but they do capture broad tendencies among OPEC members.

To consumers, stability has to do chiefly with supply. They want to know
that they can obtain sufficient oil resources in a timely manner at reasonable prices. To oil producers, stability often refers to demand. They want
to be assured of selling their product at prices that they consider reasonable. But differences exist among oil producers about what reasonable output and prices should be. OPEC doves have preferred to achieve revenue
targets by producing and selling higher volumes of oil at lower prices.
Saudi Arabia has fallen in this category, though not all Saudis view the
matter the same way. Some Saudi elites have been more willing to take
hawkish actions, even at the risk of triggering alternative energy exploration or antagonizing countries such as the United States. They have
argued that high prices should be maintained by significantly cutting production. They believe that it is more important to maximize oil revenues,
husband resources, and support the position of oil-producing nations like
Iran rather than to achieve market share by increasing production and lowering prices.

However, the House of Saud is generally reluctant to agree to high oil
production cuts, because, as the largest producer of oil, it would bear a disproportionate share of output cuts, thus allowing other producers to gain
market share. Moreover, if oil prices were to make alternative energy exploration feasible, this could hurt Saudi Arabia in the long term much more
than states such as Iran, because it has far larger reserves and sunken costs
than they do, which it wants to be able to sell at a reasonable price down
the road. Losing market share might mean that these assets would simply
waste away, especially if technology moves the world into a post-oil market
faster than is currently expected. In other words, for Saudi Arabia, the
reserve life of these resources is far longer than their anticipated economic
horizon.

By contrast, states with more limited oil reserves and an ability to expand
production have sought to achieve revenue targets by lowering production
in order to increase price. They have exhibited little interest in trying to capture expanding oil markets as a means of revenue enhancement, because
they lack the capability to expand production and face relatively higher
extraction costs p/b. In this sense, Iran and Venezuela have been relatively
more hawkish. For instance, Venezuelan President Hugo Chavez—the first
elected head of state to visit Iraq since 1990 in a sanctions-busting move—
irritated the United States in August 2000 when he called on OPEC countries
to unite as a counterweight against U.S. economic power and to maintain oil

---

[1] Interviews with OPEC officials.

quotas, at a time when Washington was trying to convince OPEC to increase production to stem rising prices.[2]

Another factor is at play. The so-called doves, such as Saudi Arabia and Kuwait, have smaller populations than their more hawkish counterparts Algeria and Iran. Price declines surely hurt the larger producers with the smaller populations, but they are far more problematic for the smaller producers with bigger populations to support.

THE SAUDI ROLE

The Saudi position, which remains roughly dovish, is vital for global oil markets. After September 11, the Saudi regime was maligned for creating an atmosphere in which the hijackers could be created, and was described by some as much more of an enemy than ally of the United States.[3] While these criticisms had some merit, Riyadh's role in global markets over time has been largely beneficial, since the 1973 Arab oil embargo, when about 90 percent of the production cuts were made by Saudi Arabia, Kuwait, and Libya.[4] In the post-embargo period, the world economy has been able to rely on two related oil norms: Saudi Arabia would oppose serious cuts in oil production within OPEC—unless warranted by depressed oil prices—and it would put more oil on the market in the event that the oil supply was threatened by crises or by a deliberate reduction by one or more oil producers. These norms are important in the story of oil stability because they work against elites in Saudi Arabia and OPEC members who want to be more opportunistic in the oil realm and they lead to real actions with positive consequences for oil stability.

In the period following the embargo, Riyadh sought to avoid an oil price spike that could cause inflation in the West and a backlash against Arab states.[5] After December 1976, in an OPEC meeting in Qatar, Saudi leaders indirectly referred to their stand against OPEC production cuts as a "present" to the President-Elect Jimmy Carter, in expectation that this act would be appreciated.[6]

---

2   See *MEED* 44 (18 August 2000), 3.
3   A briefing paper presented to the Pentagon's Defense Policy Board on 10 July 2002 viewed Saudi Arabia in this light. The Board's function is to advise DOD, which later distanced itself from the report.
4   See Dr. A. F. Alhajji, "OPEC Cannot Manage World Oil Markets with a Price Band," *World Oil* (October 2000), 136.
5   On the development of OPEC, see Jahangir Amuzegar, *Managing the Oil Wealth: OPEC's Windfalls and Pitfalls* (London: I. B. Tauris, 1999), 41–43.
6   Shahram Chubin, *Security in the Persian Gulf: The Role of Outside Powers* (New Jersey: Allanheld, Osmun, 1982), 73.

In more recent times, it should be noted that the Saudis have supported and even orchestrated production cuts, for two related reasons. The first is depressed oil prices, of which the case of 1998–99 stands out. In that period, oil prices collapsed partly because OPEC did not anticipate a steep decline in Asian oil demand caused by the currency and banking crises of 1997 and weak demand elsewhere,[7] but also because the Saudis sought to punish Venezuela for overproduction. The result was that OPEC, in what Venezuelan Energy Minister Ali Rodriguez would later call one of the "biggest mistakes in OPEC history," raised production in 1996 and 1997, creating a major over-supply by 1998.[8] In December 1998, oil prices had dropped to historic lows of $10 per barrel, a level so low that it threatened to undermine the Saudi economy and to foment domestic instability.

At the March 1999 OPEC meeting, the Saudis agreed for the first time since 1993 to a quota under eight mb/d. The key to the agreement, which followed a less effective OPEC production cut in June 1988, was a Saudi concession to Iran to absorb the larger brunt of cuts. This followed intense diplomacy in which Iran may well have exaggerated how much it had been producing. Saudi-Iranian cooperation in the oil sector had largely eluded the two states in the past.[9] The OPEC cuts, unfortunately, worked all too well, in that oil prices eventually soared well over $30 p/b. While a number of concomitant factors produced the oil price spike in addition to Saudi oil policy, the United States was troubled by the Saudi position and made its feelings known to Riyadh.[10]

The second reason at play is that states such as Saudi Arabia and Kuwait need oil revenue to meet budget targets. The oil revenues of these countries allow for large welfare states in which citizens are not taxed and receive a host of free government services. Oil revenues make these regimes, in effect, distributors of economic rent from state coffers in the form of benefits and welfare to the people—what many scholars refer to as rentier states.[11] The problem is that they built their infrastructures and systems based on pro-jected revenues at a time when oil revenues were far higher than they are today and their populations far smaller. As discussed in chapter 2, Saudi Arabia has found it harder to fund its welfare state. It relies on foreign oil sales for 40 percent of its GDP and, more important, 80 percent of its state revenue,

---

[7] See Wilfrid L. Kohl, "OPEC behavior, 1998–2001," *Quarterly Review of Economics and Finance* 42 (2002), esp. 209–13.

[8] *MEES* (3 April 2000).

[9] See, for instance, *Oil Daily* 44 (22 March 1994), 1–2.

[10] On the oil price spike, see Nawaf E. Obaid, *The Oil Kingdom at 100: Petroleum Policy-making in Saudi Arabia* (Washington, D.C.: The Washington Institute for Near East Policy, 2000).

[11] See Jill Crystal, *Oil and Politics in the Gulf: Rulers and Merchants in Kuwait and Qatar* (New York: Cambridge University Press, 1995), esp. 75–78.

making it highly dependent on oil revenues. Since domestic pressure and tradition make it difficult to tax Saudi citizens or to cut spending aggressively, the regime must depend on fluctuating oil revenues. The regime ran serious budget deficits for most of the 1990s and, more recently, a $12 billion deficit in 2002 that followed a $6.7 billion deficit in 2001.[12] Budgetary pressures have made Riyadh more interested in higher oil prices than was the case in the past, but they have not fundamentally shifted its oil policy.

While Iran and Saudi Arabia had cooperated in restricting oil production in 1998 and 1999, they still had very different oil strategies. Iran needed oil revenues for postwar reconstruction, economic growth, and military programs. In part because of this, Iran opposed the OPEC's March 2000 decision to increase output. Tehran believed that any oil increases should not exceed more than one mb/d, urging OPEC members to resist consumer pressure to raise crude oil supplies and especially to rebuff intense pressure from Washington.[13] On July 18, 2000, Iranian Oil Minister Bijan Zanganeh stated that the Clinton administration was in fact "trying to force the OPEC into increasing its production" for its own narrow national interests.[14] At the same time, the Saudis were trying to talk prices down, promising an extra 500,000 b/d if prices did not fall, a pledge made necessary by the failure of previous OPEC increases to lower prices.[15]

In September 2000, Saudi Arabia, under some pressure from Washington, which feared that higher oil prices could trigger a global recession, also took the lead role in convincing OPEC to raise production.[16] That was against objections from Iran, which disliked Riyadh's unilateral decision to increase its production by 500,000 b/d.[17]

The second norm that the world economy has been able to count on is that Riyadh would stabilize oil supply in the event of an oil disruption. The Saudis played this role in the week before and after Iraq's invasion of Kuwait.[18] Indeed, in addition to providing the U.S. military with free jet fuel

12 *Oil and Gas Journal*, "A Look at Oil Dependency" (7 January 2002), 17.
13 "Iran Favors Limited Oil Exports of OPEC," *ITAR/TASS* News Agency, 13 March 2000, www.comtexnews.com. See also "OPEC States Agree to Raise Output; Iran Stays out," *United Press International*, 29 March 2000, www.comtexnews.com.
14 Quoted in "Iran Accuses U.S. of Pressuring OPEC," *United Press International*, 18 July 2000.
15 "OPEC on top," *MEED* 44 (21 July 2000).
16 Transcript, "Clinton's Remarks on Mideast Peace Meetings and Oil Prices," 7 September 2000 (Office of International Information Programs, U.S. Department of State. www.usinfo.state.gov). On Saudi Arabia's lead role, see, for instance, "OPEC Resists Calls for Increased Oil Output," *Oil and Gas Journal*, 16 October 2000, 40. Also, Alhajji, "OPEC Cannot Manage," 131.
17 Iran Cautions OPEC Members against Oversupply of Crude," *Xinhua News Agency*, 11 September 2000, www.comtexnews.com.
18 See Lawrence Freedman and Efraim Karsh, *The Gulf Conflict, 1990–1991: Diplomacy and War in the New World Order* (Princeton: Princeton University Press, 1993), 56–57.

during the war, U.S. oil companies provided Saudi Aramco with the technical assistance and equipment to put oil on the market more quickly in the
effort to make up for the oil lost due to the invasion.[10] On August 19, 1990,
Riyadh signaled that it would increase production by 2 mb/d—over one-third
of its production level—irrespective of what OPEC decided to do. Despite
the threat of global recession, Iraq, Libya, and Iran argued that there was
enough oil on global markets already.

In late 1999, Saudi Arabia pledged that if problems were to occur and
cause supply interruptions elsewhere as the result of the Y2K bug at the turn
of the century—a widespread fear at that time—it "would stand ready to
assure the world of continued oil supply to stabilize the market."[20] In this
time period, Iraq, Iran, and Libya continued by and large to push for cuts
in oil production. Like Saudi Arabia, Tehran was split internally on how
much to push that goal, but the Saudis opposed OPEC cuts and became a
relatively lone voice in supporting production increases, recognizing the negative impact of high prices on market share.[21]

In April 2002, Iraq cut off oil supplies to the world, and, at the twenty-eighth
meeting of the Organization of the Islamic Conference, called on Arab states
to use the oil weapon in order to pressure Israel to withdraw from West
Bank towns it had re-occupied in an effort to root out Palestinian militants.
Riyadh assured global markets that it would not use the oil weapon and
would continue to supply markets in order to keep prices down.[22] Later that
month, the influential Saudi Oil Minister Ali al-Naimi asserted in Washington
that "Saudi Arabia's policy of maintaining spare production capacity is based
on its belief in the importance of price stability" and that OPEC would
increase supply to the market if it detected a supply gap left by Iraq's
unilateral embargo.[23]

Some Gulf Arab officials felt that such an embargo would hurt Arab
exporters more than the United States, while Iran argued that an embargo
would work only if all Arab producers joined, strongly hinting that Saudi
Arabia was key. The Saudis, however, ruled out the oil weapon option, and
pledged to cover any market loss of oil caused by Iraq's one-month embargo
in April 2002, which helped stabilize markets.[24] Saudi Arabian Foreign
Minister Saud al-Faisal argued that Arab countries depended on such revenues
for their development and so could not afford the losses.[25]

19   "Saudi Arabia: The Gulf Crisis," APS Review Oil Market Trends 53 (8 November 1999).
20   GCC joint statement quoted in OPEC Bulletin 31 (January 2000), 11.
21   OPEC Outlook (London: Deutsche Bank, 9 March 2002).
22   "Saudi Arabia Opposes Using Oil as Political Weapon," Xinhua News Agency (9 April 2002).
23   Quoted in "Saudis Vow to Meet Any Oil Supply Shortfall," Oil Daily (23 April 2002).
24   Fears of an Embargo Rile Oil Market (Cambridge, MA: Cambridge Energy Research
     Associates, 2 April 2002).
25   See "Market Bullishness Intact," Oil Daily (4 April 2002).

The Saudis also assured markets in January 2003, when the prospect for war in the Gulf was rising, that they would make up for some 2 mb/d of lost Venezuelan oil.[26] They had already pushed production to 8.5 mb/d by the end of 2001 to deal with a potential war in Iraq.[27] In line with earlier Saudi promises, OPEC again agreed to raise output by 1.5 mb/d to an overall 24.5 mb/d, starting on February 1, 2003, to deal with the Venezuelan and Iraq problems, though as Secretary General Alvaro Silva Calderon saw it, the effects of war were "out of our control."[28] Iran, apparently unhappy about any promises to increase OPEC production, withheld its support, arguing that there was no sign of an oil shortage on the market.[29] Zanganeh asserted that there were "no economic justifications for increasing" OPEC output and that Iran would "not endorse decisions of political connotations, [sic] and we are confident that OPEC will not make decisions regarded by the world Muslim and Arab public opinion as supportive of a U.S. military invasion against an OPEC fellow member."[30] Overall, it is the Saudis who have generally used oil production in order to moderate oil prices, of course serving their own economic interests at the same time.[31]

GLOBAL EXCESS CAPACITY

Evolving Saudi norms in the global oil arena are an important longer-run development. But at any given time oil stability will also be a function of global excess capacity. It is the amount of oil that can be put into markets in reasonable time that is not already meeting existing demand. Excess capacity is affected by many factors, one of which is the price of oil. High oil prices invite non-OPEC and alternative energy exploration, which causes OPEC oil demand to decrease. That, in turn, contributes to idle capacity—a development that was especially pronounced in the 1980s. In the 1990s, by contrast, excess capacity stayed low partly because oil companies stopped investing after years of idle capacity. The important point is that excess capacity can be viewed as part of a boom-bust cycle rather than as a trend.

[26] See Karen Matusic, "Opec Quickly Raises Ceiling to Replace Lost Venezuelan Oil," *Oil Daily* (14 January 2003).

[27] See *Oil and Gas Abacus* (Deutsche Bank, 25 September 2002), 5.

[28] Quoted in "OPEC Promises to Cover Iraqi Oil Production," *Xinhua News Agency*, 2 March 2003.

[29] "Iran Rejects OPEC Request to Increase Oil Output," *Xinhua News Agency*, 21 March 2003.

[30] Quoted in "Iran Says No 'Economic Justification' for OPEC to Boost Output," *Xinhua News Agency* (10 March 2003).

[31] *Oil and Gas Journal* (9 December 2002), 68.

Figure 3. World excess oil production capacity, 1970-2003°

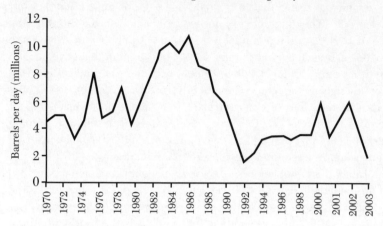

Source: Energy Information administration
° 2003 = current estimate

As Figure 3 shows, global excess capacity has fluctuated significantly over time. By 2002, it rebounded to an estimated 6 mb/d, but dropped in 2003, largely due to the Venezuelan oil strike, problems in Nigeria, and ongoing challenges in Iraq. These problems have placed pressure on states that hold excess capacity to put more of it on the market. In particular, Saudi excess capacity traditionally has accounted for more than 80 percent of global excess capacity, with other nations having significant excess capacity being Kuwait, the UAE, and Venezuela. Saudi excess capacity peaked in 1985 at approximately 10.5 mb/d and averaged less than half of that from 1982 to 2001, and by 2003 averaged approximately one-third to one-fourth of what it was in the 1980s.[32] Thus, Riyadh's ability to prevent major supply disruptions decreased, although even at this reduced level, the Saudis alone could still have replaced more oil than Iraq—whose oil sales were sanctioned—put on the market in the 1990s or than some other OPEC states produce altogether. Because even lowered Saudi capacity represents significant protection against difficult, although not worst-case, supply disruptions, the question of falling excess capacity in the market is somewhat less crucial. That said, by 2003, overall excess capacity was well off of its highs and worse off than it has been historically, which was not positive for oil stability.

Global excess capacity, however, is quite likely to increase in the near future, as estimated in Figure 4. This figure is based on several assumptions. The drop in excess capacity in 2003 was due to events that are unlikely to endure, at least not as collective problems. In addition, oil prices have been

[32]   Based on figures provided by DOE oil analyst G. Daniel Butler.

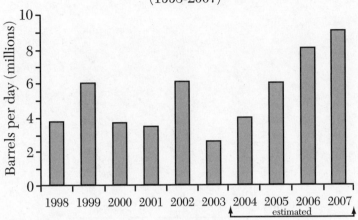

Figure 4. Projections in world excess capacity
(1998-2007)*

Source: Author's estimates
* Projections assume that oil prices will average within OPEC's $22-$28 price band.

higher from 2000 through 2003 than they were in 1998 and 1999, when they dropped significantly. If excess capacity is partly related to oil prices, relatively high oil prices should contribute to more excess capacity in the near term. Furthermore, as discussed in this chapter, greater non-OPEC oil production, as well as production from Iraq in the coming years, is likely to decrease how much excess capacity is actually put into the market from states that hold it. In turn, that should increase idle capacity levels.

On that score, the states that hold the most excess capacity have initiated policies to enhance foreign investment, which should further increase production and, perhaps, excess capacity.[33] These efforts have continued well after the Iraq war. In fact, the potential that Iraq would suck up billions in global investment pushed these states to conclude big investment deals. The Saudis announced in late July 2003 that they would form a joint venture with two European behemoths, Total and Shell, for gas exploration. It was the first time since the 1970s that the Saudis have allowed foreign companies to invest so directly in their energy sector and suggested that more could be in the offing to encourage foreign investment in the oil sector as well.[34]

[33] See Robert R. Smith, Hassaan S. Vahidy, and Fereidun Fesharaki, "OPEC's 'Quiet' Revolution of Capacity Growth," *Oil and Gas Journal* (9 July 2001).

[34] *Oil and Gas Abacus* (Deutsche Bank, 30 July 2003). *International Energy Outlook 2003* (Washington D.C.: U.S. Department of Energy, May 2003), 66–68, www.eia.doe.gov/oiaf/ieo/index.html. Obaid, *The Oil Kingdom at 100*, 53–60. "Once Bitten, Twice Shy," *Gulf Business* 4 (March 2000). David Ignatius, "Mending the Marriage with Saudi Arabia," *Washington Post*, 29 July 2003, A17.

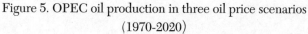

Figure 5. OPEC oil production in three oil price scenarios
(1970-2020)

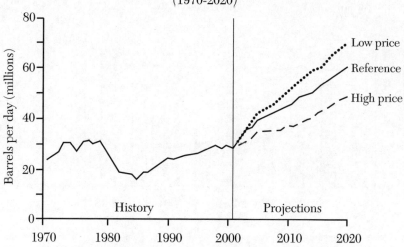

Source: Energy Information Administration, *International Energy Outlook 2002.*

NON-GULF OIL PRODUCTION

While the global economy increasingly has been able to rely on Saudi Arabia to help put oil on markets when needed, the rise of non-OPEC supply, even when compared to OPEC, is notable, as Figures 5 and 6 show.[35] North America dominated non-OPEC supply in the early 1970s, beginning a trend toward the diversification of oil supply. Mexico, Siberia, and the North Sea added to the mix as major producers in the late 1970s and early 1980s, and China, Latin America, West Africa, the Caspian Basin, and the non-OPEC Middle East came on-line in earnest in the 1990s. In part as a result of the rise of non-OPEC oil, OPEC's share of oil as a percentage of total energy consumption by the major industrialized countries has actually declined, from 55 percent in 1980 to 40 percent by 2000.[36] The Gulf states, for their part, provided only about one-third of the world's market demand by the turn of the century.

According to the U.S. Department of Energy, non-OPEC oil cannot alter the global trajectory toward increased dependence on Gulf oil, though other

[35]   *Annual Energy Outlook 2002*, 58.
[36]   On global dependence, see the statement by Saudi Minister of Petroleum and Mineral Resources Ali I. Naimi in *OPEC Bulletin* 31 (March 2000), 6.

Figure 6. Non-OPEC oil production in three oil price scenarios
(1970-2020)

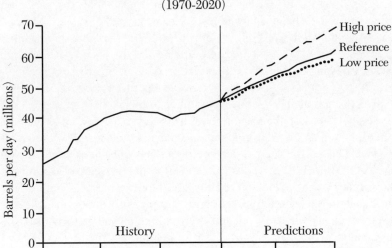

Source: Energy Information Administration, *Annual Energy Outlook 2002.*

analysts believe that it can.[37] But even if it cannot, non-OPEC supply, as the next chapter suggests, can erode OPEC power at particular junctures and dilute the effects of temporary embargoes or oil disruptions. At a minimum, it offers diversity of supply, which is qualitatively important over and beyond the amount of supply. As Daniel Yergin observes in purveying the global oil scene, "What is striking is the diversification of supply sources on a global basis."[38]

In several ways, the end of the Cold War and 9/11 produced effects that enhanced diversification. First, they created greater potential for Russia to increase its oil production and to diversify its export outlets. The fall of the Soviet Union initially produced a decline in crude oil output, but economic and political liberalization has allowed for significant production to resume. Russia and the former Soviet Union (FSU) republics produce one-tenth of

37 Oil analyst Edward Morse holds this view, for one, as he related in correspondence with the author. As the former U.S. Ambassador to Saudi Arabia notes, the notion of Russian oil replacing Saudi oil is "circulating." See Chas W. Freeman Jr., moderator, "The United States and Saudi Arabia: American Interests and Challenges to the Kingdom in 2002," *Middle East Policy* (March 2002), 12. Ambassador Richard Butler's view, "A New Oil Game, with New Winners," *New York Times*, 18 January 2002. *APS Review Downstream Trends* 58 (11 March 2002).

38 Daniel Yergin, *Persian Gulf in a Global Context* (Cambridge, MA: Cambridge Energy Research Associates, 2003).

the world's oil, and Russia and Iran account for almost one-half of the world's natural gas reserves. Russia has exhibited enough potential to produce oil that the Saudis have been annoyed over its growing market share.[39] Moscow significantly ratcheted up its oil production from 1999 to 2002, producing 7 mb/d in February 2002 compared to 6.9 mb/d for the Saudis, and appears intent on investing enough to increase its production by an estimated one-fifth by 2005.[40] Some observers go so far as to say that Russia has a "chance to displace OPEC as the key energy supplier to the West."[41]

The issue is not just about the level of Russian production but also where that production can be delivered and consumed in the world, and at what price. The share of Russian net oil exports to states outside of the FSU rose from 53 percent in 1992 to 87 percent in 2000, while the share of net exports to the former Eastern bloc and the Soviet Union decreased significantly.[42] While the shift has been toward Western Europe as an outlet, that trend is likely to extend elsewhere as well and apply to both oil and gas exports. Even if we account for the fact that Russia will consume a substantial amount of its own energy production, the changed global political landscape means that Russian energy can alter the pattern of energy delivery and offer the world greater diversity of supply.[43]

The potential for Russian energy to reach non-European markets has been driven by market incentives and possibly by Russia's interest in ingratiating itself to the West, from which it seeks favors in return. It has a strong market incentive to move its energy out of Europe, where demand is largely stagnant, to the rest of the world. European demand is expected to grow by an anemic 1 mb/d over the next ten to fifteen years compared to ten times that volume in Asia, particularly in China.[44] But Russia has lacked export pipeline capacity, a problem which it is rectifying by using increased oil revenues and by drawing on western technological support made possible by the end of the Cold War.

Russia's non-CIS export capacity has already shown some increase, albeit not a huge one, and, as Table 6 shows, is projected to grow by over 50 percent by 2007. Much of its pipeline capacity is expected to be on-line by 2005,

---

39 *Oil and Gas Journal* (4 February 2002), 5.
40 Sabrina Tavernise, "Russians to Keep Limits on Oil Exports through June," *New York Times*, 21 March 2002, W1.
41 Edward L. Morse and James Richard, "The Battle for Energy Dominance," *Foreign Affairs* 81 (2002).
42 See www.eia.doe.gov/emeu/cabs/russexp.html.
43 For instance, Russia consumed 69 percent of its own natural gas production, and exported the rest in 2000. See *International Energy Outlook 2002* (Washington D.C.: U.S. Department of Energy, 2002), 52. This document can be found at www.eia.doe.gov/oiaf/ieo/index.html.
44 See www.eia.doe.gov/emeu/cabs/caspian.html.

TABLE 6.
Russia's non-CIS export capacity projection, 1999–2007

Pipelines	1999	2000	2001E	2002E	2003E	2004E	2005E	2006E	2007E
Murmansk (Barents Sea)*	–	–	–	–	–	–	–	500	1000
Novorossysk (Black Sea)	765	765	886	886	986	986	986	986	986
Tuapse (Black Sea)	121	121	121	121	121	121	121	121	121
Odessa (Black Sea)	201	201	201	201	201	201	201	201	201
Ventspils (Baltics)	322	322	322	322	322	322	322	322	322
Butinge (Baltics)	150	150	150	150	150	150	150	150	150
Varandei Terminal (Barents Sea)	–	–	30	30	30	30	151	151	151
Sakhalin 1&2 (Okhotsk Sea)	–	–	–	–	–	–	–	150	400
Vankor Terminal (Kara Sea)	–	–	–	–	–	–	–	50	80
BPS	–	–	–	240	240	380	380	600	600
Druzhba**	1,249	1,249	1,249	1,249	1,299	1,349	1,349	1,349	1,349
Pipeline to China***	–	–	–	–	–	–	400	400	600
Russia's Total Capacity	2,808	2,808	2,959	3,199	3,349	3,539	4,600	4,060	5,960

Source: EIA, Deutsche Bank, and author's estimates.
*Proposal for pipeline faces a number of obstacles, including ultimate ownership between the government and private companies.
**on October 2000, major Russian oil company Yukos signed a $20 million agreement with the Croatian oil transport company JANAF to integrate this pipeline with the Adria pipeline. This will allow Russian oil exports to flow directly to the deep water port of Omisalj on the Adriatic Sea, which can accommodate tankers up to 500,000 deadweight tons.
***The feasibility of the China pipeline is under study.

provided Moscow can obtain sufficient investment, surmount the problem of a sclerotic bureaucracy, and remove roadblocks to private-sector pipeline and terminal construction.[45] However, once on-line, Russia's efforts are likely not only to diversify export routes but also to make energy deliverable much more economically.[46] For instance, Russia is already building an oil pipeline from Lake Baikal in Siberia to a giant Chinese refinery in Daqing in northeastern China, an effort that faces important hurdles but also underscores the potential of Sino-Russian cooperation. Moscow and Beijing are also exploring whether to build a gas pipeline along a similar route. In June 2003, Russian oil and the China National Petroleum Corporation signed a memorandum of understanding for sales via a pipeline from Anagarsk in Russia to Daqing, if it is built.[47] The two states are also involved in a consortium that is evaluating other potential projects, including a trans-China pipeline that can carry gas to Shanghai from far larger gas fields across the border in western Siberia.[48] A Russia-China oil pipeline could supply China with 26 percent of its projected 2005 imports.[49] Meanwhile, a consortium of foreign companies led by Shell began producing oil in 1999 at Sakhalin island in the Russian Far East, in the Sea of Okhotsk. It has plans to build a pipeline, with a starting date of 2005, across the North Pacific that can tap approximately two billion barrels of Russian natural gas for delivery to Japan. With significant reserves, massive exploration potential, and proximity to growing Asian markets, the region is an important non-OPEC growth arena.[50]

Privatized Russian companies, led by Lukoil, also plan to build an oil terminal at Murmansk on the Barent's Sea, which can facilitate delivery of oil to the United States and may bypass the control of Transneft, the government's oil transport monopoly. If so, it can further decrease the power of the government over how much Russian oil is exported. These decisions are negotiated between big business and the government, which controls the major export pipelines and can also influence big businesses in different ways.[51] To what extent the government will allow for privatized companies to control the Murmansk project remains to be seen. A hybrid of government and big business ownership may result—if the deal succeeds.

---

[45]   On these obstacles, see John Webb, *Choking the Boom? The Looming Shortage of Russian Crude Export Capacity* (Cambridge, MA: Cambridge Energy Research Associates, 2003).

[46]   Correspondence with Edward Morse (28 August 2002).

[47]   See www.eia.doe.gov/emeu/cabs/china.html.

[48]   "Russia Reaches for Chinese Oil and Gas Outlets," *Petroleum Intelligence Weekly* (23 July 2001), 4.

[49]   See www.eia.doe.gov/emeu/cabs/russpip.html.

[50]   See "Big Oil in Sakhalin-Can the Majors Bite into the Russian Growth?" (Deutsche Bank, Summer 2003).

[51]   Interview with Leonard Coburn.

Second, while Russia has greater potential to exploit its own resources independent of other states, its cooperation with the United States for these purposes also increased. The fall of the Soviet Union led to interaction with Washington and, in turn, has enhanced trust. Moscow is feeling less vulnerable than before in allowing the United States to help it exploit Russian oil; meanwhile, nationalist sentiment has abated as compared to the Cold War years, though it remains a factor, as discussed in chapter 6. At the Russian-American summit in Moscow in May 2002, Putin and Bush announced a strategic energy agreement. As a result of the agreement, which reflected concerns over a possible disruption of oil supplies in a U.S.-led attack on Iraq, the two sides launched a number of important endeavors into joint oil exploration and production. These efforts aimed at bringing the two governments as well as major oil companies into cooperative oil ventures and were not derailed by the lagged effects of 9/11, partly because Putin has seen the arrangements as a good way to maintain strong relations with Washington.[52]

Third, while the end of the Cold War and 9/11 enhanced U.S.-Russian cooperation in exploiting Russian oil, they also led to increased cooperation in developing Caspian Basin oil. In addition to oil in Russia proper—in particular Azerbaijan, but also Kazakhstan and Turkmenistan—the key Caspian Basin states excluding Russia and Iran account for one-third of the estimated undiscovered oil of the FSU (44 percent is in West Siberia). Azerbaijan alone may well put 750,000 barrels p/d by 2005, which would represent, after Iraq, the largest potential increase into the market.[53] The Caspian region contains proven oil reserves that are estimated at 17 to 34 bb, which is comparable to or greater than those in the United States (22 bb) and the North Sea (17 bb).

Throughout the 1990s, Russia and the United States backed different pipeline routes out of the Caspian basin. Russia and Iran were developing joint oil exploration projects, which allowed Russia to use Iran as a "partner" to limit U.S. influence and to prevent the emergence of other regional powers.[54] Russia and Iran objected to western plans to build pipelines that would bypass them and, for strategic and economic reasons, sought some control over pipeline-transported oil.[55] The lagged effects of the end of the Cold War and the September 11 attacks altered this dynamic. U.S.-Russian rivalry decreased over how oil should be produced and delivered, as well as

---

[52] Interview with Leonard Coburn.

[53] Interview with Erik Kreil.

[54] See Thomas Stauffer, "Caspian Oil and Gas: Destined to Remain Orphaned?" *OPEC Bulletin* 30 (July 1999), 4–8. On limiting U.S. influence, see "Iran Said 'Crucial Partner' in Region," in *FBIS: CEURA*, 8 March 1995, 51. "Gazprom in Deal with Iran," *Financial Times* (21 April 1997), 2.

[55] Patrick Crow, "Competition for the Caspian," *The Oil and Gas Journal* 94 (December 1996), 40; "Iran's Support on Caspian Oil Deal Seen as Ineffective," *FBIS: CEURA*, 25 May 1994, 14.

over which regional states should gain influence from such an oil regime. The United States lauded the region as a stable oil supplier, in contrast to the Middle East, and Moscow and Washington became more interested in increasing total pipeline capacity—a major constraint in the 1990s—and in fighting terrorism, which they both face.[56] In fact, U.S. and Russian companies cooperated to exploit Central Asian oil potential, as they have within Russia proper.

As with Russia, Caspian Basin energy is increasingly able to reach markets outside of traditional areas. During the Cold War, oil and natural gas pipelines in the region, with the exception of Iran, were used for energy delivery within the FSU. In the post–Cold War period, new pipelines such as the Baku-Novorossiisk, the Tengiz-Novorossiisk, and the Baku-Supsa pipelines have been constructed to increase delivery potential to the FSU, and new oil and gas pipelines are being built for delivery outside the FSU. The potential is significant because of the relative lack of export options heretofore. In 2001, less than half of Caspian exports were exported to consumers outside the FSU.[57] Most of Russia's oil, for instance, comes from western Siberia. That oil is hard not only to produce but also to deliver to ice-free ports thousands of miles away. However, dislodging the Taliban has created some potential for a pipeline that runs through Afghanistan, possibly to an outlet near the Pakistani port of Karachi, with another possible extension to India. As one U.S. energy analyst put it, it may still be difficult to get a company to risk the "human and financial capital to build and maintain it," but the chances post-9/11 have increased.[58]

It is, of course, important to note for a balanced account that oil production and foreign investment in Central Asia, and the Caspian in particular, depend on regional stability, which is uncertain. Kazakhstan, Turkmenistan, and especially Azerbaijan will have the largest control over oil fields. However, they are landlocked and will have to pipe oil across potentially noncooperative neighboring states. Several lines already exist, and new lines are being built, but still others will be mandatory to contribute seriously to global supply.[59] That requires cooperation, because even if economic incentives make agreements tempting, they may not be struck or endure.[60] Aspects of

---

56   See Sabrina Tavernise with Birgit Brauer, "Russia Becoming an Oil Ally," *New York Times*, 19 October 2001, W1.

57   See www.eia.doe.gov.emeu/cabs/caspian.html.

58   Interview with Linda Doman.

59   For instance, a 394-mile pipeline connecting Kazakhstan to the Black Sea is expected to be completed in 2003.

60   See Bülent Gökay, ed., *The Politics of Caspian Oil* (New York: Palgrave, 2001), esp. chap. 3. On relative gains thinking as an impediment to cooperation in theory, see Joseph Grieco, "Understanding the Problem of International Cooperation: The Limits of Neoliberal Institutionalism and the Future of Realist Theory," in *Neorealism and Neoliberalism: The Contemporary Debate*, ed. David A. Baldwin (New York: Columbia University Press, 1993).

rivalry among regional states, such as Iran, Saudi Arabia and Pakistan, and among outside states, including Russia, the United States, and even China, could overlap and complicate oil production.[61]

Fourth, the Soviet Union has been dissolved into states that, while still dependent on Moscow, have developed far greater independence than they had during the Cold War. U.S.-Russian cooperation on oil issues has increased, but this development has also yielded Washington greater flexibility in exploring bilateral cooperation with the FSU. This has in turn added to the potential for achieving greater diversification of global oil supply. Such potential has already been realized in the form of the Baku-Ceyhan oil pipeline, whose construction began in mid-September 2002 by a consortium led by British Petroleum and strongly supported by Washington. The trans-Caspian pipeline will run across the Caspian through Baku to the Turkish port of Ceyhan on the Mediterranean, thus reducing political dependence on either Iran or Russia, which would have influence over other pipeline routes. U.S. Secretary Abraham touted the pipeline, projected to carry 1 mb/d by 2005, as being able to give western nations "greater energy security with a diversified supply" of oil that depends less on the Middle East.[62]

Naturally, the United States does not want to alienate Russia by pushing its cooperation with the FSU states too strongly. Nor does it want to jeopardize potential influence in the FSU by inadvertently enabling Putin or subsequent leaders to reassert control in the FSU. The need to enlist Russia in the war on terrorism ran the risk of doing so. Washington gave priority to Russian relations, potentially at the expense of FSU states such as those in Central Asia.[63] However, all things considered, Washington developed greater leverage and interaction with both Russia and the CIS in the post–Cold War period.

While the United States needed to straddle the line between wooing the FSU and alienating Russia—a balancing act that will remain salient well into the future—the two efforts were not mutually exclusive. Washington could strike up a useful oil relationship with Russia while also testing the waters for oil exploration and development in Central Asia. Indeed, the improved

---

61 Even increasingly oil-dependent China seeks to gain significant influence in the Caspian and Central Asian areas, and in ways that may not be fully compatible with U.S., Russian or regional state interests. See Xiaojie Xu, "The Oil and Gas Links between Central Asia and China: A Geopolitical Perspective," *OPEC Review* 23 (March 1999). Also, on regional rivalry, see "Daggers Drawn," *MEED* (15 February 2002). On potential challenges to regional energy exploitation for Asia, see Kang Wu, "Central Asia's Potential as Asia-Pacific Oil Supplier Limited for Years to Come," *Oil and Gas Journal* (5 August 2002).

62 Quoted in Richard Allen Greene, "Work Begins on Oil Pipeline Bypassing Russia and Iran," *New York Times*, 19 September 2002, W1. Other companies in the consortium include Azerbaijan's national oil company and firms from the United States, Norway, Turkey, Italy, France, and Japan. Interview with oil analyst Edward Morse, whose company is involved.

63 Interview with Strobe Talbott.

climate of relations decreased Russian opposition to the Baku-Ceyhan pipeline, and Russia's largest oil company, Lukoil, even confirmed that it was seriously thinking about investing in it. Moreover, Russia worked with both American oil companies and its former southern provinces to transform into reality the 980-mile pipeline stretching from Kazakhstan's Caspian Sea oil fields across Kazakh and Russian territory to the Black Sea port of Novorossiisk.

Fifth, the end of the Cold War and 9/11 provided Moscow with an opportunity and an incentive to play a more important role in stabilizing global oil markets, while also making Washington substantially more amenable to pursuing Russian oil as a partial alternative to Saudi oil. Shortly after the attacks, Russia repeatedly let Washington know that it would be willing to offer its oil fields as a secure alternative to oil from the Middle East. In fact, in October 2001 President Vladimir Putin asserted that as "instability in the world directly impacts world markets, Russia remains a reliable and predictable partner and supplier of oil."[64] This sentiment continued into 2002. Shortly after Putin met Bush in late May 2002, reports surfaced that Russia had offered to make up to the United States any shortfall in oil supplies owing to a disruption of Middle Eastern oil.[65]

Reversals in these relations can no doubt occur, but it is fair to project that Washington will continue to want Russia to play an energy role after 9/11, and Russia will want to have a larger market for its energy. Insiders familiar with the negotiations and interactions between the two states see evidence that this mutuality of interests is not likely to be fleeting.[66] In fact, in the post-9/11 period the United States has understandably been quite interested in pursuing energy from states that it considers more stable, including those in other regions of the world, such as West and sub-Saharan Africa. Indeed, the end of the Cold War allowed for greater cooperation not only with Moscow but also with states in regions that before had tended to be counterproductive for global rivalry. That is a significant, even structural, shift in geopolitics with spillover effects into global oil market dynamics.

Of course, we need to put the Russia factor into some perspective. Russia and its oil companies now have the potential to penetrate some European and even Asian markets, but they cannot displace the Middle East as the world's primary supplier of oil. Russia's proven oil reserves are a fraction of OPEC's. While Russia has done much to enhance production with technology, technology has been less successful in helping it find new fields.[67]

---

64   Quoted in Michael Wines and Sabrina Tavernise, "Russian Oil Production Still Soars, for Better and Worse," *New York Times*, 21 November 2001, A3.
65   Bob Williams, "OPEC Restraint Sowing Seeds of Market Share War," *Oil and Gas Journal* (3 June 2002), 76.
66   Interview with Leonard Coburn.
67   Interview with Mohamed Hamel.

Moreover, because of its unique spare capacity, Saudi Arabia, unlike Russia, can meet global oil requirements in the case of a crisis, provided that the crisis does not affect Saudi Arabia itself. In addition, while Moscow's export capacity is improving, it remains limited compared to OPEC, as OPEC officials are quick to note, and Russia, in any case, has made it clear to OPEC for the near term at least that it understands that it is not in the collective interest to undermine OPEC.[68]

SANCTIONED STATES

In the broader oil picture, oil exports from Iraq, Iran, and Libya have been constrained by a variety of factors, including various sanctions. However, Iraq's potential in particular is significant.

The Case of Iraq

Iraq's oil potential has never been fully tapped, and it could have a greater impact on markets than Russian and Central Asian oil, which is far closer to its peak potential than Iraq's is. Iraq has 112.5 bb of known reserves, which places it second only to Saudi Arabia's 262 bb. Iraq's proven reserves are found in 73 fields, only one-quarter of which have been developed to any degree.[69] Other Middle East states such as Iran and Kuwait hold approximately 90 to 120 bb, but those fields do not have the potential yield of Iraq's because they are already producing at a high rate. Iraq possesses 11 percent of the world's proven oil reserves, yet even at its peak production in 1979, it was producing only 5.5 percent of world supply. Iraq's potential is enormous precisely because it has been hamstrung over the past twenty-five years.

The Iran-Iraq War, the 1991 Gulf War, subsequent UN sanctions, periodic American military attacks, and Saddam's own mismanagement and corruption further curtailed Iraq's potential and left its oil infrastructure in disarray. Various UN resolutions, especially UN Resolution 1284, allowed for Iraq to open its industry to foreign investors and to increase production significantly, provided that Baghdad permitted UN inspectors to rid it of WMD. But its cooperation was never viewed as satisfactory by the United Nations, much less by the United States.

Iraq's various conflicts with the United Nations resulted in a drop of production from an average of 2.0 to 2.6 mb/d from 1999 to 2001, under UN

---

68 Interviews with Javad Yarjani and Omar Farouk Ibrahim.
69 On Iraq's potential, see Vincent Lauerman, "Gulf War II: Longer Term Implications for the World Oil Market," *Geopolitics of Energy* (April 2003).

Resolution 986. It hit a high of 2.6 mb/d in 2000—3.4 percent of world supply—and dropped to 1.7 mb/d by August-September 2002.[70] With a totally
rebuilt oil infrastructure, it could increase oil production to an estimated 6
to 12 mb/d within a decade, partly because Iraq's oil is relatively underex-
plored and underdeveloped.[71] In early 1990, prior to the invasion of Kuwait,
Baghdad had planned to raise production and export capacity to 6 mb/d by
1996.[72] Since May 1997, Iraq's oil ministry has worked assiduously in producing a post-sanctions oil development plan, the latest version of which pre-
ceded the Iraq War of 2003 and had a goal of producing 6 mb/d within six
years.[73]

The United Nations lifted economic sanctions on Iraq following the
2003 war. Security Council Resolution 1483 was approved in May and not
only required that Iraq's oil profits be placed in a fund to benefit the Iraqi
people but also called on all members to assist in Iraq's reconstruction.
The United States and Britain have overseen this fund with outside mon-
itors, including those from the United Nations. However, it is quite likely
that a newly elected democratic government will ultimately make major
decisions.

Iraqi output over time will depend on a number of factors. The first factor is achieving domestic stability, an objective that Washington has found
more challenging than expected. Postwar chaos in Iraq, including looting and
pilfering at Iraqi oil production sites, civil strife, and a guerrilla-style war
have slowed down the pace.

Second, under Saddam, foreign investment from outside the Arab world
was outlawed, thus denying Iraq the knowledge, experience, capital, and
management to exploit its oil potential.[74] The United States, by contrast, will
shape most investment decisions in the near term, until Iraq's government
fully crystallizes, and will encourage massive investment. This effort is important since the repair of export facilities will be a determining factor in the
rebuilding of Iraq's capacity. As foreign investors enter, they are likely to
employ more sophisticated technology for oil exploration and production,
thus yielding lower-cost products. No one knows exactly what the impact of

---

70   "Oil prices: Short-Term Strength Masking Longer-Term Weakness," *World Oil Report*—
     2002 Issue 2 (Dresdner, Kleinwort, Wasserstein research: 24 July 2002).

71   This figure represents the average of several different estimates. On Iraq's potential, see
     Fadhil J. Chalabi, "Iraq and the Future of World Oil," *Middle East Policy* 7 (October 2000).
     Iraq could eventually triple its current production capacity. EIA, *Annual Energy Outlook
     2002*.

72   Issam Al-Chalabi, *Iraqi Oil Policy: Present and Future Perspectives* (Cambridge, MA:
     Cambridge Energy Research Associates, 2003).

73   Lauerman, "Gulf War II."

74   On how Iraq should view foreign investment and OPEC, see *Political Economy of Iraqi Oil*
     (Deutsche Bank, 1 July 2003).

such technology will be, if fully utilized, but studies suggest that it could have important consequences.[75]

Of course, American wishes could be thwarted by political realities. Political instability not only makes it physically harder to produce oil, it also deters foreign investment. Such investment tends to be irreversible, meaning that it represents sunken costs. Investment decisions are especially sensitive when investment is irreversible.[76] Instability also has implications for how contracts are perceived. Foreign investment will be deterred, especially foreign direct investment, which involves more than 15 percent of ownership of the investment assets, if the legality of contracts is unclear and nonenforceable, a problem which has long plagued Russia's oil industry and stunted its potential, at least in the short term.

Of course, I have assumed that the benefits of increased FDI generally exceed its costs for the host state, Iraq.[77] But FDI can also entail high costs. It can reduce state autonomy by giving external actors more influence over the politics of the host country than they otherwise would have, by crowding out local industries and increasing unemployment, and by allowing foreigners to exploit the host country's capital for private use, thus depriving local industry of needed capital.[78] The United States needs to work with Iraq's government and with international actors and institutions to create laws and norms that help avoid the potential costs of investment, while maximizing its benefits.

Third, inasmuch as the United States has rid Iraq of Baathists, some of whom worked in Iraq's oil industry, it will be vital to replace them with qualified individuals. Equally important will be creating leaders in the oil industry that can develop and enforce the rule of law and avoid corruption.

Fourth, after achieving these more basic tasks, the question arises whether Iraq can develop a democratic government. The Bush administration may presume that because democracy is good for America, Iraqis will also see it as good for them. But that remains to be seen. Of course, a non-democratic or quasi-democratic government can still produce significant oil.

[75] See "Technology Key to Enduring Depressed Crude Prices," *Oil and Gas Journal* (29 March 1999), 20–22. See Philip K. Verleger, Jr., *Adjusting to Volatile Energy Prices* (Washington, D.C.: Institute for International Economics, 1993), 183, table 6.4.

[76] Robert S. Pindyck, "Irreversibility, Uncertainty, and Investment," *Journal of Economic Literature* 29 (September 1991), 1110–48.

[77] On studies that find the overall impact of FDI on the host economy to be highly positive, see Robert T. Kudrlc, "Good for the Gander? Foreign Direct Investment in the United States," *International Organization* 45 (Summer 1991). On the costs and benefits, see Robert Gilpin, *The Challenge of Global Capitalism: The World Economy in the 21st Century* (Princeton: Princeton University Press, 2000), 173–81.

[78] Barbara G. Haskel, "Access to Society: A Neglected Dimension of Power," *International Organization* 34 (Winter 1980), 89–120.

Fifth, privatizing Iraq's oil industry has costs and benefits, and lessons no doubt should be learned from Russia's less than stunning experiment. But privatization is preferable to Iraq's tradition of socialist nationalism, and it is the official policy and approach undertaken by the Coalition Provisional Authority under the administration of U.S. Ambassador L. Paul Bremer III, which is aimed at installing a market economy in Iraq and "opening it up to the world."[79]

While privatization does run certain risks, what remains clear is that the more privatized Iraq is, the more likely it is that it will be able to rehabilitate itself based on more efficient market factors rather than on less efficient government dictates. That is predicated on the notion that the Iraqi government accepts the importance of privatization as an indigenous response to Iraq's economic problems and that the government is stable enough that foreign investment can help spur this effort. Privatization, moreover, could bolster oil stability because it would make it harder for Iraq to control the behavior of its oil companies. Privatized companies, less affected by pressure within OPEC, would be more likely to make decisions that maximize their own profits, and at a minimum would complicate OPEC's efforts to cut production. They would also probably attract more foreign investment, thus creating the types of economic relations that produce interdependence and a greater sense that all benefit from supply stability.

The sixth factor is Iraq's oil policy itself. If Iraq assumes a more dovish policy, then we can expect its production to be higher, especially if it distances itself from, decreases cooperation with, or outright leaves OPEC. By contrast, a more hawkish policy within the context of OPEC will likely reduce production. Iraq's relationship to OPEC and its member states will be affected by a number of factors that will be explored in the next chapter.

As it stands, it seems safe to say that Iraq's oil future under a post-Saddam government shows much greater potential than the one under sanctioned Iraq. Even in a scenario where the factors discussed above work against Iraq, it is still likely to produce 3 mb/d per day. In the best-case scenario, that would exceed 6 mb/d.

Iran and Libya

While Iraq has potential to increase production, so do Iran and Libya, either directly or through cooperation with others, though to a far lesser extent. The 1996 Iran and Libya Sanctions Act (ILSA) passed by Congress calls for sanctions on all global companies that invest more than $40 million

---

[79]   Address by L. Paul Bremer, National Press Club, C-SPAN (24 July 2003).

in Libya and Iran's oil and gas sectors.[80] ILSA has largely failed in preventing global investment in Iran's oil industry, though it has clipped American participation. The lifting of ILSA would allow for greater exploitation of Iran's energy capacity by the United States and American companies, in an area with great potential. In the summer of 2003 Iran reportedly discovered three new oil fields containing an estimated 38 bb, adding significantly to its approximately 110 to 120 bb.[81] Lifting ILSA could also spur cooperation with Tehran in the Caspian region. That, in turn, would increase the potential for Gulf energy to reach more distant markets. Lifting ILSA would allow for American businesses to help develop a pipeline that could pipe Caspian gas to Iran's southern coast, then eastward to Pakistan or more directly to the Persian Gulf. Further shipments would be accomplished by tankers.

Lifting ILSA and altering the trajectory of U.S.-Iranian relations will require changes in Iran's foreign policy behavior and in U.S.-Iranian relations overall. Given Iran's nuclear ambitions, that is not likely in the near future, although the waning of Iran's revolution and the internal push for reforms could alter this picture.

For its part, Libya, in earlier decades the poster child of international terrorism, has tried to reinvent its image from a terrorist nation to a rehabilitated political actor on the global scene. After years of foot-dragging, it offered more cooperation after 9/11 in bringing Libyan terrorists, one of whom may well be a Libyan agent, to justice for the 1988 bombing of Pan Am Flight 103 over Lockerbie, Scotland.[82] And in mid-August 2003, Libya accepted responsibility for the bombing, clearing the way for UN sanctions against Libya to be lifted formally, and pledged greater cooperation in the global war against terrorism. The United States asserted that it would not stand in the way of lifting the UN embargo, but cited Libya's pursuit of WMD, among other things, as reasons to maintain U.S. sanctions and pressure on Libya. Nonetheless, while Libya has remained problematic, it has come closer to changing its foreign policy posture than perhaps at any time in the recent past.[83]

---

80 ILSA calls for sanctions on foreign companies that invest more than $40 million in Iran's oil and gas sectors in Libya and Iran. Under the law, the President must impose at least two of the following sanctions: import and export bans, lending embargoes from U.S. banks, a ban on U.S. procurement of goods and services from sanctioned companies, and a denial of U.S. export financing. On the sanctions impact on Iran, see Jahangir Amuzegar, "Iran's Economy and U.S. Sanctions," *Middle East Journal* 51 (Spring 1997), 185–99.

81 *Oil and Gas Today* (15 July 2003).

82 On Libya's foot-dragging, see Vera de Ladoucette, "Libya: On the Slow Road to Removing Sanctions" (Cambridge, MA: CERA Decision Brief, February 2002).

83 Ronald Bruce St. John, "Libyan Foreign Policy: Newfound Flexibility," *Orbis* 47 (Summer 2003).

THE RISE OF GLOBAL OIL STOCKS

In addition to the potential for sanctioned states to put oil on the market, there is the reality of global oil stocks. Each member of the IEA that is a net oil importer, as opposed to a net exporter, is required to hold stocks equal to 90 days or more of its net imports. This can be achieved by use of SPRs, which are managed and financed by central governments for emergency situations—the stocks of the United States are a typical example of this. It can also be met with commercial stocks, which belong to companies and have been used by eleven members of the IEA to meet their total obligations, or by agency stocks, which are maintained for emergency purposes by both public and private bodies. Total global oil stocks as of mid-2000 were estimated at around 5.9 bb or the equivalent of 90 days of world consumption.[84] From 1970 through March 2003, they more than doubled in Japan, to 619 m/b; increased from zero to 66 m/b in South Korea; rose by nearly 50 percent in the United States, to 1,473 m/b; and by over 25 percent in the European members of the OECD.[85]

The United States and Japan hold the world's largest SPRs. The U.S. SPR has increased meaningfully over time, as Figure 7 shows, although the number of days of oil supply that it can cover peaked in 1985. These reserves are viewed by key energy officials as representing a "structural change" in oil markets, especially when considered as part of global oil stocks.[86]

The American SPR is an underground network of caverns in Louisiana and Texas that was created in 1975 as a delayed response to the 1973 Arab oil embargo, an event that also spawned the IEA with its detailed rules for the development and use of the strategic stocks of its member countries. The American SPR, on which the president can call in an emergency, has a capacity of 700 mb and could reach the market within fifteen days at a maximum rate of 4 mb/d. President Bush ordered the Secretary of Energy to fill the SPR to full capacity, from its November 2002 level of approximately 590 million barrels. At the 2002 rate of import consumption, the U.S. reserve would last 53 days if foreign supplies were halted. Of course, it would last far longer if it were needed to cover imports that come only from the Middle East, which, in fact, is a crucial point to appreciate, since it is the disruption of specifically Gulf oil supplies that is of particular concern.

World vulnerability to oil supply disruptions decreases as the size of SPRs increases relative to demand. Drawing on them can offset supply shortfalls

---

[84] See *Oil Supply Security: The Emergency Response Potential of IEA Countries in 2000* (Paris: OECD/IEA, 2001), esp. chaps. 1 and 2.

[85] Based on data posted by the EIA, Monthly Energy Review, July 2003.

[86] Interview with Guy Caruso.

Figure 7. Strategic petroleum reserves (1977-2002)

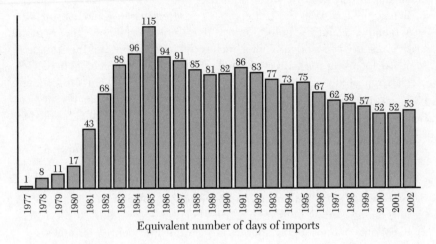

Equivalent number of days of imports

Source: Energy Information Administration

and allay market concerns. The likely effect, especially if used in conjunction with non-OPEC oil production increases, would be to limit a price shock before it caused serious economic problems. The existence of the SPRs offers a vital cushion that was absent prior to 1975.

As U.S. and world reserves became an accepted part of the oil landscape, countries have also learned to use them as a strategic tool. For instance, on the eve of the military attack on Iraq on January 16, 1991, oil prices increased, up and beyond the rise seen after Iraq invaded Kuwait on August 2, 1990. The United States, however, announced a coordinated SPR sale with Europe and Japan through the IEA, and oil prices dropped precipitously, despite the fact that America sold only half of what was announced. We can debate whether the drop in price was a function more of the SPR action or of reports that U.S.-led forces were meeting little resistance by Iraq, but there is no doubt that the SPR release played both a real and psychological role in calming oil markets.

The IEA was also prepared to announce an SPR release as Y2K approached, as some had feared it might cause economic and political disruptions on a global scale. It is safe to say that the 1991 release made the SPR a major factor in the international energy sector because it transformed it from a theoretical concept to an effective and demonstrated instrument of oil stability. Ever since 9/11, Washington has focused far greater planning on how to stabilize markets in case of a severe crisis, using the SPR as a key tool. Hence, the capability of the SPR has been matched by better planning about how it can fit into a broader energy policy. Greater strategic thinking about the SPR is positive for oil stability.

Before the Iraq War, the United States asserted that it would consult with IEA member countries before any SPR release but retained the right to make a release independently, after such consultation. However, the American standard for using the SPR was tougher than many at home wanted. U.S. officials repeatedly asserted a readiness to act quickly, but only in response to a "severe" supply disruption caused by war, and not as a market tool to decrease oil prices or as a pre-emptive measure, as a number of U.S. senators and others preferred.[87]

That debate was not really about the standard of "severe" disruption. The standard of severity is contained in Section 161 of the Energy Policy and Conservation Act, which Congress amended in May 1988 and which guides the use of the SPR. Rather, it was about how to interpret the standard. A "severe energy supply interruption" is defined in Section 3(8) of the EPCA as a "national energy supply shortage which the President determines

a) is, or is likely to be, of significant scope and duration, and of an emergency nature;

b) may cause major adverse impact on national safety or the national economy; and

c) results, or is likely to result, from (i) an interruption in the supply of imported petroleum products, (ii) an interruption in the supply of domestic petroleum products, or (iii) sabotage or an act of God."[88]

But Jeff Bingaman, the top Democrat on the Senate Energy and Natural Resources Committee, reflecting some broader opinion, asserted that the administration's failure to be clear about its interpretation of "severe" and about when it would actually use the SPR was driving oil prices up and "weighing down" the economy.[89] Others argued that the administration should have tapped the SPR in December 2002, when more than 2 mb/d of Venezuelan oil began to be lost to the market due to a strike, because that already constituted a "severe" supply interruption.[90] In fact, that amount did exceed the 7.5 percent of the 9 to 10 mb/d that the United States imports, thus meeting conditions for the release of strategic reserves according to IEA

87   Ibid.
88   *Oil Supply Security*, 299–301.
89   "Bingaman Slams Bush over SPR Policy," *Oil Daily* (4 March 2003).
90   On the SPR debate, see "Oil Falls on SPR Talk despite Imminent War," *Oil Daily* (18 March 2003).

rules. In a letter to the president, ten members of the House of Representatives asserted that high oil prices were hurting every American.[91]

The administration continued to hold to its position and to believe that the SPR needed to be used only in case the war in Iraq went awry. But the real point for the evolution of oil stability was that the SPR, as noted in the introduction of this book, did not have to be utilized despite oil supply problems in Venezuela and Nigeria, jitters over the war, and the war itself. Rather, the market largely took care of the problem itself, with active support from Saudi Arabia and other key OPEC states, and the war went well due to numerous factors, including superior American capability and regional access, that had been developed over more than two decades. Moreover, the very existence of the SPR was a real factor in stabilizing global markets because all actors knew that it could be used if ultimately needed.

For their part, the Saudis took considerable pains to convince the United States and other consuming nations that OPEC could indeed make up for supply gaps. No one could predict the outcome of the war, but Riyadh was concerned that a quick war would be followed by a price drop that would be exacerbated if its own oil and SPR releases both hit the market simultaneously.[92] In this sense, the SPR served as a cushion against an oil shock, while also giving OPEC an added incentive to ensure adequate global oil supplies, rather than to take advantage of high prices. Interviews with OPEC, American, and IEA officials strongly suggest that they had agreed that OPEC would provide oil supply to markets when they were required, while American and IEA stocks would be released only as a last-resort option.[93]

This book has attempted to assemble the story of the evolution of oil stability, chapter by chapter. Each chapter has laid out another dimension of the story, thus suggesting that oil stability is buttressed not just by one or two factors, but by a confluence of developments. This chapter has added a market element to the story. Namely, the global economy increasingly has been able to count on the fact that oil, from increasingly diversified sources, could reach the market in the effort to contain the negative effects of a supply disruption caused by political and security events.

91   "Lawmakers Ask for SPR Release," *Oil Daily* (20 March 2003).
92   "Oil Falls on SPR Talk despite Imminent War," *Oil Daily* (18 March 2003).
93   Reported in Bhushan Bahree, "Inside OPEC's Backroom Deal," *Wall Street Journal*, 29 July 2003, A1. A high-level source in the U.S. government strongly suggested that the *Wall Street Journal* story is accurate.

Chapter 10

OIL MARKET DYNAMICS AND OPEC

The potential for the use of the oil weapon, as I have tried to show, has decreased while the ability to deal with interruptions in oil supply has increased. These developments are no doubt positive for oil stability, but we still need to explore the behavior of OPEC in the broader oil market. The constraints and opportunities imposed by dynamics external to OPEC not only are important in their own right but also can affect OPEC behavior that falls short of the rare drama of an embargo and that takes place in non-crisis situations.

OPEC has become increasingly constrained by external factors. These include the rise of non-OPEC oil powers, oil industry privatization, and the realities of Iraq, which remains officially in OPEC but, given the fall of Saddam to U.S.-led forces, is something of a wild card. These developments have made it harder for OPEC to coordinate policy without broader cooperation, enhanced competition for market share, and increased the risks of cutting oil supply to raise oil prices. Moreover, rising global interdependence has created the potential that if a supply cut spikes oil prices and the global economy suffers, OPEC and oil producers suffer along with everybody else. High prices can trigger economic recession, damage the interdependent global economy, and lower the demand for oil.

THE RISE OF OPEC'S PRICE BAND

It would be useful to begin this chapter with a discussion of OPEC's price band. OPEC moved to adopt an informal price band in March 2000. Under this mechanism, automatic production adjustments would be put in effect when the OPEC basket price rose higher than $28 p/b or fell lower than

$22 p/b. An increase or decrease of one-half mb/d would result if prices exceeded the target range for twenty trading days or fell below it for ten trading days. Movement toward a price band did not represent a revolution in oil markets. Historically, OPEC has repeatedly tried to manage output. However, two points are noteworthy.

The adoption of the price band represented somewhat of a shift toward manipulating supply in order to achieve an agreed-on price target or range. For its part, Saudi Arabia, while remaining committed to supplying the global economy with adequate oil, especially in crises or potential crises, became comfortable with a higher oil price within the price band,[1] and thus generally more inclined to support oil supply cuts than it had been in the past. As discussed in the last chapter, movement toward the price band was motivated not only by the price collapse in 1998–1999 but also by the budgetary pressures facing certain governments, especially Saudi Arabia.

The second point is that, after the price collapse, tighter market conditions from 1999 to 2002 and OPEC discipline led to important successes. From the beginning of 2000, when the OPEC price band was adopted, until April 2003, the median of the price of oil had been 25 p/b. Moreover, oil prices took the form of a bell curve in this time period. They fell within the price band during 85 percent of the days, despite a number of shocks to oil markets including Nigeria's political turmoil, the Venezuelan oil strike, the September 2001 terrorist attacks, and the Iraq War.[2] Not surprisingly, OPEC officials, including the Secretary General, have stated confidently that the price band serves global markets and OPEC's member states by decreasing the volatility of prices. But they also believe that its success will entice non-OPEC producers to cooperate and that we can now view the price band as likely to endure.[3] Obviously, that remains to be seen.

All other things equal, the price band makes lower production and higher prices more likely than they otherwise would be. Indeed, the price band was adopted in response to falling prices, with the unambiguous goal of ensuring OPEC discipline and price stabilization. In February 1999, the oil price of the OPEC basket was around $10 p/b, pushing the OPEC 10 (excluding UN-sanctioned Iraq) to cut production by 1.716 mb/d, with pledged support from Mexico, Russia, Norway and Oman.

We can debate over what level of oil supply and corresponding price is most sensible for oil stability, but suffice it to say that the Aristotelian mean is for prices not to rise too high or move too low. The OPEC price band is

---

[1] On the manipulation of supply, see Nordine Ait-Laoussine, "OPEC: The Need To Reform The Current Pricing System," *MEES* 39 (25 September 2000).

[2] Based on data assembled by Adnan Shihab-Eldin, Director of OPEC research, and provided to this author (Vienna, Austria: 19 May 2003).

[3] Interviews with Alvaro Silva Calderon, Adnan Shihab-Eldin, and Nadir Gürer.

positive inasmuch as it can militate against extremes in price. Exceedingly low oil prices decrease investment in global oil, which for several reasons would be problematic in the long run. The U.S. Department of Energy has projected in its analysis through 2020 that oil supply will keep up with rising oil demand. But the Gulf states in particular do need to plan better to increase their production and export capacity in order to hedge against the potential of a tighter future market and unexpected oil shocks. This is because current projections suggest that global demand will increasingly be met by these states. A low oil price environment makes that less likely in the Gulf and elsewhere.

Oversupply and much lower oil prices can cause another problem. They remove the incentive for increasing energy efficiency, investing in oil exploration, finding non-oil alternatives, and taking environment-friendly measures. Such measures are tied fundamentally to the economic incentive provided by the price of oil. Longer-term energy stability may depend on such measures and on ongoing research into oil alternatives.

The United States, for its part, and other states with a major energy industry do not want prices to drop too significantly, because that can hurt their industries and cause economic dislocation. The collapse of oil prices from late 1997 to early 1999 led to a major decrease in oil exploration and development in the United States and approximately 51,400 lost jobs.[4]

Very low oil prices can also generate political instability in states such as Saudi Arabia. While chapter 2 argued that Saudi Arabia is more stable than it might appear, extended depressed oil prices could alter the domestic milieu and produce unpredictable effects. Such risks are better to avoid, at least from the standpoint of global oil stability.

THE REALITIES OF MARKET COMPETITION

The OPEC price band supports the argument of this book inasmuch as it adds resistance to oil supply cuts when prices are near or exceed the price band. But the effect of the price band is more complicated than that. In fact, it creates the potential for several problems. In particular, oil stability can be threatened if OPEC underestimates global demand, especially at a time when the price of the OPEC basket is at the higher end of the price band and when a political, economic, or military crisis hits. In such a case, supply would be restricted and prices would jump seriously. Moreover, it is

---

[4] "Editorial: Oil Prices and Layoffs," *Oil and Gas Journal* 97 (29 March 1999). For instance, drilling activity in North America decreased by more than 25 percent in 1998 from the previous year. DOE, *International Energy Outlook 2002*, 32.

possible that a successful price band can motivate OPEC states to push for the price spread to be increased, or that the discipline exacted in maintaining the price band can also be misused in the event that some members want to use oil as a political weapon. These developments do not preclude the possibility that OPEC will try to raise the price band, but they militate against the success over time of such an effort. The developments are also important for oil stability in their own right.

The Role of Non-OPEC Actors

Chapter 9 explored the diversity and increased production offered by non-OPEC actors, but production is just part of the story. Non-OPEC producers also enhance oil stability because OPEC increasingly has had to try to coordinate with them—a feature which OPEC officials largely agree is much more a genuine trend than a makeshift response to temporary global conditions.[5] Scholars who study cooperation widely believe that the greater the number of actors involved in making decisions, the more difficult the prospect of cooperation becomes[6] and, in the case of oil, domination by one or a group of actors.

States such as Russia, Angola, and Oman have recently been invited to ordinary OPEC meetings and even to extraordinary ones in which crucial decisions are made. And, recognizing the pressures of global change, OPEC is committed, according to Secretary General Alvaro Silva Calderon, to strengthening coordination with non-OPEC producers.[7] While such coordination can decrease price volatility, OPEC has increasingly recognized that it is difficult to accomplish.[8] That was exemplified, for instance, in January 2002, when it implemented cuts in production of 1.5 mb/d in an effort to maintain oil prices, contingent on a non-OPEC decrease in oil exports of 462,500 mb/d.

Russia was supposed to execute 150,000 mb/d of these cuts, but ultimately failed to do so. Probably for political reasons, OPEC leader Chakib Khelil described the cuts by Russia as "very small" but "significant from a symbolic perspective," underscoring the idea of OPEC and non-OPEC cooperation.[9] Other observers were less sanguine, arguing that Russia had increased rather than decreased production, a form of non-OPEC "quota-busting" by Russian oil companies that disdain export constraints.[10] For his part, Putin had

---

5 Interviews with Adnan Shihab-Eldin and Mohamed Hamel.

6 Kenneth A. Oye, ed., *Cooperation under Anarchy* (Princeton: Princeton University Press, 1986).

7 Interview with Alvaro Silva Calderon.

8 "OPEC S trives to Keep New Alliance Together," *Oil Daily* (31 December 2001). Interview with Nader Sultan.

9 Quoted in "OPEC Continues to Court Russia," *Oil Daily* (19 February 2002).

10 See *Oil and Gas Journal* (25 February 2002), 5.

Figure 8. Saudi versus Russian oil production (1996-2002)

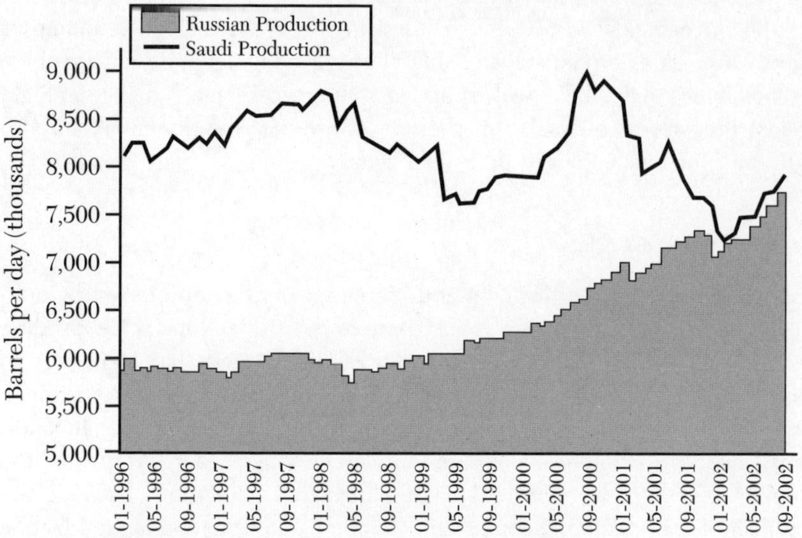

Source: Data drawn from Energy Information Administration.

observed following September 11 that Russia would not play along with OPEC production cuts, as a show of "solidarity with the antiterrorist coalition," in which Russia plays the role of an "alternative source of energy to the unstable Middle East."[11]

Russia and its companies appear to be planning for more production than the 3 percent growth that the markets may be able to support or that OPEC can tolerate.[12] And it is questionable whether the Saudis would ever drop production below 7 mb/d in the face of Russian increases in production; as Figure 8 suggests, Riyadh has, in fact, sought to match Russia at that level.[13]

OPEC's courting of Russia highlights a key change in global oil markets. As Javad Yarjani, head of OPEC's petroleum analysis department, pointed out, the decrease in OPEC's share of oil as a percentage of total energy consumption among major industrialized states from 1980 to 2000 can help "explain why OPEC cannot manage the market on its own and needs help from non-OPEC producers."[14] Of course, Saudi Arabia more than any other state could undercut competitors like Russia. Saudi oil is extremely cheap to

[11] Quoted in Daniel Schorr, "Cheap Fill-Ups? Thank Russia," *Christian Science Monitor*, 30 November 2001.
[12] *Global Energy Wire* (Deutsche Bank, 29 May 2003).
[13] Deutsche Bank originated the thesis that the Saudis would try to match Russian production.
[14] Address to the Conference on Oil and Gas Investment Opportunities in West Asia, www.opec.org/NewsInfo/Speeches/sp2002/spYarjaniOmanApr21.htm.

produce, at about $2 p/b, compared to costs that are seven or so times as much for new production oil. And Saudi excess capacity, though diminished in comparison with the 1980s, has averaged around 2.5 and 3.5 mb/d and is increasing; this could be used to maintain or capture market share. More than any other state, Saudi Arabia has been able to meet revenue targets by playing the volume strategy. That is, it could produce and sell more oil in order to make up for lost revenues due to lower prices. The regime has hinted at using that capacity to maintain market share, if it were significantly threatened by Russian production.[15]

However, while the Saudis could price the competition temporarily out of the market, that would not hurt oil stability as defined in this book unless it allowed Riyadh to capture and keep greater market share. Greater supply to the market is positive for oil stability, but longer-run shifts in market share toward one state may not be positive, even if the state is a responsible producer, because we can never be assured of the stability of its supply. Yet, in particular, the rise of non-OPEC oil and Iraq's post-Saddam potential should make it harder for the Saudis to capture significantly more market share down the road until demand moves notably higher.

Meanwhile, Russia sees some advantages in coordinating with OPEC, but it also wants to become its own power center in the global oil arena. OPEC officials claimed that they are not especially concerned about longer-run Russian or even increased Iraqi productivity, because world oil demand is projected to increase, allowing the market to take care of the issue.[16] But, even if such projections prove true, the real question for oil stability is not just whether supply and demand will balance out over time, but whether the instruments and policies are in place to make them balance at critical junctures when they otherwise might not balance. It is especially in this context that OPEC sees a balancing effort with Russia as important to preventing serious pressures on the price band.[17]

The Privatization Factor

Another dimension of this complex puzzle is also important to note. National oil companies rose in influence in the 1970s, slowly overshadowing the Seven Sisters. Until the 1970s, they had little influence, yet by 2001 they controlled three-quarters of the oil sold in world markets, adding new and important players to the market.[18] For its part, privatization has contributed to a diffusion of power in oil markets. The control of oil is much less concentrated

15 Patrick E. Tyler, "Power Politics," *New York Times*, 4 August 2002.
16 Interview with Omar Farouk Ibrahim.
17 Interview with Nadir Gürer.
18 Øystein Noreng, *Crude Power: Politics and the Oil Market* (New York: IB Tauris, 2002), 163.

now than it was in 1953 or 1972.[19] Moreover, privatization has shifted some power away from nation-states toward oil companies, thus adding even more actors to the market.

Privatization is an important development in oil markets, for two key reasons. The first is that many non-OPEC oil producers, be they states or oil companies within states, largely prefer to put more oil on the market, even at lower prices. Non-OPEC states are not as dependent on oil for meeting budget targets, and privatized companies are even less concerned with how revenue affects the welfare state.

While OPEC's price band is between $22 and $28, Russia's de facto price band has been roughly between $18 and $22, although it is higher than that if we account for the appreciation of the OPEC basket.[20] Some Russian oil companies have said that they can make a profit at $11, though Finance Minister Alexei Kudrin said in mid-November 2001 that the economy would suffer if the price fell below $14.[21] Further restructuring of Russian oil companies and expectations of significantly increased oil production from them led one economic adviser to President Putin to predict on January 10, 2002, that oil prices would eventually fall to $10 p/b, leading OPEC to be "historically doomed."[22] That is highly doubtful, but it suggests that the potential exists for the OPEC price band to fall eventually to $18 to $21 or, according to some estimates, even lower than that.[23] In early 2002, when oil demand dropped, OPEC was especially concerned when Russian oil production exceeded 7 mb/d, and Kuwait's Oil Minister was widely quoted in the press as warning that oil prices could fall to $10 p/b if non-OPEC countries did not cooperate.[24] Russia, to be sure, cannot replace or even compete effectively with OPEC, but even OPEC analysts acknowledge that it could be a more serious competitor if "private industry penetrates non-OPEC nations."[25]

Second, while privatized companies are more likely to put their own oil on the market at lower prices, they are less likely than states to cooperate with OPEC to curb production and to boost prices.[26] Even in states such as Norway, Mexico, and Venezuela, the government dictates how much oil will be produced. In Russia, Putin wields enormous power, and he has periodically

[19] For a graph and analysis, see Michael C. Lynch, *Oil Market Structure and Oil Market Behavior* (Riyadh, Saudi Arabia: 7th International Energy Forum, 17–19 November 2000), 12.

[20] See Lynne Kiesling and Joseph Becker, *Russia's Role in the Shifting World Oil Market* (Cambridge, MA: Harvard University, Caspian Studies Program Policy Brief Series, May 2002).

[21] "The Russian Connection," *MEED* (4 January 2002).

[22] Kiesling and Becker, "Russia's Role," 6.

[23] Correspondence with Edward Morse.

[24] Quoted in Wilfrid L. Kohl, "OPEC Behavior, 1998–2001," 223.

[25] Interview with Omar Farouk Ibrahim.

[26] "Russia's Oil Majors: Engine of Radical Change," *Oil and Gas Journal* (27 May 2002), 20–32.

called in the CEOs of major oil companies to excoriate them for not abiding sufficiently by his view.[27] However, by and large, the major oil companies compete with each other, chart their own production schedules, and have different perspectives on key foreign policy issues, including how much oil Russia should put on the market and what oil prices should be. Even if the Russian government wanted to decrease overall oil production, it could not simply make an agreement to do so without significant efforts to entice or coerce its companies to cooperate. This works in favor of lower oil prices, which are not in the interest of OPEC.

The near-term trajectory of privatization, which was made possible by the end of communism, is unclear. This is because Moscow's major oil companies, as well as potential foreign investors, still face serious hurdles.

Moscow has lost some control over domestic oil companies, but it has sought to retain some influence over them. This struggle is partly a function of sporadic power struggles between the executive and influential oil companies, but it also stems from rivalry between pro-western free market advocates and those who are suspicious of western capitalist practices and foreign companies. When the latter prevail and their interests happen to coincide with those of Putin, that contributes to government efforts to control the oil companies.

For instance, in October 2003, the government arrested the CEO of Russia's second largest oil company, Yukos, and seized his multibillion dollar stake in Yukos, on the charges of fraud and tax evasion. The CEO, Mikhail B. Khodorkovsky, had become powerful in Russia and his firm was quite innovative. Many close observers in Russia believe that Putin used the legal system to restrain either Yukos as a company, its increasingly powerful CEO, or both.[28] Naturally, no one can preclude the possibility that Russia will revert back to aspects of communism, which could stunt the growth of its oil sector, or to a more hard-line position in its foreign policy, which could damage foreign cooperation. In summer 2002, the government did threaten, though not clearly and strongly, that it might nationalize the oil industry. While the threat was quickly withdrawn, it suggested at least some potential for such an outcome.[29] But the effects set in motion by the end of the Cold War and by marketization seem strong enough to survive major setbacks to privatization; in fact, they could spur it along, if oil companies slowly gain in strength and freedom to maneuver.[30]

---

[27] Interview with Strobe Talbott.
[28] Sam Fletcher, "U.S.-Russian Oil Supply Ties Deepen with Cargo to Texas," *Oil and Gas Journal* (5 August 2002), 23–25.
[29] *Oil Market Outlook: OPEC's Balancing Act* (Deutsche Bank, September 2002), 47.
[30] This paragraph is based on an interview with Leonard Coburn, who explored the issue with Yukos and Russian officials. See *Oil and Gas Journal* (28 July 2003), 30–31.

Privatization also faces the difficulties of infighting among Russia's oil companies. They do not have a tradition, as do western oil companies, of sharing control over oil projects, much less playing second fiddle to western companies. Other challenges include bureaucratic sloth and the absence of a reliable set of laws governing investment.[31] A case can be made that these problems are not as serious in relatively mature areas where the infrastructure already exists and the ability to produce and generate revenue is established, as they are in Russia where terms of agreement are nascent.[32] These issues will have to be surmounted for successful cooperation in the coming years.

Of course, the restructuring of oil companies at the domestic level has not taken place in a global vacuum. It has coincided with Russia's post–Cold War reorientation at the global level. During the Cold War, Moscow was largely self-sufficient in oil production. Thus it was less concerned about global oil prices, because it had the power to regulate its own energy prices. If anything, it might have viewed higher prices as useful for weakening its western adversaries in the Cold War. After the Cold War, however, not only did Russia move away from seeing world affairs in zero-sum terms, its economy also became increasingly tied to western economies. Thus it had greater interest in assuring oil stability, an interest that was not transient so long as it felt that it had a serious stake in the health of the global economy. Moreover, while Moscow might struggle for power with Russian oil companies or their increasingly influential CEOs, it must at least consider that the world is watching and that it will suffer some costs if it makes a habit of cracking down on these companies. Such constraints, while not an outright deterrent by any means—especially not when domestic factors are intensely motivating—cannot be dismissed as was the case during the Cold War.

Iraq after Saddam

While privatization is a factor that OPEC must consider, another factor more speculative in nature is Iraq. Chapter 9 examined the potential for Iraqi oil production post-Saddam, but the Iraq factor is about more than the quantity of oil. As memories of the 1998–99 price collapse fade and as Iraq starts

---

31   On bureaucratic sloth, see A. M. Samsam Bakhtiari, "Expectations of Sustained Russian Oil Production Boom Unjustified," *Oil and Gas Journal* (29 April 2002), 24–26. For a succinct piece on improvements in, and challenges to developing, investment laws, see Andrei Konoplyanik, "Would Russian Oil Companies Really Like to Have a PSA Regime in Russia?" *Oil and Gas Journal* (23 December 2002), 22–26.

32   See Sam Fletcher, "U.S.-Russian Summit Spotlights Need for Russian Oil Law," *Oil and Gas Journal* (7 October 2002), 27–29.

to put enough oil on the market in the next decade to take market share away from other OPEC members, it may be harder to maintain OPEC discipline.

The fall of the Baathist regime has created the potential for a major shift in global oil markets. In the best-case scenario, the fall of Saddam would trigger a domino-like effect of democratic, stable, western-leaning governments across the Middle East and a moderate Iraq determined to rehabilitate its dilapidated oil infrastructure. Short of such empyrean outcomes, postwar Iraq will do more to complicate OPEC coordination and to put downward pressure on oil prices than Iraq under Saddam Hussein.

One reason for this likelihood is that Iraq will slowly put more oil on the market and create greater competition among OPEC members. Of course, it will probably take Iraq several years to ramp up to a level of production (its implied 3.5 mb/d ceiling) where it can start to threaten the market share of other OPEC members.

However, like Saudi Arabia, Iraq is one of the few countries in the world that could benefit from a market-share strategy in a low-price environment. In the future, Iraq may well push the case that its resources are so large that it is entitled to a larger OPEC quota or, irrespective of OPEC, greater production. Fearful of losing market share, the OPEC doves might push for greater production, thus further putting downward pressure on price or at least on the OPEC price band.

The Saudis probably want to see Iraq rebuilt, but they do not want to see it ramp up to the point that it could threaten Saudi market share. Since Iraq has the second-largest potential surplus capacity after Saudi Arabia, it could generate such a threat, especially because, once rehabilitated, it would combine huge untapped reserves with comparatively low oil production costs.[33] Indeed, serious market share competition may well be likely at some point in the future, barring unexpected increases in demand, because there is not enough market share to easily include Iraq's expected increases in supply.[34] Depending on the extent of the threat and numerous other factors, Riyadh may decide to flood the market, collapse oil prices in the short run, and hurt Iraq's ability to draw investment for boosting production and capture market share, or force Iraq to negotiate on quota limits. Of course, such tensions over a finite market could cause oil prices to fall or even trigger Iraq's departure from OPEC, which is a second reason that Iraq could put downward pressure on price.

[33] Imad Jabir, "The Prospects for the Oil Sector in the Iraq Economy after Sanctions," *OPEC Review* (September 2002).

[34] Vincent Lauerman, "Gulf War II: Longer Term Implications for the World Oil Market," *Geopolitics of Energy* (April 2003), 11–12.

To be sure, several factors work against Iraq leaving OPEC. OPEC was founded in Baghdad in 1960 by Iraq, Saudi Arabia, Iran, Kuwait and Venezuela, a fact in which Iraq takes considerable national pride. Moreover, Iraq's immediate neighborhood consists of OPEC members, with which Iraq would want to have positive or at least acceptable relations. Staying in OPEC gives Iraq a platform from which it can reintegrate itself into the Arab world. Baghdad may also see value in operating within OPEC, where it can influence decisions while cheating on quotas if it does not like the decisions that result. Leaving OPEC could also make Baghdad look like an automaton under American control, wound up to undermine an organization that some view as a greedy cartel.

However, while unlikely, the potential of Iraq's withdrawal has been seriously considered by OPEC members and the United States.[35] Venezuelan President Chavez went so far as to assert that "what is happening in Iraq is very dangerous for the world" and that U.S. domination in Iraq threatens the unity of OPEC.[36] If Iraq were to withdraw, this would further complicate OPEC's ability to coordinate with non-OPEC producers. Iraq's potentially massive oil production capacity could be transferred to managers who are dismissive of OPEC objectives and seek to gain market share through lower prices. Such a position could easily be based on the notion that Iraq needs monies to fund reconstruction and, given its reserves, has a vested interest in lower oil prices that pre-empt alternative energy exploration. In such a case, the competition with OPEC would be even more significant. In either case, since Iraq is likely to want to achieve market share over price maximization, it will be more likely to contribute to lower oil prices, rather than higher ones.

GLOBAL INTERDEPENDENCE AND OIL MARKETS

While chapters 6 and 7 discussed the role of global interdependence in influencing U.S.-Russian and Sino-American relations and, in turn, oil stability, interdependence also adds complexity to market phenomena. It may well worsen oil price volatility because events in one area of the world are more sensitive to events in others under conditions of high interdependence. However, this works against oil instability, which, as discussed in the introduction of this book, is different from oil price volatility.

The first way that it works against oil instability is by making it harder for OPEC to control the market without coordinating with others.[37]

---

[35] "Few Expect Iraq to Quit Opec despite Suggestion," *Oil Daily* (20 May 2003).
[36] Quoted in J. Michael Waller, "How to Break the OPEC Cartel," *Insight on the News* (27 March 2003).
[37] Interview with Nadir Gürer.

Interdependence implies mutual dependence and connections in reality among states and issue areas, but it also means that policies and, more important, their many effects are also linked. They cannot be made in isolation of each other because they can more easily be at cross-purposes when the realities that they affect are tied together. That is a constraint on OPEC structurally imposed by the international system.

The second way is that it gives oil producers and consumers a vested interest in oil stability, because it ties them together in its tangled web. The higher the price of oil, the less the level of growth is in the world economy. That is problematic for OPEC because it wants a large market for its oil. Thus, it may want to raise oil prices high enough to yield profits and meet its members' budget targets, but not so high that the loss of market share offsets the revenue from higher oil prices.

In an interdependent world, moreover, the Saudis and other oil exporters would not want to harm global growth because they have investments all over the world. Saudi investments in the United States, for instance, have increased to possibly over one-half trillion dollars over the past two decades, though an exact accounting seems impossible. Global interdependence means that if the global economic boat sinks, it will take many actors with it, including the oil producers. Global interdependence has added special impetus to the need to maintain oil revenues at predictable prices and to avoid politicizing global oil.

Global interdependence doesn't concern OPEC states only, though, so it makes other parties interested in assuring market-friendly policies. Indeed, exceedingly high oil prices carry boomerang costs for states that are tied to U.S. economic health, like Mexico. The United States is Mexico's largest trading partner and also provides it with support through policies on immigration. If oil prices hurt the U.S. economy, that will spiral back to hurt Mexico as well. Such a factor was less prominent in the past, and global interdependence has made it more important.

The United States as well is linked to the global economy through interdependence and the argument that it imports far less oil from the Middle East than do states in Europe or Asia is a modest distinction. Global interdependence means that a severe interruption in oil supplies is likely to have a similar price effect across regions. This might be different if the global oil market—like the market for natural gas—were not integrated and if oil were not fungible as a commodity. But as it is, the United States would not shield itself from global dependence on oil or from the vagaries of Middle East politics, even if it radically reduced the amount of oil that it imports from the Middle East. Global interdependence increases its proclivity to use the range of foreign policy tools in order to ensure oil stability.

FUTURE OPEC COOPERATION AND THE PRISONER'S DILEMMA

Drawing on the foregoing discussion, OPEC's ability to cooperate and to maintain the current price band in the near future will be a function of several key conditions, all of which have changed over time.

The first condition is the number of actors that influence oil decisions. As we have seen, non-OPEC actors and privatized oil companies are more involved in affecting critical oil decisions than in the past. That works against OPEC because it makes coordination harder and largely puts downward pressure on price, ceteris paribus.

The second condition is global productive capacity, which likewise does not appear to favor OPEC, in the near term at least. Iraq will likely ramp up in the coming years, though when is quite unclear; production pressures are mounting from Algeria, Libya, and Nigeria; and now that its labor problems appear to have abated, Venezuela may come fully on-line. The Russia factor cannot be discounted, especially given privatization, and non-OPEC production outside Russia is also important. Meanwhile, Azerbaijan may contribute perhaps the most significant influx of oil into the market—after a rehabilitated Iraq—at approximately 750,000 b/d by year 2005.[38]

While it is hard to predict to what extent the price band will succeed in the future, it may falter due to the complexities of global energy dynamics and OPEC quota allocations.[39] The Al Saud are likely to face a choice between cutting back on their quota to allow others a greater share or face quota-busting and intra-OPEC rivalries. Such problems would not develop if the market pie could accommodate all actors. But a strategy of chasing volume as opposed to price is mutually exclusive and thus is sure to produce tension among OPEC producers.[40] In the absence of serious institutional cooperation or high demand, joint gains are unachievable and a zero-sum logic takes hold, wherein one's market share increases only at the expense of others, even if the overall pie is expanding.

The third condition is excess capacity, which differs from productive capacity in that it is held in reserve. Thus far the OPEC price band has performed quite well, but historically such cooperation has failed, complicated by higher excess capacity.[41] As explored in chapter 9, excess capacity is a cyclical factor in markets, but there is strong reason to believe that it will increase substantially in the coming years. When excess capacity significantly exceeds demand, as it did in the 1980s, producers have a greater incentive

[38] Interview with Erik Kreil.
[39] On the history and complexity of the OPEC quota allocation debate, see Nordine Ait-Laoussine and John Gault, "OPEC's Delicate Balancing Act," *MEES* (24 September 2001).
[40] Interview with Nader Sultan.
[41] Interview with Nadir Gürer.

to offer price discounts in order to utilize their excess capacity, sell their oil, and maintain market share. If each producer fears that others will strategize in this manner and be more inclined to cheat, they will be more likely to cheat as well, so as to avoid being the one left out. The result could precipitate a dynamic of competition, driving prices even lower.

The fourth condition is Saudi policy, because Riyadh would have to absorb the brunt of supply cuts to placate OPEC and non-OPEC members. This factor is hard to assess because of unpredictable world events. Moreover, the Saudis have supported the OPEC price band, but at the same time they have questioned its price spread. When Venezuela originally proposed the idea of an OPEC price band of $22 to $28 p/b, Saudi Oil Minister Ali al-Naimi expressed his personal preference that it be from $20 to $25, though in March 2001 he asserted that he was satisfied with the "different OPEC" that has evolved and with the higher-level commitment in cutting and raising production.[42] Yet that did not stop him from asserting in March 2002 that he would be happy with a price of $20 a barrel in the medium term, which was not far from the OPEC price consensus of a rock-bottom minimum.[43] Under more difficult circumstances, it is not clear where Riyadh would stand, especially if it came under pressure from the United States and the other importers on which it depends for a variety of purposes.

The fifth condition is obviously crucial: demand. This is something of a wild card in the near term. Oil demand is expected to increase, but forecasts of demand are subject to great change. The potential for a spike in demand notwithstanding, the foregoing analysis suggests that the concept of the price band may well endure but that major supply cuts that would raise prices above the price band are unlikely. In fact, the band's price range is more likely to decrease than to increase. That would not be a historical anomaly, either for OPEC or for any organization. Studies show that agreements to stabilize the prices of commodities, including those governing oil, have usually failed, given enough time.[44]

Structurally, OPEC can only be as good as the collective actions of its members. Even under good conditions, it is challenging to get individual actors to pursue collective goals voluntarily when their individual preferences may be to cheat or, in OPEC's case, produce beyond their quotas. Although OPEC is an important institution, it suffers, like other international institutions, from a lack of verification and enforcement that can enhance compliance.

Under challenging conditions, OPEC members may start to behave in ways akin to the Prisoner's Dilemma. The Prisoner's Dilemma is a basic game theory

42 Quoted in Wilfrid L. Kohl, "OPEC Behavior, 1998–2001," 216, 219.
43 "Cautious Confidence Hides the Cracks," *MEED* (15 March 2002).
44 Philip K. Verleger, Jr., *Adjusting To Volatile Energy Prices* (Washington, D.C.: Institute for International Economics, 1993), 109–31, 167–68.

concept that yields an interesting insight. In the absence of a sovereign that can enforce agreements, actors are inclined to cheat on agreements on the assumption that others will do the same, rather than to cooperate while others cheat and to risk being, in Prisoner's Dilemma parlance, the "sucker." Yet when actors pursue their own individual best strategies (such as cheating on OPEC oil quotas), all actors involved are worse off than would be the case had they cooperated (because cheating produces a greater supply of oil and lower oil prices).

Such an increase on supply may not benefit OPEC. But it is in the interest of oil-consuming states and benefits oil stability, provided that the price of oil does not drop too low.

Of course, we might argue that OPEC interaction resembles iterated Prisoner's Dilemma (repeated play) rather than Prisoner's Dilemma (one-time play). Because the actors are part of an institution, they perceive that they will interact with each other in the future, and thus will be more likely to consider that present cheating can be punished by others in the future, while present cooperation can be rewarded by others in the future. Experimental evidence suggests that this dynamic of expectations in iterated play increases the likelihood of cooperation.[45]

I would argue, however, that OPEC interaction really resembles a mix of single-play Prisoner's Dilemma and its nicer iterated version. Whether it leans much more one way or the other depends largely on existing conditions, such as those explored above. Based on them, we may see some Prisoner's Dilemma–like fireworks in the coming years. As al-Naimi has pointed out, should "OPEC open the taps and the oil prices falls straight off, then it would be very difficult to instill discipline again [sic]."[46]

The market and political dynamics explored in this chapter add another element to the story of oil stability. Serious supply manipulations, be they independent or collective, political or economic in motivation, are less likely to occur and less likely to succeed over time if they do occur. The risks of such action have risen over time, due to developments ranging from the rise of non-OPEC oil and oil industry privatization to the reality of global interdependence. These developments, while surely not precluding OPEC opportunism in the near term, have made it harder for OPEC to coordinate policy without broader cooperation and have increased competition for market share, while global interdependence has tied the fortunes of OPEC to the health of the global economy. Adding to the constraints on OPEC and to oil stability in their own right are global environmental pressures and the realities of high technology, to which we now turn.

[45] Oye, ed., *Cooperation under Anarchy*, 13. Robert Axelrod, *The Evolution of Cooperation* (New York: Basic Books, 1984).

[46] Quoted in "Saudis Vow to Meet Any Oil Supply Shortfall," *Oil Daily* (23 April 2002).

Chapter 11

GLOBAL OIL, HIGH TECHNOLOGY, AND
THE ENVIRONMENT

This book has explored how global and regional developments, market dynamics, and the oil strategies and policies of major oil producers affect oil stability. But little has been said about the role of high technology and global environmental pressures as they relate to oil stability. Threats to oil stability can be viewed partly as a function of the inability to discover, produce, deliver, and conserve oil, and to produce alternative sources of energy. While such threats are less central to what we may traditionally think of as oil stability, they are important because they affect how much stress is placed on oil supply.

High technology has enhanced the potential for increasingly cost-efficient and fast oil discovery, production, and delivery, and for the development and use of partial substitutes for oil products, thus decreasing pressure on supply at key junctures and over the long term. Environmental pressures have motivated greater use of high technology and energy efficiency and have raised consciousness about the costs of the oil era. These factors have placed some constraints on the extent to which oil supply can be cut, because high oil prices can motivate non-oil investment more easily in the face of cost-efficient technology and environmental pressures. These factors also create some potential that the rise in oil demand can at least be decreased in its pace. In 2002, the Department of Energy (DOE) projected increasing dependence on world oil, but its models did not account appreciably for policy changes driven by factors such as environmental concerns and technological breakthroughs, or the types of global political changes, such as interdependence, discussed earlier in this book.[1]

---

[1]   They conduct regressions on the accomplishments of technology in the past and assume that it will continue at that level and presume present policy and rules, rather than potential changes in laws on emissions standards, for instance.

HIGH TECHNOLOGY AND OIL DEPENDENCE

Technological progress is not easily suppressed or reversed, and it has often been underestimated or gone altogether unforeseen in history. Yet high technology advances, while both the bane and the energizers of change in the twentieth century, have done much for and are likely to continue to contribute to oil stability.

The first major effect of high technology is that it can create potential substitutes for oil products. As Nader Sultan, CEO of Kuwait Petroleum Corporation, points out, the energy industry was dominated by coal until World War I, which opened up the era of oil, but the "coal age did not end because of a lack of coal"—similarly, the oil age will not end because of a lack of oil.[2]

Such scenarios are hypothetical, but we would be unwise to dismiss their potential. Short of major technological breakthroughs, we do know that renewable energy has increasing potential and could show rapid growth (admittedly, from a low base), though this is not likely to happen for some time, barring major changes in consumer appetites and government policies.[3] The potential, however, is important to note and derives partly from technological advances, which have diminished the costs of producing renewable energy. For instance, estimates suggest that if this trend in renewables continues, non-hydropower renewable energy will account for 2.8 percent of total U.S. electricity generation by 2020. While oil accounts for only about 3 percent of electricity generation, renewables are expected to contribute to a decline in that number.[4] Thus far, oil and other fossil-fuel energies have enjoyed such high efficiencies that it has been hard for solar and other forms of energy to compete. But advances in technology are changing that dynamic, although the extent to which substitute energies can become economically feasible depends very much on the type of energy.[5] This positive effect of technology is augmented, like other effects of technology, by learning processes. They are rarely factored into models of technological impact that focus on the costs of alternative energy relative to oil, but they are demonstrably important.[6]

[2] Interview with Nader Sultan. See "Implications of September 11 for Middle East Energy Supply," APS Review Downstream Trends, 11 March 2002.
[3] On renewables, see a study from the Royal Institute of International Affairs, www.riia.org/publications.
[4] National Energy Policy (Report of the National Energy Policy Development Group, May 2001), 1–9.
[5] For instance, on solar power advances, see Ron R. Luoma, "Catch the Fire," Discover 24 (August 2003).
[6] See Nebojsa Nakicenovic, "Technological Change and Diffusion as a Learning Process," in Technological Change and the Environment, ed. Arnulf Grubler, Nebojsa Nakicenovic, and William D. Nordhaus (Washington, D.C.: Resources for the Future, 2002).

Figure 9. Energy use per capita and per dollar of GDP
(1970-2020) (Index, 1970=1)

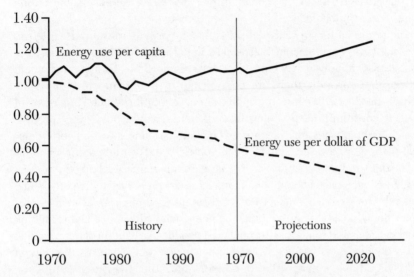

Source: Energy Information Administration, *Annual Energy Outlook 2002.*

The second major effect of high technology is greater energy efficiency. For example, technological advances have allowed the United States and other countries to decrease what is referred to as "energy intensity," or the amount of energy used per dollar of GDP. As Figure 9 shows quite clearly, from 1970 to 1986, U.S. energy intensity decreased by an annual rate of 2.3 percent, in response to oil price increases. Lower oil prices led to a lower, but still significant, rate of decrease of 1.5 percent per year from 1986 to 2000. Overall, while U.S. consumption of energy has increased, energy intensity has decreased by more than 30 percent since 1970. Had it remained constant since 1972, consumption would have been about 74 percent higher by 1999; in fact, while the American economy has grown 126 percent since 1973, energy use has increased by only 30 percent.[7] Energy intensity for industrialized countries and developing countries is expected to decrease by 1.3 and 1.7 percent per year, respectively, between 2001 and 2025.[8]

Most energy demand forecasts fundamentally account for energy efficiency improvements, but forecasts differ widely on how important they

---

[7] Luoma, "Catch the Fire," 1–4.
[8] *International Energy Outlook 2003* (Washington, D.C.: U.S. Department of Energy, May 2003), 2. This document can be found at www.eia.doe.gov/oiaf/ieo/index.html.

are.[9] For its part, the DOE forecast projects technological growth as a uni-linear development. It assumes that it will continue to play the role that it has played. Yet, free of the constraints of modeling, we have some reason to be more optimistic.

The potential for a positive effect is major, partly because much is left to be done.[10] Energy efficiency is especially important in the transportation sector because it now drives and will increasingly drive future oil demand growth, and currently there are no available fuels to compete significantly with oil products. Because transportation accounts for about 70 percent of U.S. oil consumption, doubling fuel efficiency would be a "very positive step."[11] Technologies for this purpose include gasoline-electric hybrid vehicles, hydrogen-powered and fuel-cell vehicles, and various approaches for enhancing the fuel economy of existing gasoline-engine technology.

Increasingly, major automobile companies are preparing for a post-oil era. General Motors rolled out its Hy-wire car in September 2002 at the Paris Motor Show, a car that runs on environment-friendly hydrogen and is built on a fuel-cell chassis. Honda and Toyota have introduced a handful of experimental fuel-cell vehicles, as has nearly every other major company. Cars that run on fuel cells produce energy from pure hydrogen rather than from petroleum, and thus emit only water and heat as waste. Major Japanese firms such as Honda and Toyota have also developed cars driven by hybrid engines, which are easier to produce than fuel-cell engines. Volkswagen has produced a two-seater hybrid that gets 239 mpg, compared to 15 mpg for a sports utility vehicle, and its composition of magnesium, titanium, and aluminum make its safety rating equal to that of a racecar. In addition to energy-efficient cars, developed high-speed rail corridors between major American cities could also increase efficiency, as they already have in Japan, Germany, France and Italy.

To be sure, numerous challenges exist. Foremost among them are the costs of building the infrastructure to support and integrate such cars, a challenge that makes a "huge breakthrough in transportation unlikely until around 2020" in the absence of an intense commitment to do so.[12]

Indeed, political will and leadership is needed to put tens of thousands of energy-efficient vehicles on the road. That would impose costs on consumers and governments and will require a shift in the consumer culture. Studies show that culture plays a key role in consumption habits and in

[9] Improvements that are not induced by energy price movements are referred to as "autonomous energy efficiency improvements." See *Global Energy Outlook* (Riyadh, Saudi Arabia: OPEC, 7th International Energy Forum, 17–19 November, 2000), 7.

[10] On new technologies, see Adnan Shihab-Eldin, "New Energy Technologies: Trends in the Development of Clean and Efficient Energy Technologies," *OPEC Review* 26 (December 2002).

[11] Interview with Lowell Feld.

[12] Interview with Mohamed Hamel.

conditioning the preferences of consumers.[13] Thus, to shift culture and, in effect, to alter the paradigm of energy consumption, leaders will have to think creatively, offer economic incentives, and change the discursive environment that shapes how we think about energy and the environment. Efforts to move toward fuel-efficient cars will matter little if they are left to the voluntary appetite of consumers or if done in a piecemeal fashion. However, they can make a major difference if done with pressing incentives and penalties, and in mass numbers.[14]

For instance, introducing a carbon tax aimed at reducing car pollution can encourage market penetration by alternative cars, such as hybrid or fuel-cell vehicles, by making them economically more appealing. Evidence does suggest that taxation can be effective and beneficial to the environment. An OECD study has suggested that a broad energy tax on carbon content in fuels would lead to a reduction in the use of oil and, in turn, in carbon emissions of over 10 percent, a result confirmed by a subsequent OPEC Secretariat study. Further, if this is combined with other approaches, the reduction in greenhouse gases mandated by the 1997 Kyoto Protocol could be met.[15] In this sense, the Kyoto Protocol could represent a breakthrough for restrictions on oil use motivated by environment-related taxation.[16] However, even more significant taxation as well as special regulations and even the mandatory introduction of biofuels may be required to bring about major changes in oil consumption and engender more serious development of advanced technologies such as solar and fuel cells.[17]

Thus far, the United States, with the exception of the state of California, has not done much to increase fuel efficiency. Secretary of Energy Spencer Abraham and other officials have stressed the importance of energy efficiency and conservation to reduce energy consumption.[18] The Bush administration has also spearheaded an effort to bring about a hydrogen future and sought to speed up the development of commercially available hydrogen-powered cars and the energy infrastructure to support them. But we will

[13] See Gary Becker, *Accounting for Tastes* (Cambridge, MA: Harvard University Press, 1996) and Robert Settle and Pamela Alreck, *Why They Buy: American Consumers Inside and Out* (New York: John Wiley, 1986), 224–32.

[14] Projections on the potential of such technology to offset oil dependence vary widely.

[15] On these studies, see *Global Energy Outlook*, 26.

[16] Øystein Noreng, *Crude Power: Politics and the Oil Market* (New York: IB Tauris, 2002) 183–85.

[17] Christian Azar, Kristian Lindgren, and Bjorn A. Andersson, "Global Energy Scenarios Meeting Stringent CO2 Constraints: Cost-Effective Fuel Choices in the Transportation Sector," *Energy Policy* 31 (2003).

[18] See "U.S. Officials: Policy Should Promote Secure Oil Supplies," *Oil and Gas Journal* (1 July 2002), 27. And the national energy report calls for increased efficiency, including the passage of CAFE standards. See *National Energy Policy* (Report of the National Energy Policy Development Group, May 2001).

have to see how serious the administration is about this initiative and whether future administrations will advance it.

What we do know is that the U.S. Senate has had chances to improve car fuel efficiency and has been less than enthusiastic about it. For instance, on March 13, 2002, the Senate rejected the Corporate Average Fuel Economy (CAFE) requirement standard, an effort to increase fuel efficiency standards by 50 percent over thirteen years.[19] Some estimates suggest that passing the CAFE standards would decrease oil consumption by 2.5 mb/d, while other estimates are more optimistic.

Given that the United States is projected to import approximately 25 mb/d by year 2020, it certainly needs to develop a coordinated and determined plan for efficient energy use.[20] Such a plan, as the National Energy Development Group has pointed out, is both missing and pressing.[21] As one energy analyst put it, it will take "fairly heroic efforts to get U.S. import dependence down by even 25 percent, and Washington is not as oil dependent as many other states."[22] As a result, such an energy strategy would have to be planned in concert with other nations. This is because the health of other economies such as Japan's, which obtains nearly 90 percent of its oil imports from the Middle East despite efforts to diversify away from oil dependence, fundamentally affects the growth of the American economy in an interdependent world.[23] Energy independence would not insulate America from an oil shock and its effects on the overall global economy.[24] These challenges notwithstanding, the potential exists for decreasing oil dependence, and environmental pressures, which were not as present in 1979, are more likely to continue to rise than to decrease.

The third effect of technology is to make the exploration and production of oil and gas cheaper and faster. High technology is especially important to the viability of non-Gulf oil production. It is well known that rational actors are unlikely to sink money into oil exploration and production if the marginal

---

[19] President Clinton's Partnership for a New Generation of Vehicles program, which aimed at developing high automobile efficiency, also failed for a variety of reasons.

[20] Interview with G. Daniel Butler. For discussion of the options available, see *Domestic Oil and Gas Producers: Public Policy When Oil Prices Are Volatile* (CRS Report RL30290).

[21] *National Energy Policy* (Report of the National Energy Policy Development Group, May 2001), 1.

[22] Interview with G. Daniel Butler. Note that U.S. oil resources have been tapped for decades and are largely mature.

[23] For data, see "In Search of Security," *MEED* (14 December 2001).

[24] In fact, the United States is required to share imports under the monitoring of the International Energy Agency (IEA) as the representative of consumer countries. This is mandated if a disruption of petroleum supplies of at least 7 percent of IEA supplies occurs, and if a majority of the IEA Governing Board votes for import sharing. While such circumstances have not existed since the IEA sharing mechanism was formulated, they could develop in the future.

costs of doing so are high, especially compared to alternative choices.[25] Commercial producers are aware that energy prices can only rise so high before competition is set in motion. Economically, Gulf oil has had major advantages over most non-Gulf oil in terms of quality and lower extraction costs. Newer discoveries, partly due to exploration costs and economies of scale, have been far more costly to bring to market than those in the Gulf arena, where the problem of diminishing returns is much less significant.[26] In areas where oil resources have been depleted, such as in the North Sea, it is especially expensive to find and extract new oil because of diminishing marginal utility.

However, non-OPEC production has been fueled by new technologies that allow for the exploration and enhanced recovery of oil in heretofore cost-prohibitive places. Thus, for many years, certain reserves in the Gulf of Mexico were not viable for exploitation due to high production costs, but technological breakthroughs which allowed for the more efficient use of very large oil platforms changed this picture.[27]

High technology has also facilitated deep water oil and gas exploration, which has made it commercially feasible at lower oil prices. For instance, until a few years ago, it was assumed that deep water production beyond 1000 feet of water would be possible only at prices of $30 p/b or more, but in March 2002 Shell's URSA field started producing oil at a cost of $3.25 p/b in 4000 feet of water.[28]

On the whole, development costs, according to a major study by Deutsche Bank, have fallen by 50 percent from the 1980s to the present, and one prediction is for deep water exploration, viewed as the growth play in the oil industry, to add 4 mb/d to global oil supply by 2008 or nearly twice the average amount of oil that sanctioned Iraq put on the market.[29] Estimates vary on its potential from predictions that it could represent 7 to 9 percent of total global oil and gas production in 2010 (up from 2 percent in 2002), to much more optimistic projections of a long period of continuous growth.[30] Deep

---

[25] Most commercial producers have models that show that at certain levels, the price of energy can trigger investment in the exploration and production of gas and oil, and in developing and using certain technologies. For instance, gas-to-liquids technology may prove quite useful in the production of stranded gas, partly by enabling it to be delivered in liquid form. However, models show that the use of such technology becomes financially feasible only when oil prices exceed $30 p/b.

[26] See Peter Kassler, "Developments in the Global Energy Market and the Implications for Gulf producers," in *Managing New Developments in the Gulf*, ed. Rosemary Hollis (London: Royal Institute of International Affairs, 2000), 17–18.

[27] Interview with Nader Sultan.

[28] Ibid.

[29] See *Deep Water Oil and Gas: Taming the Monster* (Deutsche Bank, 2 August 2002), esp. 10, 23.

[30] On the costs and benefits of deep water exploration, see Ivan Sandrea and Osama Al Buraiki, "Future of Deepwater, Middle East Hydrocarbon Supplies," *Oil and Gas Journal* (17 June 2002).

water exploration technology offers the means, and the end of the Cold War has offered the improved global environment, for increased production in various places, including the Atlantic Basin; Nigeria, whose potential may exceed its OPEC quota; and sub-region Africa more broadly, which may be able to rival the production of some major OPEC producers.[31] The president of Vanco Energy Corporation, which is the largest deep water license holder operating off the coast of West Africa, asserted that the African sub-region, which produces around 3.7 mb/d, will by 2008 produce more than Saudi Arabia at around 8 mb/d, partly due to deep water exploration, and become "fantastically important to oil economy in the U.S."[32] That is very unlikely. However, high technology makes substantially increased production there quite possible, as it does in other otherwise economically infeasible and often ignored ventures. These include heavy oils buried in sand deposits, among other places, which have been located especially in Canada and Venezuela. Some analysts see their potential as vast enough to extend the oil century well into the future, but extracting and producing them requires special and very costly efforts.[33]

Global political change has also increasingly opened Russia up for business. U.S. technology can help the Russians engage in deep water exploration and oil retrieval, and it may help them unlock Russia's potential, while foreign firms can execute such efforts on their own, loosely cooperating with Russian firms. Onshore drilling into deep water areas requires sophisticated technology that allows for oil to be retrieved from long distances, but doing so gets around the problem of needing oil tankers to retrieve oil from ice-locked drilling rigs. Foreign firms and governments have planned to spend well over $10 billion over the next several years to build pipelines, onshore drilling rigs, airports, and roads for the exploitation of oil and gas in Russia, with some of the gas being liquefied so that it can be shipped on tankers. The potential here is immense.

The integrated use of high technology may produce synergies that no single technology could muster independently and that models cannot predict. The Digital Oil Field of the Future—a concept in development—may well revolutionize exploration and production by using technology to make it much more targeted, exact, and cheap. Precision-guided exploration, to borrow a term from the lexicon of the American military, could in the next five to ten years expand existing oil reserves by 125 bb—more than the entire proven reserves of Iraq.[34]

31 "Oil Production: West Africa May Overtake Saudi Arabia," *Africa News Service*, 24 November 2002.

32 Quoted in ibid.

33 For data on these oils, see *Oil and Gas Journal* (28 July 2003), 21–27.

34 Daniel Yergin, "Global Energy Security" (Cambridge, MA: Cambridge Energy Research Associates, 2003), 4.

High technology and political sensibilities may still be wedded to provide further impetus to alternative and non–Middle East energy exploration. While the Senate rejected CAFE standards, it has recognized in the post-9/11 period the importance of getting oil and gas from areas other than the Middle East.[35] If such political realizations heighten, whether after another major terrorist act or by virtue of concerted, creative, and indefatigable leadership, they can constitute an additional non-economic incentive to exploiting technology for non–Middle East energy development.

The fourth effect of technology is an offshoot of the third. If production, exploration, and delivery are made cheaper and more effective by technology, that also means something more broadly for oil stability. It suggests that energy from non-Gulf areas could reach markets more quickly than in the past. This effect is heightened by the fact that technological advances substantially decrease the timeline for finding and developing oil. Thus, both speed of delivery, which is especially crucial in crises, and discovery have been enhanced.

The fifth effect of high technology, as suggested earlier in this chapter, is that it has increased the chances that using the oil weapon for political reasons or seriously cutting oil supply for economic reasons will result in a loss of market share. The rise of oil-relevant technology is important because it can lower the costs of exploration, as noted earlier, but also because it affects expectations. All players must understand that technology increases the potential that high prices will generate alternatives to oil. That was not the case two decades ago, but today it represents an invisible ceiling beyond which oil price increases will generate unacceptable risks.

ENVIRONMENTAL PRESSURES AND POLICY CHANGES

It is fair to project that policy changes that meaningfully decrease demand for oil are possible. Environmental pressures make alternatives to oil energy more pressing and promising. Environmentalists highlight the importance of cutting fossil fuel consumption in order to deal with central problems such as global warming. Indeed, oil accounts for an estimated 40 percent of global carbon emissions, which in turn are approximately 80 percent of greenhouse gases—the gases that exacerbate global warming.[36]

The DOE recognizes that environmental efforts could decrease the projected rise in future oil demand, but its predictions do not account for the potential impact of the Kyoto Protocol or any other proposed climate change

---

[35] Maureen Lorenzetti, "Secure Supplies," *Oil and Gas Journal* (12 May 2003), 27.
[36] John V. Mitchell, "Energy and the Environment" (Riyadh, Saudi Arabia: 7th International Energy Forum, November 17–19, 2000), 8–9.

policy measures. This is because binding agreements for such measures, including the Kyoto Protocol, which the United States did not join, were not in play when these projections were made. However, if the Kyoto Protocol became effective and industrialized states sought to reduce emissions by cutting fossil fuel consumption, significant reductions in such consumption would be necessary, which is quite possible.[37]

OPEC officials are quick to note that OPEC is committed to sustainable development, and that OPEC is not against environment-friendly use of energy and even renewable energy technologies. From OPEC's perspective, however, these approaches are still in their infancy and cannot support global economic development, which is driven by petroleum and which helps less-developed countries advance from pre-industrial to industrialized economies.[38]

While this may be true, OPEC does see the Kyoto Protocol as a threat, because it would significantly reduce the demand for OPEC oil if taxes are raised to a level that shifts consumer preferences and if states seriously commit to the Protocol's mandated limits on emissions.[39] As suggested earlier in this chapter, taxation has decreased oil demand. At the outset of the 1980s, taxation on oil products was either nonexistent or constituted a minimal portion of oil prices. By 1998, this picture had changed dramatically in OECD states, thus causing a major decrease in oil demand.[40] Since OPEC states, and especially big oil producers in the Gulf, have large reserves, they are dependent on ensuring that there is longer-run demand for oil.

The Kyoto Protocol has received the most attention, but other environmental efforts are also important. The European Union, while not embracing renewable energy with great vigor, still pushed a plan that ensures that renewable energy sources, such as solar and wind power, would account for 15 percent of the world's total energy production by 2010. Wind power provides 28 million Europeans with electricity, based on increasingly sophisticated and effective turbines that now produce 250 times more electricity than the turbines of twenty years ago.[41] And some studies show that it has great potential to play a larger role in the global energy mix.[42]

37 DOE, *International Energy Outlook 2002*, 14. Interviews with DOE analysts, July-August 2002. On how environmental concerns may decrease oil demand, see Shihab-Eldin, "New Energy Technologies," esp. 279–83.
38 Interviews with Mohamed Hamel, Alvaro Silva Calderon, Omar Farouk Ibrahim.
39 Noreng, *Crude Power*, 185.
40 For supporting data, see Shihab-Eldin, Lounnas, and Brennand, "Oil Outlook to 2020."
41 Marlise Simons, "Wind Turbines Are Sprouting off Europe's Shores," *New York Times*, 8 December 2002, A3.
42 Suzanna Strangmeier, "Wind Power Share of Global Energy Mix Growing," *Oil Daily* (23 August 2002).

The E.U. states, driven partly by polls that show significant public interest in environmental issues, have been more environmentally conscious than most other states. For a variety of reasons, major producers of fossil fuels like the United States, Saudi Arabia, and Canada have taken issue with the European plan and the Kyoto Protocol. The United States has questioned whether the Kyoto Protocol is the most cost-effective way to reduce greenhouse gases. Moreover, it has argued that the Kyoto Protocol would disproportionately impact its large and growing economy by reducing demand for energy products and requiring demand-reduction policies. It has also said that developing nations, especially China and India, should not be exempt from the Kyoto Protocol, because the biggest increase in carbon emissions will come from their growing economies.[43] Along with other oil-producing states, the United States, Saudi Arabia, and Canada in fact blocked an effort by the E.U. to put specific 15-percent targets in effect at the World Summit on Sustainable Development in South Africa in September 2002. While they did agree to promote an increase in renewable energy, which was important, the failure to adopt 15-percent targets disappointed environmentalists and states that pushed in that direction.

The Kyoto Protocol and other environmental efforts have faced serious implementation challenges.[44] However, there is little doubt that efforts to develop environment-friendly policies will continue. They may even produce tipping-point consciousness changes over questions involving oil and the environment. These pressures will be continued by non-governmental organizations (NGOs), by mounting scientific evidence, and by governments and leaders seeking to behave more responsibly. Indeed, there has been an explosion in environmental NGOs, and their pressure and watchdog tactics have been aided by global communications and the Internet. Reflecting this growth, the World Wild Fund, with 570,000 members in 1985, had exploded to 5.2 million only ten years later.[45]

Because of such pressures—and for reasons of their own—political and business leaders have also gained greater appreciation for the importance of protecting the environment. One study of 200 major companies found that those with better environmental performance had higher returns on investment than their competitors, even after accounting for sales, growth, and

---

43   Interview with Guy Caruso. On the disproportionate impact on the United States, see
     William Nordhaus and Joseph Boyer, "Requiem for Kyoto: An Economic Analysis," *Energy
     Journal* (1999 special issue), *International Energy Outlook 2003*, 157–66.
44   For a good analysis of the challenges of putting Kyoto into practice, see Mitchell, "Energy
     and the Environment."
45   Lester R. Brown, *Eco-Economy: Building an Economy for the Earth* (New York: W. W.
     Norton, 2001), 265–69.

market position, suggesting that oil companies and fund managers are under greater pressure to consider social and environmental issues in their business plans.[46]

British Petroleum, Conoco, and Phillips Petroleum have addressed in their annual reports the strong potential that climate politics and regulations could affect future business operations. They have gone to some trouble, partly for public relations purposes but also because it is increasingly viewed as good business, to establish that they are concerned about the environment and to meet their own targets for reducing greenhouse gases, without hurting business prospects.[47] In fact, John Browne, CEO of British Petroleum, who believes that governments will soon be regulating greenhouse gases, pointed out that his company not only met its targets but also saved $600 million in doing so, thanks to energy efficiency measures.[48]

Global leaders have also put an increasing spotlight on the environment, focusing on the longer-term implications of failing to act. In assailing America's failure to join the Kyoto Protocol, President Jacques Chirac of France asserted in September 2002 the not uncommon feeling that "climate warming is still reversible. Heavy would be the responsibility of those who refused to fight it."[49]

In the United States, the Senate, as noted earlier, rejected CAFE standards. But a majority of Americans do believe that sport utility vehicles should have to meet the same mileage standards as cars.[50] This indicates some potential public support for tougher fuel-efficiency standards. Renewable energy sources are not expected to become economically feasible compared to oil, but that could change with government policies that encourage their widespread adoption.[51] On February 14, 2003, the DOE launched President Bush's Climate VISION program, which aims to meet the president's goal of reducing U.S. greenhouse gas intensity by 18 percent by 2012.[52] Although a step in the right direction, the program is a voluntary,

[46] *Should Big Oil Turn Green?: Responses to the Energy Puzzler* (Deutsche Bank, 11 November 2002), 13.
[47] See, for instance, the analysis and the statement of Lord Browne of Madingley, Group Chief Executive, British Petroleum, *Environmental and Social Review* (British Petroleum, April 2002).
[48] See George Packer, "The Liberal Quandary over Iraq," *New York Times Magazine*, 8 December 2002, 102.
[49] Quoted in Richard L. Swarns, "Compromise Brings Accord on Renewable Energy Closer," *New York Times*, 3 September 2002, A3.
[50] Based on an Associated Press poll. See Will Lester, "Poll Shows Public has Mixed Opinion about SUVs," *Associated Press*, 3 July 2003.
[51] *International Energy Outlook 2003*, 4.
[52] Ibid., 163–64.

public-private partnership. That status raises questions about how effective it can be and to what extent its spirit will motivate reductions in or more efficient use of oil resources.

For their part, U.S. senators have become more aware of environmental pressures as well. They have, for instance, pushed increasingly to determine whether the Securities and Exchange Commission has done enough to make corporations disclose the environmental risks that could potentially cost investors millions.[53] This type of pressure may bring slow change.

While the U.S. government has dragged its feet on the Kyoto Protocol, the state of California, which would be the fifth-biggest economy in the world if it were a sovereign nation, did take important measures to cut emissions in the summer of 2002. These measures put the state light years ahead of the federal government. If the bill signed by since-banished Governor of California Gray Davis is followed, it should spur auto companies to get moving on the project of improving miles per gallon.[54] And if it is true that California sets trends, then other states may very well follow suit, which, in turn, will push the federal government to take more serious action.

We need to be realistic about the potential for changes in consumption habits and for the effective development and use of alternative energy. Most estimates are not especially optimistic about blockbuster breakthroughs. Other reports are more optimistic and emphasize that energy dependence is at least partly a choice open to us.[55] In either case, we can temper sober accounts of our oil future with some counterarguments that at least deserve consideration. On that score, technology often has outstripped our imaginations, and it may do so in the oil arena as well. In the current age, we have special motivations for using technology to advance energy exploration and development. Indeed, we have faced multiple wars in the Middle East—not to mention 9/11—and the perception is that it is all connected to global rivalries and jockeying over how to protect or influence Middle East oil supplies. Decisions about pursuing alternative energy are related to the cost of existing energy, but they are also influenced by this broader geostrategic set of issues and hardening perceptions that it is important to ensure alternatives to Gulf oil.

Future acts of terrorism will only highlight the importance of alternative and non–Middle East energy sources, while concern for the environment

---

[53] Ibid., 7.
[54] Interview with Lowell Feld.
[55] See the range of United Nations publications at www.un.org/publications.

will more likely rise over time than flag. For its part, the broader world economy has at least a chance to count on real and potential technological capabilities and environmental pressures to slow down the projected rise in oil demand or to be able to deal with it more effectively. That is important. In. ʒed, only one or two decades ago, the world surely seemed headed for *increased* dependence on Gulf oil. The difference between then and now is that the world back then lacked such real and potential abilities, which were largely locked in the nascent genie of energy technology and science.

Chapter 12

TWENTY-FIRST-CENTURY THREATS
TO GLOBAL OIL STABILITY

Like any complex drama, the tale of the evolution of oil stability is hardly unvarnished, nor is it absent some of the stirrings of turmoil that could become more significant down the road. But while threats to oil stability no doubt exist, it is not as hostage as we may think to the caprice of Middle East, global, and oil market events and politics. Rather, it has multiple anchors forged on the anvil of longer-run developments, each with its own center of gravity.

The body of this book sketched these developments, but has not done much to show what they mean when considered together. While each of them is important in its own right, when combined they also create synergies; should one weaken or falter, the others can still play a stabilizing role. This aspect, described in the introduction as "complex stability," is crucial to understanding the evolution of oil stability. In this chapter, I will briefly present some of the existing and potential threats to oil stability, and then pick up themes elaborated on in the book to show how these longer-term developments work together to deter, check, and diminish some of them.[1]

IRAQ'S TURMOIL AND OIL FUTURE

Following the Iraq War, U.S. forces faced a guerrilla war, which at first seemed unorganized but by July 2003 appeared much more coordinated. Saddam Hussein and his sons, the latter of whom were killed by U.S. forces in late July, appeared to be directing some of these attacks. At a minimum, they were

---

[1] One comprehensive study argues that the chances of an oil supply disruption are higher than at any point in the last two decades. Report of an Independent Task Force, *Strategic Energy Policy: Challenges for the 21st Century* (New York: Council on Foreign Relations, 2001), 2.

encouraged by audiotapes supposedly recorded by Saddam, which were periodically released by Al Jazeera. The guerrilla war unnerved many Iraqis who feared Saddam's return and generated the impression that the United States was unable to control Iraq. Saddam's capture in mid-December 2003 eliminated concerns that he might somehow return to power and created greater hope for American-led nation-building efforts. Iraq, moreover, has undergone an important process of de-Baathification and Saddam's removal should facilitate the elimination of more opposition to U.S. forces. However, remaining Baathist elements may continue to support this guerrilla movement or undermine the government through other means. Iraq's population also includes anti-colonial and anti-American elements who see the Iraqi Governing Council as an American quisling, Islamic extremists within and from outside Iraq who could seek Taliban-like or possibly more enlightened clerical rule, and nationalist and some democratic forces that appreciate the American liberation of Iraq but want to be free of American control. The Shia despised Saddam more than the Sunnis, but several key Shia clerics with large followings denounced the Iraq Governing Council shortly after it was formed in mid-July 2003, calling for a new council that could serve Iraq's interests better.

Of course, the oil factor looms prominently. Oil is wrapped up in Iraqi nationalism and Iraqis want control over it. Many of them doubt America's intentions, adding yet another element of potential resentment, should America be perceived as taking or unduly influencing Iraqi oil.

At the regional level, both Iran and Turkey have interests in Iraq. Turkey wants to ensure that Kurdish rebels do not operate from Iraq, that the Kurds do not develop their own autonomous state that can destabilize Turkey, and that they do not gain influence over Iraq's northern oil fields at Kirkuk. For its part, Iran would like to gain influence over Iraq's southern Shia, though it is vital to note that the Shia of Iraq and Iran are quite different, making such a goal difficult to achieve.[2] In fact, the Iran-Iraq War heightened the Arab-Iranian distinction among Iraq's Shia even more.[3]

Adding to the uncertainty, America's commitment to Iraq is not ironclad. Polling information shows that public support for the war decreased sharply in the three-month period following the war. Seventy-three percent believed that going to war in Iraq was a good idea on April 16, 2003, whereas 56 percent said so in late June. Eighty-six percent thought that things were going well for the United States in Iraq on May 7, 2003, a figure that dropped to 70 percent by June 1 and to 55 percent in late June.[4] Even under positive

---

[2] Yitzhak Nakash, *The Shi'is Of Iraq*, 2nd ed. (Princeton: Princeton University Press, 2003).

[3] A. William Samii, "Shia Political Alternatives In Postwar Iraq," *Middle East Policy* 10 (Summer 2003), 93–101.

[4] USA Today/CNN/Gallup poll, 28–30 June 2003. Richard Benedetto, "Confidence in War Effort Slips; Bush Support still Strong," *USA Today*, July 1, 2003.

circumstances, Americans may question more forcefully why the United States is spending so much money on Iraq when it has problems at home. American domestic politics in the coming years could take unpredictable turns, especially given the potential for another terrorist strike at home, which could generate pressure to remove the U.S. presence from the Middle East.

Global pressure for an American withdrawal could also mount. In a July 2003 report distributed to Security Council members, UN Secretary General Kofi Annan began to push for an American timetable for withdrawal, noting that Iraqis do not want democracy imposed from above. An American withdrawal at some point would be prudent, but a premature withdrawal could leave a power vacuum that would invite enduring rivalry.

All this does not mean that Iraq will be a failed effort in nation-building. The most likely scenario remains that the United States will stay committed to a troubled Iraq, help it rebuild possibly with greater international support, develop at least some nascent elements of democratization, and put it on a slow, tortuous path to far higher oil production. However, one or more of the following scenarios are important to consider in the story of oil stability.

In the first scenario, the U.S. commitment to Iraq wanes and American forces, under attack and increasingly disliked, withdraw from Iraq. With American forces largely gone, Iraq could conceivably descend into chaos or splinter into multiple countries. From the sixteenth century to approximately 1920, the area today known as Iraq was under Ottoman rule. It consisted of three provinces: Mosul in the north, Baghdad in the heartland and Basra in the south. By 1920, control over Iraq devolved to the British. When Iraq achieved independence in October 1932, Mosul, Baghdad, and Basra united into one state.[5] Saddam kept Iraq unified with brute force and sheer terror, but the United States cannot play a comparable unifying role in perpetuity because it cannot use Saddam's draconian measures.

In a second scenario, Washington remains fully committed to Iraq but fails to stabilize the country effectively and continues to face a guerrilla war and sporadic attacks on Iraq's government and civil structures, oil pipelines, and oil production facilities. We would have an ongoing drama in which Iraqis are uncomfortable with the American presence but cannot evict U.S. forces and the United States is uncomfortable with its commitment to Iraq but sees withdrawal as a worse option. In both of the first two scenarios, Iraq would break down into areas of warlord or tribal conflicts that crisscross the religious divide between Shia and Sunnis.

---

[5] Charles Tripp, *A History of Iraq*, 2nd ed. (Cambridge, U.K.: Cambridge University Press, 2002), chap. 1.

In the third scenario, Iraq is largely stabilized but the democratic process produces a regime that eventually becomes anti-western and autocratic. This could occur based on a one-person, one-vote, one-time outcome in which the elected government proceeds to undermine the democratic system in order to maintain power. Or it could occur simply because such a position reflects the popular views of Iraqis. A coup by certain elements in Iraq's population is also possible

Another scenario is also plausible. Iraq makes the transition to a quasi-democracy and genuflects toward the West, but remains riddled with domestic corruption, a dubious set of legal norms, incompetence, and sporadic political instability that deters investment and the government's ability to rehabilitate its oil industry.

Of course one or more of these scenarios may transpire, not to mention other scenarios that are hard to fathom. But the longer-run developments sketched in this book, on balance, make such damaging scenarios less likely.

First, the U.S. commitment to the region has increased significantly since 1980. This is crucial because Iraq's challenges will test the national will, especially if American casualties continue to mount and the goal of establishing a stable Iraqi government proves elusive. Even if the American commitment begins to flag, Washington may move to incorporate peacekeepers from other nations to help stabilize Iraq, drawing on its global economic leverage to develop such a force.

Second, as chapter 4 showed, Washington has become increasingly capable of handling various scenarios in the region and, more specifically, in Iraq. One could easily argue that it should have put more forces into Iraq for the postwar period and done much more to train the military or a policing force for the job of nation-building. Disbanding Iraq's regular army was also a bad idea because it left tens of thousands of men unemployed, angry and more likely to join the opposition. However, these are not arguments about whether America had the capability to stabilize Iraq, but rather about its planning and strategy. America clearly has developed the capability to handle such contingencies, and in fact is currently operating in multiple theaters of operation, including Afghanistan and Asia.

The United States also has developed significant regional access in multiple states and through offshore platforms. That enhances its ability to maneuver in the region. Such capability could prove vital in a truly worst-case scenario, in which a radical anti-western regime gains control in Baghdad or utter chaos threatens Iraq's oil supply. The United States and its willing allies, one could surmise, would probably not allow this supply to come under hostile control, barring extreme and uncontrollable anti-American agitation in the population, which spilled over into Iraq's oil production areas.

To be sure, seizing oil centers, even in a drastic worst-case scenario, would be costly. The images of colonialism and infidel invaders would be prominently featured around the world, and anti-American tensions would rise, as might transnational terrorism against U.S. regional forces and Americans around the world. But the United States may well countenance that cost, and oil-dependent states around the world would likely tolerate it as a stop-gap measure, at least behind the scenes, until a better alternative could be found.

Third, even if a reactionary, anti-western regime takes control over time, it will still likely want to sell lots of oil. After all, Iraq possesses the second-largest oil reserves in the world and thus has a vested interest in using these resources to avoid their obsolescence down the road. Moreover, Iraq's leadership should have some interest in gaining oil revenues with which to rebuild the country, after decades of war and conflict, and to show the people that it can provide basic services. Just because a government is reactionary or anti-western does not mean that it can or would want to ignore certain needs of its domestic constituency. Moreover, as history shows, even corrupt leaders would still prefer to line their pockets with money from oil than to leave it in the ground.

Fourth, the changing distribution of power in the region is also important. In 1979, Iran sought to undermine Iraq's government by subverting the Shia. This is one of the reasons that Iraq attacked Iran. Yet, at the outset of the twenty-first century, regimes in Iraq's neighborhood are less able and willing to meddle in Iraq's affairs than they were in the past. Iran's revolution has mellowed and, while Iran would like to affect Iraq's future, it may not want to take major risks to do so.

Fifth, beyond the fact that Washington has developed the capability to deal with multiple security contingencies, other stabilizing factors have also developed. They would be crucial for a worst-case scenario in Iraq or in any event-driven oil crisis. As laid out in chapters 8 through 10, the global economy has increasingly been able to count on sources of oil that can be put on the market to contain the negative effects of a supply disruption caused by political and security events. In addition, non-OPEC oil, as well as SPRs and global commercial stocks, have become sizable enough to replace a temporary cutoff of oil from the Middle East. Technology and experience have made it easier to deliver and use those alternate sources effectively. Rising U.S. capability and political cooperation with Arab Gulf states has further enabled this development, as reflected in the joint U.S.-Saudi response to the 1991 Gulf crisis, in which they cooperated not only to contain Iraq militarily but also to put oil on the market quickly.

We can compare 1980 with 2003. In 1980, Saddam was firmly entrenched in power. His absolute rule ensured domestic stability under a stifling, oppressive regime. But he would also proceed to militarize his society and repress its energies, thrust it into horrific wars, cut oil supply to the world economy, face a UN embargo that further cut the supply, and ultimately put Iraq into chaos.

PREVENTING A ROYAL FALL

Turmoil in Iraq could infect the House of Saud, whose future has been doubted seriously by many thinkers. The Saudis have faced in the 1990s and continue to face some unprecedented economic and political problems. We cannot predict how Saudi Arabia will navigate modernity while seeking to preserve tradition, how it will integrate a restless generation and diversify its oil-dependent economy without causing profound socioeconomic chaos, or how it may negotiate entry into the global economy and manage its increasingly educated citizens in a world where high technology allows access to global information.

A new regime arising through a coup or other means that is less disposed to the West could prove quite problematic for regional and oil stability. It could limit U.S. relations in favor of a regional approach to security, undermine Middle East peace efforts, align more closely with Iran, eschew antiterrorist measures, and decrease oil production or outright embargo the West. The nature of the regime would largely determine the extent to which such measures are taken, but even succession within the royal family could produce some movement in this direction.

While the fall of the regime is possible, the Saudis, as discussed in chapter 2, are more adept at self-preservation than many believe. They have handled significant domestic problems in the past and could continue to do so, or at least well enough to avoid major upheaval. In fact, the regime is arguably not less stable than it was in 1979 but rather demonstrably better off at the inter-state level, especially when we compare it to Iran and Iraq—two states that short-circuited each other's ambitions in the quixotic pursuit of regional hegemony.

However, changes at the regional level are just part of the evolving story. The United States has increasingly enhanced its ability to protect the regime. Although the two states do not trumpet this connection, Washington has played a central role in organizing, equipping, training, and coordinating the Saudi Arabian National Guard—the regime's internal security force—making it crucial to Saudi internal stability.[6] U.S.-Saudi cooperation has also put

[6]   Anthony H. Cordesman, *Saudi Arabia: Guarding the Desert Kingdom* (Boulder, CO: Westview Press, 1997), chaps. 6–8.

significant technological, intelligence, and financial tools in the regime's disposal, and American oil companies in Saudi Arabia have had a similar effect.[7] Would-be coup plotters, and outside states that might aid them, must be aware that it is committed to the regime, thus raising the potential costs of subversion and decreasing the prospects for success. To be sure, it would not be sensible to assume that the United States could save the Al Saud against a determined, grassroots movement. It might even stand back if the movement appeared broad and popular, and not driven by radicalism. After all, the United States has trumpeted democratization in the Middle East, a message that might restrain its options against a bona fide grassroots movement, even if it wanted to intervene. But Washington could help deter and possibly help reverse a coup attempt engineered from within. To be sure, the well-known Catch-22 is that the greater the U.S. profile in the region, the more annoyed that some in Saudi Arabia and elsewhere will become. That can be counterproductive by fostering nationalist agitation, the disdain of the religious community, and anti-American sentiment deriving from the U.S. commitment to Israel. Until mid-2003, Riyadh balanced effectively the goals of assuring U.S. support without antagonizing domestic elements, albeit through some odious forms of domestic suppression and appeasement of extremist elements. And since then Saudi Arabia has announced that American troops will no longer be based in the country, thus making this balancing act easier to manage.

At the economic level, U.S. efforts to help the regime diversify its economy are also at play and of fairly recent origin. They can help Riyadh reduce its dependence on oil exports, decrease its destabilizing unemployment problems, and ease its transition from a massive welfare state—one that it may not be able to afford in the future. Failure to make this transition could leave the regime vulnerable to domestic discontent and less able to play a crucial role in oil stability.

While it would not be sensible to assume that Washington could deal with a grassroots revolution, it would be equally mistaken to believe that Saudi Arabia could easily turn into another Iran. As discussed in chapter 2, little potential appears to exist for the type of grassroots populist movement that overthrew the Shah. Moreover, the opponents of the regime or of its ties to the United States do not have much influence in the decision-making process, except indirectly insofar as the decision makers cannot ignore the Arab Street or important tribal leaders and other elites. Saudi leaders will have to strike a careful balance between appeasing their critics at home and satisfying the United States, but it appears that they have the wherewithal to do so, at least in the near term.

---

[7]   Thus, the senior Saudi leadership was not reluctant to bring them back into the kingdom. Nawaf E. Obaid, *The Oil Kingdom at 100: Petroleum Policymaking in Saudi Arabia* (Washington, D.C.: The Washington Institute for Near East Policy, 2000), 53–60.

Of course, we should also consider the potential U.S. role in a scenario where the royal family falls to a radical regime with ties to transnational terrorism. In such a scenario, the United States would likely have the military capability, intelligence resources, regional and global backing from important actors, and local royal family support on the ground to overturn a coup attempt. More important, perhaps, as a last-resort option it could consider seizing and holding the Saudi oil fields, irrespective of whether or not it would be sensible to oust the radical regime. Of course, this would be difficult because of the geography and ethnography of the eastern al-Hasa oil province, an area whose predominantly Shia population marched in demonstrations against the royal family in 1979, some exhibiting support for the Ayatollah Khomeini. It would also be difficult to oversee and protect the installations, especially if radical forces gain control over some of the regime's sophisticated weapons, and if the Arab Street is agitated over the seizure, which could easily play into every colonial and imperialist conspiracy theory. The Congressional Research Service did consider such a scenario following the 1973 Arab oil embargo. The report emphasized how difficult seizing the oil fields would be, especially because of the potential of Soviet intervention—a factor that is probably irrelevant in the post–Cold War period.[8] In any event, before taking such drastic action, global oil stocks, including the SPRs, could buy Washington some time to see how a new regime behaves, and to plan worst-case options.

The foregoing discussion allows us to offer a contrast with 1980. At the regional level, the Saudis faced a revolutionary Iran bent on overthrowing Gulf monarchies. For its part, Iraq was clearly a growing threat whose potential was constrained only by its war with Iran. At the domestic level, the most serious anti-regime demonstrations the royal family would face broke out in eastern Saudi Arabia. In terms of global affairs, even the United States had serious doubts about Saudi stability, after the fall of the Shah of Iran, and the Saudis had doubts about Washington's ability to help them. Meanwhile, fears existed that the balance of power in the region and at the global level was shifting in Moscow's favor and, in turn, in favor of the region's less moderate states.

PREVENTING A RADICALIZED SAUDI FOREIGN POLICY

While Iran and Iraq pose some direct threats, a threat also exists that the Saudis will lean more toward the interests of Iran or, in the distant future an Iraq gone awry, over those of Washington. As discussed earlier in the

---

8   Robert Baer, *Sleeping with the Devil* (New York: Crown, 2003), 208–9.

book, Riyadh has shown a strong, albeit sporadic, proclivity to seek security more by accommodating its adversaries than by opposing them strongly.

To be sure, accommodating threatening actors can make sense. Even Washington blessed the Saudi-Iranian rapprochement that began in late 1997 and early 1998.[9] But the real question is under what conditions such a rapprochement benefits regional stability. I argue that it is served when these two states are not antagonistic, and when Saudi Arabia can act as a conduit for better U.S.-Iranian relations. But stability is undermined if Iran, rehabilitated politically and resurgent militarily, slowly brings Riyadh to sympathize with the more radical aspects of its foreign policy orientation. This is because Iran has been more likely to want higher oil prices, threaten oil embargoes, seek WMD capability, aim to eject U.S. regional forces, and hinder Middle East peace efforts than has Saudi Arabia.[10]

While the course of Riyadh's regional orientation will depend on innumerable factors, some unpredictable, it is likely to be related to the factors explored in this book. Scholars who study alliances have shown that states are more likely to appease than to oppose a state that threatens them if they are weak and lack effective allies.[11] The fact that Saudi Arabia has risen in power, compared to Iran and Iraq, that the United States is more capable in the region, and that states inside and outside the region are more asymmetrically interdependent on the United States at the turn of the century than in the past is crucial. All these developments have made, and are likely to continue to make, the Saudis less inclined to drift slowly toward a regional orientation influenced by Iran over a more pro-western one.

Rising U.S. credibility and power after Desert Storm helped undermine Iran's dogged efforts to convince GCC states that their security would be better served by relying less on the United States and more on indigenous force structures that included Iran. Iran's repeated official response to the Damascus formula for stabilizing the region was that it was wrong-headed because it counted on states outside the Gulf and excluded Iran. As Iran's UN Ambassador put it in 1994, Iran has tried its "best" to convince the GCC states to join with Iran rather than Washington for secure regional stability.[12]

By way of contrast, in 1980 U.S.-Saudi relations were very strained, the Saudis were weak at home and not influential in the region, and they lacked

---

9   Shireen T. Hunter, "Outlook for Iranian-Gulf Relations: Greater Cooperation or Renewed Risk of Conflict?" in *Iran, Iraq, and the Arab Gulf States*, ed. Joseph A. Kechichian (New York: Palgrave, 2001).

10 This has largely been its policy since the revolution. For a good statement of Iran's view, see "Tehran, Voice of the Islamic Republic of Iran," August 24, 1990 in BBC Summary of World Broadcasts/Middle East (August 27, 1990).

11 Stephen M. Walt, *The Origins of Alliances* (Ithaca, NY: Cornell University Press, 1987), esp. 29–31.

12 "Interview with U.N. Ambassador," *Middle East Policy*, 128.

military capability. Washington's regional position, moreover, was in tatters, and Riyadh had not yet developed in full the norm of protecting oil stability against OPEC hawks. Meanwhile, Iran and Iraq had a far greater ability to use their potentially significant threat potential in order to obtain Saudi compliance on a range of economic and security issues. Clearly, as the balance of the analysis in this book has shown, this set of circumstances would change by 1990 and even more by 2002.

TRANSNATIONAL TERRORISM

Saudi Arabia and transnational terrorism have been inextricably woven together in the popular mind by the September 11 attacks. Thus far, terrorism has not affected oil stability significantly. The attack on the U.S. barracks at the Khobar Towers in Saudi Arabia in 1996 did kill nineteen Americans; the attack on the USS *Cole* in 1999 was also deadly, as were the Al Qaeda attacks on sites in Saudi Arabia in 2003. However, as tragic as these events were, one or two such attacks are not the real threat, save for an effort like something out of a James Bond movie to explode WMD over the major oil refineries in the region, thus rendering them temporarily out of commission. Short of that incandescent nightmare scenario, the real threat would more likely result from a sustained effort to use more modest acts of terrorism to drive the United States from the Gulf or scale back its presence. U.S. leaders such as Secretary of Defense William Cohen asserted before 9/11 that "no act" of terrorism would drive the United States from the region. However, even if terrorism did not achieve that, it could still make regional leaders less likely to support U.S. regional efforts or undermine them altogether.[13]

Such a sustained effort might be highlighted by sporadic, dramatic acts of terror to hinder the free flow of global oil. While it is hard to predict how this might happen, it is possible that terrorists would try to close down the Strait of Hormuz, a fear that arose after the 9/11 attacks; assassinate an Arab leader whose regime has influence over Persian Gulf oil; or attack key oil fields directly.[14] Terrorists could hit sensitive points in Saudi Arabia's eight most significant oil fields, both onshore and offshore, and cause major problems in supply that could last months. Loading terminals, such as the one at Ras Tanura, and oil pipelines could also be hit along the broader Saudi oil system. The Abqaiq extra light crude complex, with a capacity of 7 mb/d, is

---

13 Quoted in Gerry Gilmore, "Cohen Visits, Reaffirms UAE, Qatar Ties," *American Forces Press Service*, 20 November 2000.

14 On concern about the Strait of Hormuz, see Neela Banerjee, "Fears Again, of Oil Supplies at Risk," *New York Times*, 14 October 2001, section 3, 1.

the "Mother of All Processing Facilities" and therefore a grand target, because a moderate to severe attack could create a loss of oil equal to that of the 1973 embargo.[15] Terrorists could also hit large oil reservoirs such as Kuwait's Burgan Field, which was crippled by Iraq's invasion in 1990.[16]

In fact, it is quite likely that Al Qaeda has targeted such facilities. Speaking on condition of anonymity, U.S. intelligence officials revealed that Al Qaeda has sought volunteers for precisely such attacks.[17] The bombing of the French-flagged supertanker Limburg in the Arabian Sea off Yemen's southeastern Hadramaut coast on October 6, 2002, was further evidence of such intentions. Tanker attacks can only do so much damage to the flow of oil and to perceptions of its reliability, but attacks on Kuwaiti and Saudi oil fields are another matter altogether. On the same day that the Limburg was attacked, the Al Jazeera network in Qatar broadcast a Bin Laden audio recording in which he warned that Islamic forces were preparing to attack the crusader's "economic lifeline."[18]

It is also conceivable that terrorist groups will seek to disrupt global energy, not within the Middle East context, but at other chokepoints. These range from Texas oil refineries to the Alaskan and other pipelines around the world. The United States alone has over 200,000 miles of oil and gas pipelines and numerous storage facilities. The National Infrastructure Protection Center, which became part of the U.S. Department of Homeland Security, issued information bulletins on February 7 and February 12, 2003, that warned that the energy sector should be considered an Al Qaeda target. Terrorist acts against American and global oil facilities, especially if simultaneously conducted in different areas, could produce significant spikes in oil prices.[19]

The American and global power grid could also be attacked, which would indirectly affect oil stability. Such attacks could shut down key oil refineries and other relevant facilities around the world that run on electricity, causing massive economic problems. Of course, we saw the real potential for these types of attacks in August 2003, when the United States and Canada faced major blackouts after the electrical grid failed.

The September 11 attacks and other events since then also raise the potential that terrorists may use WMD, possibly in connection with a major blackout that disrupts security, against targets linked to their key perceived adversaries. In fact, Bin Laden claimed on November 10, 2001, that he had nuclear and chemical weapons and that he would use them in retaliation if

---

[15]   Baer, *Sleeping with the Devil*, prologue.
[16]   Neal Adams, *Terrorism and Oil* (Tulsa, OK: Pennwell Corporation, 2003), 102.
[17]   "Report: Al Qaida May Sabotage Saudi Oil," *United Press International* (11 March 2003).
[18]   "Tanker Terror," *The Middle East* (December 2002).
[19]   "Big Oil Ready for Possible Terror Strike," *Oil Daily* (18 February 2003).

the United States used WMD in its war in Afghanistan.[20] American and Pakistani officials doubt that Al Qaeda has this capability, but it is possible that in the future, it may obtain it, as may another terrorist group.

As noted earlier in the chapter, the high U.S. profile generates some resentment against the regimes that enable it and could produce political problems for the Arab monarchies that Washington seeks to support. But the rising U.S. presence is not without its benefits. Washington has helped in antiterrorism efforts and can use force against states that sponsor terrorism, which may deter them from doing so if the force is used effectively. Moreover, while the potential for terrorism against the global oil infrastructure has grown over time, so has the ability to prevent and contain it. Governments as well as major oil companies have taken major actions on this front.[21] Overall, however, transnational terrorism represents part of the story of oil stability that has clearly worsened over time, and its future trajectory is very hard to predict.

BLOCKING THE STRAIT OF HORMUZ

While transnational terrorism poses a rising risk, the security of the Strait of Hormuz must also be considered. It has been crucial to global trade for ages, and for ages great powers have understood that influence over it could allow them to disrupt the trade of other great powers and gain leverage. Indeed, in its effort to build empire in the fifteenth and sixteenth centuries, Portugal identified the strait as precisely such a global chokepoint, as did the British in the seventeenth century when they viewed its security as pivotal in preserving their lifeline to their crown jewel, India.

Three hundred years later, the strait is even more crucial as a global energy chokepoint. Much of the world's oil travels through its two-mile-wide channels for inbound and outbound Gulf tanker traffic. Closure of the strait would require the use of alternative routes—if available—such as the Abqaiq-Yanbu pipeline across Saudi Arabia to the Red Sea. But that would impose higher transportation costs and greater lag times for delivery.

Iran has posed the central potential threat to the Strait of Hormuz. Its ability to interdict or shut down oil traffic is enhanced by anti-ship missiles and submarines, by its long coastline dominating the strait, and by its position on the Greater and Lesser Tunbs and Abu Musa, which are islands near the strait over which it asserted control in 1992.[22] Prior to the 1987 U.S.-led

20   CNN, 10–11 November 2001.
21   "Big Oil Ready for Possible Terror Strike."
22   On the threat, see Lawrence C. Kumins and Kenneth Katzman, *Iranian Military Buildup: What Sort of Threat to Persian Gulf Oil Supply?* (Washington, D.C.: Congressional Research Service, 1995).

reflagging of Kuwaiti tankers, Iran harassed tankers to prosecute the war against Iraq. Later, in November 1994, Iran began increasing troop strength and deploying anti-aircraft missiles on the Gulf islands near the strait, in ways that threatened oil traffic.[23] It also tripled the number of missiles deployed on its Gulf coast and began fitting Chinese-built cruise missiles on its naval boats in 1995 and 1996, which U.S. military officials saw as heightening the threat.[24] Iran has regularly conducted major military exercises in the strait.[25]

To be sure, Tehran must recognize that disrupting Gulf shipping would produce profound political and military countermeasures, chiefly by the United States, and also cut off its own oil. Yet Iranian Deputy Foreign Minister Abbas Maleki asserted that while Iran supports the stable flow of oil, it reserves the option to shut down the strait if threatened.[26] Such an act might also result from a non-government sanctioned act or from irrational behavior.[27]

The Strait of Hormuz scenario needs to be considered, but several factors suggest that it has become harder to interrupt Gulf shipping. Iran remains war-weary and militarily weakened, despite its nuclear program. The United States is far more able and willing to use military capability and political influence to protect Gulf shipping, as it did during the reflagging mission. By the end of 1987, U.S. forces stopped frequent attacks on Gulf shipping and actually escorted twenty-three convoys without attack from either Iraq or Iran.[28] Washington may also pre-empt, deter, or punish efforts by Iran to close down the strait and bring political pressure to bear on outside states in order to decrease the flow of arms to Iran. That has proven to be a difficult task in Iran's case, but one marked by some successes, as noted in chapters 6 and 7, and one that global dependence on Washington can facilitate.

WEAPONS OF MASS DESTRUCTION

In addition to threats against the Strait of Hormuz, WMD represents an indirect threat to energy stability, one that has become modestly less serious from 1979 to 2003. Global intelligence services widely believed that Iraq

23 *Paris AFP* in FBIS: NES, 2 March 1995, 64.
24 "Remarks by Secretary of Defense William H. Perry to the Washington State China Relations Council," *Defense Issues* 10 (Washington, D.C.: DOD, Office of the Assistant Secretary of Defense, 1995). "U.S. Navy: Iran Triples Gulf Deployed Missiles," *Reuters*, 20 July 1996.
25 For instance, *Xinhua News Agency*, "Iran Ends Naval War Games in Strait of Hormuz," 8 February 2001, www.comtexnews.com.
26 Cited in *World Oil Market and Oil Price Chronologies: 1970–2000*, www.eia.doe.gov/emeu/cabs/chron.html.
27 On threats to the strait, see Dagobert L. Brito and Eytan Sheshinki, "Alternatives to the Strait of Hormuz," *Energy Journal* 19 (April 1998), 135–48.
28 *Jane's NATO Handbook*, "Naval Co-operation in the Gulf War" (1988–89), 198.

nearly developed nuclear capability prior to the Gulf War, and evidence suggests that it remained interested in obtaining it after the war.[29] Of course, at least by the late 1990s, Iraq's threat was diminished by war and U.S.-led containment—much more than had been previously believed—and then all but eliminated by the demise of Saddam Hussein's regime. We will probably learn more about the status of Iraq's programs over time as information is obtained from the capture of former Iraqi officials, including Saddam.

For its part, Iran is capable of completing the design and manufacture of a nuclear weapon, but for the acquisition of fissile material, which could take it years to produce on its own or which may be obtained through a transfer.[30] The use of a nuclear weapon by Iran is a worst-case and almost unimaginable scenario. The Middle East is a fairly small neighborhood, meaning that such use could produce fallout or negative consequences on all states, including the attacker. Under most circumstances, that alone would likely be a deterrent. Moreover, if Iran threatened to use a nuclear weapon, it would invite a pre-emptive Israeli or United States attack. The use by Iran of a nuclear weapon, thus, is extraordinarily unlikely.

Nonetheless, the GCC states must factor that possibility into their calculations, as must Israel and the United States, no matter what they see as the potential for correct relations with Iran. Even the most remote chance cannot be ignored. A nuclear-armed antagonist with a functioning delivery system could destroy any target or city within its target range, which would include the GCC states and possibly large oil fields. Since Riyadh, for instance, is the vulnerable heart of Saudi Arabia, the Saudis would be facing an existential threat. Biological and chemical weapons could also present serious threats to population and command centers.

WMD could also be used for brinkmanship or coercion, either directly or because others are aware of their existence. Under some scenarios, this could facilitate efforts by Iran or, in the distant future, Iraq to coerce other OPEC states into lowering oil production, launching an embargo, or undermining the United States. Such weapons could also make it harder for the United States to deploy regional forces.

States, of course, seek to build WMD for many reasons. WMD offers domestic and regional prestige, global notoriety, an offensive regional threat, and a deterrent. But while many motivations exist, the rise of U.S. regional standing has, on the whole, decreased prospects for proliferation. The United States has used economic statecraft to constrain Iran and Iraq

---

29   On Iraq's systematic and repeated efforts to conceal its weapons programs, see Anthony H. Cordesman, *Iraq and the War of Sanctions: Conventional Threats and Weapons of Mass Destruction* (Westport, CT: Praeger, 1999), esp. tables 10.1, 10.2, and 10.3.
30   David Albright and Corey Hinderstein, "Furor Over Iran," *Bulletin of the Atomic Scientists* (May-June 2003).

in general, as well as UN sanctions and potential UN inspections to impede Iraq's WMD development. In addition, the Cooperative Defense Initiative, as referred to earlier in the book, has reduced the vulnerability of the GCC states to "WMD coercion and to the effects of WMD use."[31] Furthermore, Washington is much more able now than in the past to destroy WMD facilities, by use of such capabilities as special forces, unmanned aircraft, satellite and other intelligence monitoring, stealth aircraft, and smart weapons. That is important because, for instance, Iran's facility at Natanz is housed in huge underground buildings, built to a depth of 75 feet and intended to be able to withstand aerial attack, and Iran's facilities, unlike the Osirak reactor that Israel destroyed in Iraq in 1981, are widely dispersed.[32]

The United States increasingly has developed the capability and commitment to try to prevent any regional state from becoming a serious nuclear threat. Asked about Iran's nuclear progress, President Bush asserted in late July 2003 that the development of nuclear weapons was not in the interest of Iran and that "all options remain on the table."[33] Whether or not the United States and others around the world can prevent Iran from obtaining nuclear weapons remains to be seen, but Washington is likely to pursue this goal doggedly.

Some observers might argue that WMD were less of a threat in 1980 than in 2003. This is in part because the intellectual infrastructure of Iran and Iraq for developing WMD was less developed. It may also be because the Soviet Union had more control over fissile materials and its scientists were not nearly as inclined to sell their services abroad. That said, we should also consider that in 1980 Iraq was not in the military, political and economic box that would constrain it throughout the 1990s, did not face significant international scrutiny into its WMD, and was a powerful military actor with much political influence in the Arab world. Moreover, Baghdad was far closer to developing the bomb in 1980, before Israeli aircraft destroyed the nearly-operational Osirak nuclear reactor in 1981, than in 2002 after a decade of war, UN sanctions, global scrutiny, and intrusive UN inspections. Of course, the Iraq War toppled Saddam altogether.

In 1980, Iran also had not yet been weakened by sanctions, revolution, and war. Nor did it face a set of constraints imposed by its war-related economic predicament and the need to have economic support from the international community that were absent in the bipolar period of the Cold War.

---

[31] *Cooperative Defense Initiative against Weapons of Mass Destruction in Southwest Asia* (Washington, D.C.: Department of Defense, United States Central Command, 2002).

[32] On the Natanz facility, see Albright and Hinderstein, "Furor over Iran."

[33] Quoted in Douglas Frantz, "Iran Appears to be Zeroing in on Building Nuclear Bomb," *Los Angeles Times*, 4 August 2003.

Furthermore, Washington lacked the military ability, the global connections, and the leverage to address the WMD threat, not to mention a post-9/11 U.S. citizenry far more willing to support efforts to contain WMD.

TERRITORIAL AGGRESSION

The Persian Gulf has faced the potential that serious territorial aggression by Iran or Iraq could overturn the status quo and leave either state predominant in the Gulf region and possibly in the entire Middle East. Iraq, of course, has been slowly cut down to size in the past two decades, and trimmed altogether for the foreseeable future. It is possible that in the distant future, though, it may reconstitute itself as a major regional threat. After all, many Iraqis still regard Kuwait historically as part of Iraq.

The longer-term developments discussed in this book have clearly helped contain Iran and Iraq. The rise of U.S. regional power and commitment, as laid out in chapter 4, has been crucial in its own right but also because it meant that the Saudis and other regional states had a strong partner at the global level. As chapter 5 showed, the development of regional access for U.S. projection forces also accelerated and diversified from 1979. Iran and Iraq also became less likely, because of the Iran-Iraq War, to coordinate, even sporadically, on regional and global issues or to pressure actors such as Saudi Arabia on military or economic issues. Such coordination is hard to fathom now but history could have taken a different turn, with negative consequences for oil stability. The changed global context also yielded the United States more leverage with China and Russia, both of which have needed Washington far more economically in the 1990s and into the twenty-first century than they had in past decades.

Overall, we can offer a brief contrast between 1979 and 2002. In 1979, Iran and Iraq were the two clear power brokers in the region: no state in the Gulf region could challenge them, no outside state could contain them, and each had the potential to dominate the Middle East or parts of it politically and in some measure through war-related territorial gains. That would change. The region would move toward tripolarity, with an evolving U.S. capability and commitment above it, and increasing coordination over two decades between regional and global actors. Meanwhile, the opportunistic forces of radicalism, which drove regional rivalry and bolstered threats to oil resources, would become far weaker; their counterparts would rise in influence. Thus, both in terms of the material balance of power and of the balance of ideas between moderation and radicalism, the region has become more stable, rather than less. Subsequently, Saddam's fall produced a range of implications, some of which were assessed earlier in the chapter and some of which continue to unfurl.

OIL STATECRAFT

As sketched out in chapter 8, two or more states could push for or initiate an oil embargo within or outside the context of OPEC or the Arab League. Short of an oil embargo, one or more OPEC states could also seek to decrease production in order to raise prices significantly or fail to put more oil on the market in case of an interruption. Yet, while such scenarios certainly cannot be dismissed, they have been diminished in part by some of the longer-term developments analyzed in this book.

Saudi Arabia has gained in relative regional power, which has been important to the dynamics of OPEC and, in turn, to oil stability. The rise of U.S. standing has also been relevant to ensuring moderate oil policies. In 1979, the Saudis and Kuwaitis were far less dependent on Washington than they would become in the years to come. And the United States had far less influence by virtue of its relations with them to deter or contain an embargo or higher oil pricing policies. Meanwhile, OPEC had not yet started to ebb in power. By 1990, these states depended on Washington not only for protection but also for arms, spare parts, technical training and support at the heart of their defenses, and aid in the effort to diversify their economies. That made them more likely to attach importance to American, and, in turn, global energy interests, and placed some limits on how far they could go to satisfy Iran or on how far Saudi price hawks who sought greater production cuts could rail against Saudi moderates.[34] For their own reasons, the Saudis have exhibited a developing norm to put more oil on the market in periods of potential or real crisis. Moreover, while they have become more likely in the past five years to support and even spearhead production cuts in OPEC, due chiefly to budgetary pressures, they are willing to take such efforts only so far.

Another factor is that coordination for decreasing the oil supply is complicated not only by the rise of non-OPEC oil, which OPEC increasingly has had to consider in its decisions, but also because OPEC hawks have become less likely to align significantly for extended periods. This is partly for market reasons, but also because of political factors, which include tensions and mistrust among OPEC members, a lack of charismatic leadership, and pressures from an ascendant United States. At a minimum, the rise of U.S. capability and the improvement of U.S.-GCC interaction over two decades represents a further constraint on enduring OPEC opportunism, though none of these developments are enough to prevent it, especially in any particular period. Rather they are tendencies which decrease the probability of hawkish behavior over time.

[34] See Ali Naimi, "Richardson Agrees on Need for Stability in Global Oil Markets," *OPEC Bulletin* 31 (March 2000), 15. See also "Iran: The OPEC Factor and Price Prospects," *APS Review* 56 (9 April 2001).

At the global level, OPEC actors face the sheer complexity of acting under conditions of global interdependence, where the interests of states and non–state actors are linked. In such a global economy, they are forced to seek elusive non-OPEC cooperation and cannot raise oil prices to the point that global economic growth falters and they lose market share. High technology and environmental pressures have only accentuated the risks of higher oil prices by increasing the potential for cheaper, non-Gulf oil exploration and for future oil substitutes. At the same time, while budgetary pressures create incentives to avoid price collapses and to manage the market artificially, they also militate against major cuts in production that could spike oil prices and provoke alternative energy exploration and loss of market share, which the Saudis cannot afford down the road. This leaves the Al Saud in particular with little leverage to use oil as a weapon.[35]

At the regional level, war between Israel and Arab states is possible. However, I would argue that war is less likely than it has been since the first major Arab-Israeli War in 1948. This is largely because of changes in the regional and global balance of power, the weakening of the Arab rejectionist front, the fall of Saddam's regime, and increasing economic dependence on Washington. These factors decrease the incentive to make war with Israel and make defeat more likely. The decreased potential for a long-lasting Arab-Israeli war is positive for oil stability.

By way of a brief contrast, the potential in the 1970s for Arab states to use the oil weapon or coordinated price hikes was far higher than it was in 2003. The Arab-Israeli peace process was nonexistent, except for the peace accord between Egypt and Israel, for which the Arab world ostracized Egypt. Yasser Arafat and others in the PLO leadership had yet to be estranged from Kuwait and Saudi Arabia by his support of Iraq during the Gulf crisis. Iraq and Libya were more influential in the Arab world and thus over OPEC pricing. And Saudi Arabia was far weaker and more likely to mollify Iraq and the so-called rejectionist front. For its part, Washington was far less able to translate its global and regional position into influence in oil markets, because that position was demonstrably far weaker.

The threats to oil stability discussed in this chapter are real and could become problematic, especially if more than one of them were to develop simultaneously. Together, they may trigger a tipping point, after which maintaining oil stability becomes increasingly difficult.

At a minimum, a constant tension exists, and will continue to exist, between forces that work in favor of oil stability and those that work against

---

[35] See "Market Bullishness Intact," *Oil Daily* (4 April 2002).

it. But amid the many threats to global oil stability that have alarmed leaders worldwide, and amid the seemingly immutable instabilities that occur in a world that is quasi-anarchic, there does appear to be some good news. Longer-run developments have enhanced oil stability. They have not been, nor are they likely to be, unilinear. But they do represent central and vital changes in the complex mosaic of the story of the evolution of oil stability. Some of them have been slow enough in their evolution to escape much notice in terms of their various effects. But they have been generated and sustained partly across the global-regional space and have worked independently and together to add needed bedrock to the fault lines of global oil dynamics. Taken together, they paint a picture that contrasts starkly with the fears and concerns about oil stability that are periodically expressed in various circles.

Indeed, this book illustrates that stability may exist within chaos; within political currents that are hard to predict; within conflicts that at some level still smolder; and under the sheer weight of global anarchy, with its negative impact on trust and cooperation among states. All this is not to say that we can fruitfully find order and stability within any seeming chaos—no matter where we look—or that such a venture would always be sensible. But it does demonstrate, in this rather tough test case, that it is useful to train our eyes on multiple phenomena, and on those that jibe with our preconceptions about the world as well as those that clash with them.

In the future we may count on the thumbnail-size semiconductor or other unimaginable gizmos to save us from our global oil dependence. We may turn to solar or geothermal power or place our bets on nuclear cold fusion, which could possibly turn water into gasoline one day, provided we are able to control and channel its force. We might even place hope in our capacity to conserve energy, despite the global population boom and a proclivity to revert to old habits. But all signs indicate that we will depend on oil and on the numerous by-products of the "Age of Oil" for quite some time. Thus, it is good for us that we can tell a story of the evolution of oil stability, rather than of the evolution of oil instability.

But to say that the stability of oil supply has increased does not mean that the aggressive pursuit of alternative energy sources is unimportant. Quite the contrary. In closing, I would emphasize that alternative energy is germane for a variety of reasons that lie outside of the central purview of this book.

Namely, we must consider that there is a chance that oil may run out sooner than projected. Indeed, some well-respected experts believe that, especially with growth trends in China and India, oil production worldwide is already near its peak.[36] The exhaustion of global oil resources in the absence of other sources of energy could spell disaster. In such a worst-case scenario, the stability of supply would matter little. In addition, whether or not one accepts the central argument of this book, non-oil energy is much more environment-friendly than oil, and we should be concerned about the longer-run effects of damaging the environment.

Moreover, dependence on Middle East oil, while inevitable in the short run and, if policies do not change, in the long run, is undesirable no matter how stable the supply of oil in the region and globally. Trying to ensure oil stability has real and hidden costs, direct and indirect. These costs include loss of human life; alliance-building expenditures in which Washington offers side payments to others, such as debt relief or political favors, in exchange for cooperation; and non-wartime expenditures, which some estimate have averaged $32 billion per year for defending oil supplies.[37] Of course, the nation-building effort in Iraq has been even more costly, at approximately $4 billion per month, if not more. The U.S. military presence is not only very expensive but also offensive to those in the region who see foreigners as infidels or imperialists. As such, it contributed to transnational terrorism. The use of force has also complicated U.S. global relations.

In addition to direct and indirect costs, another downside is the potential, even probable, connection between oil monies and authoritarian rule.[38] States that use oil monies to provide free services to the population do not depend on the consent of taxpayers. Nor are these taxpayers especially involved in the affairs of the state. The state becomes such a dominant force that it can expand its control at the expense of individual freedom. For those who believe that democratization is important, it is worth considering that the oil era has probably impeded rather than promoted democracy. But this is a subject that is beyond the scope of this book and is in need of much further study.

The fact that oil is so central in global commerce also puts substantial monies in the pockets of oil sheiks, kings, and princes. These monies can eventually help fund terrorism, whether or not that is the intent of oil-rich benefactors.[39]

[36]   See A. M. Samsam Bakhtiari, "2002 to See Birth of New World Energy Order," *Oil and Gas Journal* (7 January 2002), 19. Also, see *APS Review Gas Market Trends*, 58 (11 March 2002). See Cyrus H. Tahmassebi, "Effective U.S. Energy Policy," *Oil and Gas Journal* 99 (2 April 2000), 21. Report of an Independent Task Force, *Strategic Energy Policy: Challenges for the 21st Century* (New York: Council on Foreign Relations, 2001), 2.

[37]   On this average of estimates in the literature, see Patricia S. Hu, *Estimates of 1996 U.S. Military Expenditures on Defending Oil Supplies from the Middle East: Literature Review* (Prepared for the U.S. DOE under contract DE-AC05–960R22464, August 1997).

[38]   On this connection, see Terry Lynn Karl, *The Paradox of Plenty: Oil Booms and Petro-States* (Berkeley: University of California Press, 1997).

[39]   Gilles Kepel, *Jihad: The Trail of Political Islam* (Cambridge, MA: Harvard University Press, 2002).

In a post-oil era, or one in which oil were less vital in global trade, these monies would decrease and, in turn, so would monies that can likely reach terrorists. To what extent that would diminish terrorism is another question.

Clearly, the oil era is vulnerable to a litany of rallying cries enumerated at the outset of this book. If the good news is that the supply of oil to the global economy has become more stable over time, the bad news is that we have much work to do on the pothole-ridden road out of the oil era.

Appendix A

LIST OF INTERVIEW SUBJECTS

Al-Tayyeb, Muhammad. Head, Data Services Department, OPEC (Vienna, Austria: May 19, 2003).

Bandar, Prince. Saudi Ambassador to the United States (Washington, D.C.: October 12, 1997).

Bishara, Abdullah. Former Secretary General, Gulf Cooperation Council (Kuwait City, Kuwait: August 5, 1998).

Butler, G. Daniel. Senior International Oil Analyst, DOE(Washington, D.C.: April 1, 2002).

Calderon, Alvaro Silva. OPEC Secretary General (Vienna, Austria, May 21, 2003).

Caruso, Guy. Director, U.S. Energy Information Administration, DOE (Washington, D.C.: August 8, 2003).

Coburn, Leonard. DOE Russia expert (Washington, D.C.: August 8, 2003; March 6, 2001).

Doman, Linda, DOE Energy Analyst (Washington, D.C.: March 6, 2001).

Feld, Lowell, DOE Energy Analyst (Washington, D.C.: August 8, 2003).

Freeman Jr., Chas W. Former U.S. Ambassador to Saudi Arabia (Washington, D.C.: March 7, 2001; by phone, April 12, 2003).

Grummond, Steven. Former National Security Council official (Washington, D.C.: March 6, 2001).

Gürer, Nadir. Associate Director, Research Division, OPEC (Vienna, Austria: May 19, 2003).

Haass, Richard. Special Assistant to the President for Middle East Affairs (Washington, D.C.: February 19, 1999).

Hamel, Mohamed. Head, Energy Studies Department, OPEC (Vienna, Austria: May 19, 2003).

Ibrahim, Omar Farouk. Head, PR & Information Department, OPEC (Vienna, Austria: May 20, 2003).

Kagan, Edward. State Department Analyst (By phone, multiple times: May 2002).

Kessler, Chris. Director, Congressional & Public Affairs, Bureau of Nonproliferation, U.S. Department of State (Washington, D.C.: March 6, 2001).

Kreil, Erik. DOE International Energy Analyst (August 8, 2003).

Murphy, Richard. Former U.S. Deputy Secretary of State (By phone: August 10, 1996).

Pelletreau, Robert. Former U.S. Deputy Secretary of State (Washington, D.C.: October 1, 1999; March 7, 2001).

Pickering, Thomas. Former U.S. Ambassador to the United Nations (Washington, D.C.: March 2, 2001).

Scowcroft, Brent. National Security Advisor (Washington, D.C.: February 19, 1999).

Shihab-Eldin, Adnan. Director of Research, OPEC (Vienna, Austria: May 19, 2003).

Sultan, Nader. CEO, Kuwait Petroleum Corporation (Via email: September 11, 2002).

Talbott, Strobe. Former Deputy Secretary of State (By phone: August 12, 2002).

Webster, William. Director, Federal Bureau of Investigation (Washington, D.C.: March 1, 2000).

Yarjani, Javad. Head, OPEC Petroleum Market Analyses Department, Research Division (Vienna, Austria: May 19, 2003).

Note: Several officials from the United States, Russia, China, and France provided vital information and insights, but asked not to be cited because they are currently in service.

Appendix B

THE MIDDLE EAST AND GLOBAL ENERGY:
A CHRONOLOGY, 1973–2003

October 6, 1973	Israel attacked by Arab states
October 19–20, 1973	Arab oil embargo begins
March 18, 1974	Arab oil embargo ends
April 9, 1975	Twenty-four OECD members sign an agreement to establish a $25 billion lending facility to provide assistance to industrial nations hurt by high oil prices.
June 13, 1975	*Business Week* publishes controversial comments by U.S. Secretary of State Henry Kissinger hinting at military action against oil exporters in case of "actual strangulation."
January 16, 1979	Shah of Iran departs Iran
Spring 1979	OPEC raises prices nearly 30 percent
November 4, 1979	Iran takes American hostages
December 24–27, 1979	Soviets invade Afghanistan
September 23, 1980	Iran attacks Iraq
1980–1988	Iran-Iraq War
1981	Saudis flood market with inexpensive oil, forcing unprecedented price cuts by OPEC members.
1982	OPEC reaches an agreement to keep the price of crude at $32 per barrel through the end of the year and sets an ultimate price ceiling of $38 per barrel.
June 10, 1982	Iraq declares a unilateral cease-fire, but Iran demands war reparations and the trial of Saddam Hussein.
July 13, 1982	Tehran launches first attack into Iraq

1983	Oil glut takes hold. Demand falls as a result of conservation, use of other fuels, and recession. OPEC agrees to limit overall production and cuts prices by $5 to $29 per barrel.
March 27, 1984	Tanker war begins in which 44 ships are attacked in a nine-month period by Iranian and Iraqi warplanes or are damaged by mines.
1986	Average world oil prices fall by over 50 percent
1986–1987	Iran captures the strategic Faw Peninsula and threatens to win the war against Iraq (February). OPEC fails to reach accord on a production cut until December 19, when it cuts production by seven percent for the first six months of 1987, but the accord begins to deteriorate in early 1987.
1988	Iran finally accepts a cease-fire (July). OPEC reaches another six-month production accord in November to raise prices.
August 2, 1990	Iraq invades Kuwait. Crude and product prices soar.
August 1990–February 1991	Market prices plunge as OPEC nears informal agreement to increase output to cover the shortfall due to the Gulf crisis (August 27). Oil prices fluctuate according to various regional events and reports of increasing Saudi production.
November 29, 1990	UN Security Council approves U.S.-sponsored resolution authorizing the use of force against Iraq if it does not withdraw from Kuwait by January 15, 1991.
January 16, 1991	U.S.-led coalition begins Operation Desert Storm with air attack on Iraq. President Bush orders a drawdown of the Strategic Petroleum Reserves which results in 3.75 million barrel release.
January 22–February 28, 1991	Kuwaiti oil facilities are destroyed by Iraq and its oil fields are lit afire as Iraqi troops retreat and the "100 hour" ground war ends.
April 2, 1991	Resolution 687 mandates full disclosure of all of Iraq's ballistic missile stocks and production facilities (over 150 kilometers range), all nuclear materials, chemical and biological weapons and facilities, and cooperation in their destruction.
November 1991	U.S. Senate filibuster causes withdrawal of an Alaska Wildlife Refuge pro-leasing bill.
December 1991	Soviet Union collapses.
October 1992	OPEC production reaches highest level in more than a decade at 25.25 mb/d.

July 1993	Oil prices plunge due to speculation that Iraq will accept UN missile test site inspection and receive approval to resume oil exports.
February 28, 1995	Pentagon announces that it has monitored Iran's installation of surface-to-air Hawk missiles in the Strait of Hormuz.
May 20, 1996	Iraq and the United Nations agree to UN Resolution 986, which provides Iraq with the opportunity to sell $1 billion of oil for 90 days for a 180-day trial period.
June 30, 1996	Iran tests a new anti-ship missile near the Strait of Hormuz. It reportedly has a range of 60 miles and is thus viewed as a threat to U.S. naval forces.
August 6, 1996	President Clinton signs a new bill imposing sanctions on non-U.S. companies that invest over $40 million a year in the energy sectors of Iran or Libya. Under the law, the president would be required to impose at least two of the following sanctions: import and export bans; lending embargoes from U.S. banks; a ban on U.S. procurement of goods and services from sanctioned companies; and a denial of U.S. export financing.
September 5, 1996	U.S. cruise missile strikes on Iraqi military facilities push crude oil prices up.
February 20, 1988	The UN Security Council votes unanimously to more than double the amount of oil Iraq can export under the UN oil-for-food program. Iraq can export $5.26 billion over six months rather than $2.14 billion.
March 30, 1998	To address depressed oil prices, OPEC agrees to production cuts of 1.245 million barrels per day. Another round of cuts is announced in June.
February 10, 1999	U.S. Energy Secretary Bill Richardson visits Saudi Arabia to discuss potential U.S. investment in the kingdom's oil and gas sectors. His visit comes several months after a meeting between U.S. oil companies and Saudi Crown Prince Abdallah and Oil Minister Ali Naimi, during which they requested proposals from the companies on the development of Saudi oil reserves.
March 23, 1999	OPEC decides to cut production by a combined 2.1 million barrels per day. Low oil prices resulted in OPEC crude oil export revenues falling by 30 percent from the previous year.
September 22, 1999	OPEC decides to maintain production cuts until March 2000, despite the fact that crude oil prices have doubled since early 1999.

October 4, 1999
The UN Security Council agrees to raise the monetary ceiling on Iraqi oil sales from $5.26 billion to $8.3 billion. This is a one-time adjustment, with the option of being extended.

November 18, 1999
Turkey, Azerbaijan, and Georgia sign an agreement to build a $2.4 billion pipeline for the export of crude oil from the Caspian Basin.

December 31, 1999
Vladimir Putin becomes Acting President in Russia, after a surprise resignation by Boris Yeltsin.

March 28, 2000
OPEC agrees to increase oil production quotas by 1.452 million barrels per day, excluding Iran and Iraq, although Iran indicates its intention to raise production in order to avoid loss of its market share.

May 17, 2000
The EIA releases a study indicating that the Arctic National Wildlife Refuge, which is off-limits to oil exploration, has between 5.7 and 16 billion barrels of recoverable oil.

June 21, 2000
OPEC agrees to raise crude oil production quotas by 708,000 barrels per day.

September 10, 2000
OPEC agrees to raise crude oil production quotas by 800,000 barrels per day.

September 22, 2000
President Clinton authorizes the release of 30 million barrels of oil from the Strategic Petroleum Reserve over 30 days to bolster oil supplies, particularly heating oil in the Northeast.

October 12, 2000
Oil prices rise sharply after news of a terrorist attack on a U.S. warship, the USS *Cole*, in the Yemeni port of Aden, as well as escalating violence between Palestinians and Israelis.

March, 2000
OPEC ratifies the price band such that if basket prices rise higher than $28 p/b or fall lower than $22 p/b, this would trigger automatic production adjustments.

Late March–early April, 2001
The Bush administration emphasizes that the United States is facing a serious energy crisis and calls for less dependence on oil from the Middle East.

September 11, 2001
Terrorists strike the United States.

Fall 2001
The Saudis refuse to allow the United States to use their bases in the Afghanistan war of 2001 which removed the Taliban from power.

January 29, 2002
President Bush's State of the Union address officially launches a war on terrorism, foreshadowing a potential war with Iraq when he identifies Iran, North Korea, and Iraq as part of an "axis of evil."

March 13, 2002	The U.S. Senate rejects the Corporate Average Fuel Economy requirement standards.
April 2002	The Saudis put more oil on the market after Iraq suspends oil shipments.
May 2002	Putin and Bush announce a strategic energy agreement at the Russian-American summit in Moscow.
September 2002–January 2003	The Bush administration threatens to attack Iraq and generate regime change if Iraq does not comply fully with UN resolutions.
November 8, 2002	The UN Security Council passes UN Resolution 1441 by a vote of 15–0. It requires Iraq to admit inspectors from the UN Monitoring, Verification, and Inspection Commission and the International Atomic Energy Agency. Baghdad accepts the resolution on November 13 and, on December 7, 2002, provides the United Nations with an unsatisfactory 12,000–plus page report.
January 2003	OPEC decides to increase oil output by 1.5 million barrels per day in response to the oil strike in Venezuela and the potential war with Iraq.
March 19, 2003	The United States and its "coalition of the willing" attack Iraq.
April 2003	Saddam's regime falls.
May 12, 2003	Al Qaeda suicide bombings on western residential compounds in Riyadh kill 35 people. Saudis accelerate domestic crackdown on Al Qaeda elements.
May 2003	UN Security Council passes resolution 1483. It requires that Iraq's oil profits be placed in a fund to benefit the Iraqi people and calls on all members to assist in Iraq's reconstruction.
April-August 2003	The United States cannot find actual weapons of mass destruction in Iraq, raising questions about whether it had trumped up charges against Iraq to justify the war.
July-August 2003	Apparently authentic tape recordings from Saddam are released, calling for jihad against American forces.
July 14, 2003	An Iraqi Governing Council is erected officially and could be considered Iraq's first postwar government.
July 23–25, 2003	Saddam Hussein's sons, Uday and Qusay, are killed by U.S. forces. In a separate incident, some of Saddam's personal bodyguards are captured, sparking speculation that Saddam's days are numbered as well.
August 14, 2003	The UN Security Council approves by a vote of 14–0 a resolution recognizing the Iraqi Governing Council, although Syria abstains, following an August 4 Arab

League decision to refuse recognition until Iraq is led by an elected government.

August 19, 2003   A 1500-lb. truck bomb destroys part of UN headquarters in Baghdad, killing and injuring over a hundred people. The bombing raises questions about U.S. ability to provide security in Iraq, despite the fact that the United Nations preferred not to count on U.S. force protection at its headquarters. The UN commitment to Iraq, however, does not waver.

August 27, 2003   The United States officially withdraws from Saudi Arabia, thus removing a major source of agitation in the region.

August 28, 2003   Facing ongoing attacks on American forces and on Iraq's infrastructure, the United States initiates more serious discussions at the United Nations about a potential United Nations role in Iraq.

INDEX